CATCHING
THUNDER

About the Authors

Eskil Engdal and Kjetil Sæter are both feature journalists at the Norwegian broadsheet *Dagens Næringsliv*. They have both been recipients of the prestigious SKUP Award for Investigate Journalism, in addition to numerous other awards and distinctions.

About the Translator

Diane Oatley is a writer, independent scholar and translator. Originally from the United States, she transferred to the University of Oslo in 1983, completing an MA in comparative literature there in 1990. She is a member of the Norwegian Non-fiction Translators Association and the Norwegian chapter of PEN.

CATCHING THUNDER

THE TRUE STORY OF
*THE WORLD'S LONGEST
SEA CHASE*

ESKIL ENGDAL AND KJETIL SÆTER

TRANSLATED BY DIANE OATLEY

ZED

Catching Thunder: The True Story of the World's Longest Sea Chase
was first published in 2016 by Fagbokforlaget, Norway,
under the title *Jakten på Thunder*.

First published in English in 2018 by Zed Books Ltd,
The Foundry, 17 Oval Way, London SE11 5RR, UK.

Published by agreement with the Kontext Agency.

Translated by Diane Oatley.

www.zedbooks.net

This translation has been published with the financial
support of NORLA.

Typeset in Haarlemmer MT and Akzidenz-Grotesk Pro
by Swales & Willis Ltd, Exeter, Devon
Cover design by David A. Gee

A catalogue record for this book is available from the British Library

ISBN 978–1–78699–087–7 pb
ISBN 978–1–78699–089–1 pdf
ISBN 978–1–78699–090–7 epub
ISBN 978–1–78699–091–4 mobi

Printed and bound by the CPI Group (UK) Ltd, Croydon CR0 4YY

CONTENTS

CONTENTS

CONTENTS

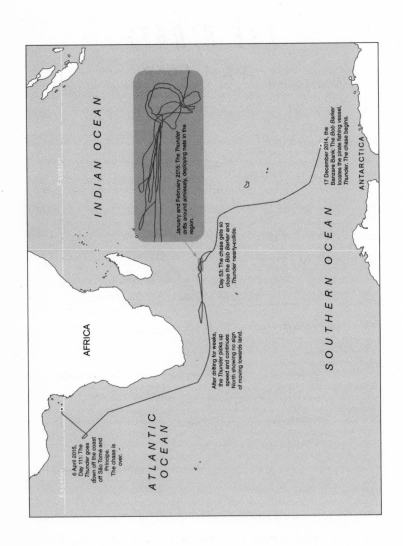

AFRICA

INDIAN OCEAN

ATLANTIC OCEAN

SOUTHERN OCEAN

ANTARCTICA

Equator

6 April 2015, Day 111: The *Thunder* goes down off the coast of São Tomé and Príncipe. The chase is over.

After drifting for weeks, the *Thunder* picks up speed and continues North showing no sign of moving towards land.

January and February 2015: The *Thunder* drifts around aimlessly, deploying nets in the region.

Day 53: The chase gets so close the *Bob Barker* and *Thunder* nearly collide.

17 December 2014, the Banzare Bank: The *Bob Barker* locates the pirate fishing vessel, *Thunder*. The chase begins.

1

THE PIRATE
APRIL 2016

He hasn't slept in the past 24 hours, he says.

The rain is beating down against the large window panes of the airport terminal. He is standing in the arrival hall and holding a sign bearing our names, as if we were meeting for a conference or a safari.

There is nothing distinguishing him from the cluster of taxi drivers battling their way through the tiny group of travellers who have just landed in the provincial town, the name of which he has asked us not to reveal.

"Who gave you my phone number?" he asks over and over again on our way out to the waiting car.

He feared it was a trap – that it was the past that had brought down the plane's landing gear.

"These people are capable of murder to protect their name and their profits."

His sole motivation for wanting to meet us is greed, the same motivation that sent him on mission after mission to the Southern Ocean. He is demanding a considerable amount of money for telling his story, along with the assurance that we will disclose neither his identity nor that of the city, the country or even the continent where we meet.

Every morning he arrives, trudging dutifully to the hotel, listing names and places, trying to untangle the various poaching expeditions, to remember details that time has erased from his mind. He is neither well-spoken nor particularly observant. Now and then the stories are choppy waves that suddenly break – and then spill out into a large, uniform mass.

As soon as he is done with his story, he hurries off to the day job that has kept him alive since he was forced to go ashore from the *Thunder*. His only friends appear to be some neighbourhood dogs and a young nephew.

When he signed on with the *Thunder* in Malaysia, the ship had been wanted by Interpol for one year. On the way from land in the dinghy that transported him through the darkness to the *Thunder*'s anchoring site, he had an uneasy feeling that something terrible was going to happen.

2

"THE BANDIT 6"
HOBART, AUSTRALIA, DECEMBER 2014

The Shadowlands. There is no evidence of it on any map, but Captain Peter Hammarstedt sets the ship's course for this region on the afternoon of 3 December 2014. He sails the MY *Bob Barker* down the River Derwent, towards the capricious Storm Bay and out on a 15-day voyage to an out-of-the-way purgatory with the worst winds and the highest waves of all the oceans in the world.

He is headed into no man's land. There he will bring down a mafia operation. There are very few people who believe he will succeed.

His boyish haircut and reluctant beard growth make the Swedish-American shipmaster seem younger than his 30 years. Despite his youth, he is already a veteran of the militant environmental movement Sea Shepherd. The target is a fleet of vessels that are poaching the Patagonian toothfish, a deep sea delicacy that can be just as profitable as narcotics or human trafficking. The trawlers and longline fishing vessels operate in a region so inhospitable and inaccessible that the chances of locating them are negligible.[1] Should he find the vessels, he will chase them out of the Southern Ocean, destroy the fishing gear and hand the crew over to the coast guard or port authorities.

Before setting out from the Tasmanian capital of Hobart, Hammarstedt studied the target of his search in depth. He scrutinized the maps of the regions where the fleet of illegal fishing vessels had formerly been observed by research vessels and surveillance planes. Now he is trying to think like a fisherman, studying the underwater topography and the banks where large concentrations of Patagonian toothfish might be found. In the Ross Sea, the bay cutting into the continent of Antarctica, there are a number of legal fishing vessels. The area is also regularly frequented by Navy vessels, which makes it less likely that fleets of poachers will be found there. Instead, he decides to sail towards the Banzare Bank – an underwater plateau jutting up out of the plunging depths of the Antarctic. It is this region that Hammarstedt calls the "Shadowlands". He is pleased with the term; he came up with it himself. It sounded edgy, almost a little *Pulp Fiction*-ish, he thinks. It will take him two weeks to sail there. From there he will start the search.[2]

Eventually, as the *Bob Barker* nears the 60th parallel and the northern border of the Southern Ocean, he has the crew of 31 men and women do training drills. In "the Screaming Sixties" the clear blue surface of the ocean can rise up without warning and transform into deep green, ferocious walls of water and hurricanes are so common that they are never given names. The volunteer crew practises "man overboard" procedures,

4

evacuation, confrontation tactics and the use of shields in the dinghies.

When Hammarstedt engaged in close combat with Japanese whaling ships, he met with aggressive resistance, but he knew that they would not undertake any actions leading to the loss of human lives. With a pirate fleet he can't anticipate what lies in store. The illegal fishing activity taking place in the Antarctic constitutes one of the most lucrative fish poaching operations in the world and Hammarstedt has prepared the crew for the possibility that the pirates can resort to the use of weapons.

On the starboard side of the bridge he has posted a laminated sign in A4 format. The words "Wanted – Rogue toothfish poaching vessels – The Bandit 6" are printed on it in blood-red letters against a sandy-brown background. The culprits are the ships the *Thunder*, *Viking*, *Kunlun*, *Yongding*, *Songhua* and *Perlon* – a fleet of battered trawlers and longline fishing vessels that have been plundering the valuable Antarctic Patagonian toothfish stock for years.[3] All the vessels have been blacklisted by CCAMLR, the organization that manages the living marine resources of the international maritime zone surrounding Antarctica.[4]

The 64-year old *Perlon* has been blacklisted by the authorities since 2003. The *Yongding* has been looting the Southern Ocean for at least ten years. The *Kunlun* is the smallest, but perhaps best known and is affiliated with a Spanish mafia network. Then there is the large *Songhua*, with the characteristic low deck afore, which has being fishing illegally in Antarctica since 2008.

At the very top of the poster are photos of the two ships Hammarstedt has been daydreaming about. The *Viking* – a rusty hulk that glides silently in and out of Asian ports with its illegal cargo – the first fishing vessel ever to be wanted by Interpol. And then the Norwegian-built trawler the *Thunder*, also wanted by Interpol.[5] The owner is to have earned more than EUR 60 million on the plundering of the Antarctic. It is the *Thunder* he wants most to find.

Hammarstedt has put copies of the Interpol notices on a shelf on the bridge. If he finds one of the vessels, he will pose by the railing with the mafia ship in the background and the laminated Interpol notice in his hand. Then the ship's photographer will take a picture of him.

After nine days at sea, at 61 degrees south, they spot the first icebergs: two towering ice cathedrals with dripping facades and ephemeral spires. Hammarstedt guides the *Bob Barker* around the icebergs so the crew can dwell upon the landscape, as a hint of what lies in store.

The first person to sail into the Antarctic Circle, James Cook, had a terrified and freezing crew on his hands, who later described the frozen wasteland as the forecourt of Hell. "The whole scene looked like the wrecks of a shattered world, or as the poets describe some regions of hell; an idea which struck us the more forcibly, as execrations, oaths, and curses re-echoed about us on all sides," the scientist George Forster wrote, a crew member on Cook's second journey.[6]

For the crew of the *Bob Barker* the Antarctic is an idea of the world as they wished it to be: pristine, peaceful and timeless. Beneath them lies a lost continent, the Kerguelen Plateau – an enormous land mass that was formed by a series of volcanic eruptions 110 million years ago. The continent was three times larger than Japan; tropical flora and fauna were presumably to be found here. And then, 20 million years ago, the continent slowly began sinking. Today it lies hidden more than one kilometre beneath the ocean's surface. The only dry remains of the lost continent are Kerguelen, McDonald and Heard Islands with mountain peaks higher than any to be found on the Australian mainland and named after French explorers, Australian scientists and Norwegian whalers. Norwegian Bay. Mount Olsen. Mawson Peak.

In the depths between the continental shelf and the conti-nental slopes lives the Patagonian toothfish, a petulant and repulsive giant that can grow to a weight of 120 kilos and live more than 50 years.[7] It starts its life in the shallows close to land and it is not until the age of six to seven years that it sets out to swim down into the ice-cold darkness of 1,000 to 2,000-metre depths. After a specimen was caught and described at the end of the nineteenth century, it lived in oblivion until it was rediscovered by chance and served at restaurants in the USA in the 1980s. The fatty, pearly white and boneless meat created a gastronomic sensation. The flavour of the tooth-fish resembled a mixture of lobster and scallops, and some called it the best tasting fish in the world. A British restaurant critic offered his readers the following advice: "It is seriously endangered, so you'd better eat as much as you can while stocks last."[8]

The hunt for "the white gold" generated hidden fortunes, cost hundreds of lives in shipwrecks and accidents at sea and came close to wiping out the slow-maturing delicacy.

On the eve of 16 December, the *Bob Barker* sails into the southern part of the Banzare Bank. The ocean around him seems untouched by time, but on the map Hammarstedt can read fragments of the continent's history. He sees remnants of greedy ambitions and incredible heroism: stretches of open sea, hills and mountainsides that have been named after wives and mistresses, rulers, patrons, heroes who froze to death, or sheer hallucinations.

The Banzare Bank was discovered and named by the Australian polar hero Douglas Mawson. On his first large-scale expedition to Antarctica, Mawson spent two winters at a stony outpost that turned out to be the windiest place on earth. During a sledding trip he lost two members of his team. When Mawson set out on his next expedition from Cape Town in October 1929, the "heroic" era of explorations of the Antarctic had come to an end. But there were still large white patches on the map.

The Banzare expedition's express objective was scientific, but in reality it would undercut "aggressive" Norwegian expeditions and territorial claims.[9] In January, Mawson met the Norvegia expedition led by the Norwegian pilot and polar pioneer Hjalmar Riiser-Larsen. The two agreed to explore the Antarctic, each on their respective side of the 45th parallel, an agreement that is considered to be the first international treaty in Antarctica.

Peter Hammarstedt's hope is that clear regulations and agreements will also be imposed on modern day fishing and environmental protection – and that somebody will ensure their compliance.

The Swedish captain guides the ship into the shelter of an ice tongue to protect it from the swells rolling in from the west. He will commence the search from here. First, he will sail directly into the middle of the bank and then cross it from west to east. It will take two weeks to cover the entire area, the radar will pick up on each and every movement within 12 nautical miles, and the light of the Antarctic summer will allow him to search around the clock. Hammarstedt knows the fishing vessels he is chasing have probably also posted a sentry who is monitoring the radar and that the *Bob Barker* could be detected long before they gain any actual visual contact with a vessel. He has, however, studied the six ships thoroughly and believes the *Bob Barker* with its 3,000 horsepower is faster than they are.

When he assembles the crew in the lounge, a number of them are wracked with seasickness.

"We will start the search from the west. Then we'll go south towards the ice. We could come across a ship at any time. Crow's nest watch starts tonight. Action station drill after lunch and first aid training after that," Hammarstedt says.

The search will probably take several weeks.

The banks of fog rising from the ocean thicken. Every half hour Hammarstedt is on the bridge checking the radar image. It is covered with a scattering of dots – icebergs that have broken away from the Amery Ice Shelf, a gigantic platform of ice extending out from the Antarctic land mass. The only thing distinguishing an iceberg from a ship on the radar screen is the speed. If a vessel is fishing, it will move slowly, perhaps at the same pace as the icebergs. For that reason Hammarstedt wants an additional pair of eyes that can decipher the objects picked up by the radar.

The weather hits harder in the crow's nest than anywhere else on the ship. The person standing at the top of the mast has nothing more than a thin steel shield for protection from the wind. This individual must constantly scan the water surface in search of ships and net floats. One is more likely to spot something from the corner of the eye than straight ahead in one's field of vision. Most of the crew members volunteer for a shift in the crow's nest; everyone wants to be the first one to spot the *Thunder*.

Forty to fifty objects are now visible on the radar. It's like staring at a pepperoni pizza and the bridge sentry calls up to the watchstander in the crow's nest constantly, reporting the direction and distance to whatever cannot be identified on the radar. But the only thing in sight is the glassy ocean and an iceberg drifting in and out of the fog. One day after they have commenced the search, the *Bob Barker* is located 300 nautical miles from Davis Bay and 150 nautical miles from the ice edge.

"We could find them at any minute," Hammarstedt says.

On the radar, Hammarstedt suddenly sees one of the slowly floating dots move in the opposite direction, away from the icebergs' sluggish trajectory. It is maintaining a speed of six knots on a course headed southwest. It has to be a ship. Has the ship seen the *Bob Barker*? Should he change course to cut them off or will that attract attention?

A few minutes later, in the crow's nest, the seaman Jeremy Tonkin spots three orange, interlinked fishing buoys bobbing in the ocean on the starboard side of the *Bob Barker*. It is very likely that they belong to an illegal fishing vessel, Hammarstedt thinks. As soon as there is visual contact from the bridge with the unknown vessel, he tells the crew to stand by.

The ship is enveloped in fog when he first catches sight of it.

"That's a fishing boat," Hammarstedt says.

"Oh yeah," first mate and second-in-command Adam Meyerson confirms. "It looks very much like the *Thunder*, Peter. It's got the same paint configuration and the forward bridge."

From photographs Meyerson is able to recognize the outline of the vessel now emerging out of the mist, its protruding wheelhouse and the characteristic steep stern of the old trawler.

The jovial first mate grew up with the sea as his neighbour in San Francisco. He sailed from California to Hawaii in a small, single-mast sailboat as a 27-year-old and has been a mate in the employ of Sea Shepherd for five years. At his most intense, he resembles Jack Nicholson's character in *The Shining*, when he pops into room 237 of the Overlook Hotel.

The news begins to spread on the ship. Soon the wheelhouse is filled with crew members and Hammarstedt orders one of them to take note of their position. Then he pulls down the window of the wheelhouse and lifts his binoculars to his eyes. The ship is partially hidden behind an iceberg. Through the binoculars he can see flocks of seagulls diving for the fish waste being thrown overboard. The net floats hang over the rails, ready for deployment into the ocean.

From the bookshelf furthest back in the wheelhouse, Hammarstedt takes down the red folder containing pictures and descriptions of "The Bandit 6" and rapidly leafs through the pages to the picture of the *Thunder*. Meyerson hangs over his shoulder.

"That's the *Thunder*," Hammarstedt says. He smacks the palm of his hand into Meyerson's and presses the alarm. Five short blasts. That is the signal to the crew for everyone to prepare themselves.

They have found the ship that nobody has seen for two months, and which has been wanted all over the world by New Zealand, Australia and Norway for extensive poaching of fish. The vessel is the most notorious of them all, the vessel that ministers, bureaucrats and criminal investigators from four continents are hunting for. It has been mentioned in speeches and discussed at seminars, its movements recorded in strategic documents and investigation protocols, and it has been blacklisted and hunted for eight years.

The *Thunder* is the evasive ship that turns up only to suddenly vanish again, as if it didn't really exist, but was merely a folktale, Hammarstedt thinks. He knows that the analogy might seem melodramatic, but in the course of recent months, the *Thunder* has become his own Moby Dick.

"17 December 2014, 2118 hours," Hammarstedt notes in the ship's log.

He then sets the ship's course for his prey.

3

OPERATION ICEFISH
FRANKFURT, 2012/
VERMONT, 2014

May 2012. After having presented his identification to the security guard, Peter Hammarstedt was led behind the walls of the more than 100-year-old, high security prison Preungesheim. He had been asked to come right away; therefore only a few hours passed from the time he boarded the flight from Stockholm until he was standing before the prison on the outskirts of Frankfurt city centre.

In one of the cells was his boss.

Paul Franklin Watson had been on his way from Denver to the film festival in Cannes, but when he stopped over in Frankfurt, he was taken aside by the German police and placed under arrest. During the almost 40 years that had passed since he founded Sea Shepherd, Watson had had his regular altercations with the law. While in custody, Watson learned that Costa Rica had circulated an arrest warrant for him through Interpol due to a dispute between Sea Shepherd and a shark fishing vessel ten years earlier.

While the red carpets were being rolled out in Cannes, the Hollywood darling Watson was sitting in solitary confinement in the old prison. To be sure, the activist and former *Baywatch* star Pamela Anderson was also on her way to show her support, demonstrations were taking place outside German embassies and one of the group's supporters had offered to pay Watson's bail, but the Sea Shepherd leader was at risk of being extradited to both Costa Rica and Japan. It was the thought of a legal battle in Japan that frightened him the most.

When Watson came out of the cell to meet Hammarstedt, he sat down at the tiny table in the visitors' area and glanced up at the walls, which were decorated with children's drawings. Hammarstedt thought Watson appeared collected and un-worried.

"In the time ahead, you will represent me in the media and at all events. If anyone should question it …," Watson said, and then stopping mid-sentence, he pushed a small piece of paper across the table. The text was written in longhand.

"Peter will represent me. Paul Watson."

Hammarstedt was already a loyal veteran. He had taken part in all of Sea Shepherd's large-scale campaigns since 2003. For ten Antarctic summers he had chased Japanese whaling ships through Antarctica, and had spent almost five years at sea. He always obeyed the lines of command and had proven fearless. When he left the prison, Captain Peter Hammarstedt was Sea Shepherd's new front man – the Commander.

After eight days in prison Watson was released on bail in the amount of EUR 250,000 and placed under house arrest in a flat in the Bornheim district of Frankfurt. Every morning at noon he walked over to report to the local police station. He stepped down from his positions of president of Sea Shepherd USA and the captain of the flagship SS *Steve Irwin*. Now he had received a tip that Japan wanted him extradited and he was convinced that the nation would not give him a fair trial. There were also rumours circulating that the mafia in Costa Rica had put a price on his head of 25,000 dollars.

Watson killed time in the evenings by walking along the bank of the Main River. And planning his upcoming escape.

One evening in August he shaved off his beard, dyed his chalk-white hair and disappeared in a car over the border to the Netherlands. He felt ill and weak from an infection in his leg, had neither a passport nor a cell phone, and didn't dare use his credit card.

On the coast of the Netherlands Watson was met by the sailboat the *Columbus*. The Sea Shepherd logo was covered up so the boat wouldn't attract needless attention. After the *Columbus* had sailed out into the English Channel and onward into the Atlantic Ocean, four months would go by before Paul Watson appeared again in public.

In the Southern Ocean.

When the German police realized that Watson had escaped, Japan also requested that Interpol issue a Red Notice – the type of notice issued for war criminals and murderers. With two Interpol notices hanging over his head, Paul Watson had extremely limited freedom of movement.[1]

In the summer of 2014 Watson lived on a farm in Woodstock, Vermont – an unreal place, a rolling, green landscape surrounded by maple trees, and classical farmhouses with colonnades and big windows in a resplendent New England style. In the midst of all this there was a Japanese Zen garden, a teahouse and a Buddhist meditation temple that was a meeting place for a group of resident monks. On an open field a cluster of standing stones had been arranged in a circle – a copy of Stonehenge. From the property Watson could see all the way to the majestic White Mountains in New Hampshire. There was also a small lake on the property, in which nobody was allowed to swim since the guests' suntan lotion could harm the frogs that lived there.

This surprising corner of the American dream was owned by the billionaire Pritam Singh – born Paul Arthur Labombard in an impoverished industrial town in Massachusetts. After having run away from a neighbourhood fraught with alcoholism and poverty, he reappeared as a radical student activist and later as a spokesperson for Sikh rebels in northern India. Back in the USA, on borrowed money and with a powerful desire to accomplish something, he fought his way up the ladder of the construction industry. Before long, the left-wing radical with clear blue eyes, a bristly beard and turban was one of the largest property developers in Key West on Florida's southern tip.

There, by chance, he met Paul Watson. Pritam Singh was quickly incorporated into the movement's entourage of high-profile celebrities. He part-financed Sea Shepherd's flagship the *Steve Irwin*, named after the Australian environmentalist and crocodile hunter who was killed by a stingray, and took the position of vice president of the Sea Shepherd Conservation Society. Paul Watson understood the value of connections with celebrities from the business and entertainment worlds. They had the power of seduction mixed with wealth. Or as Watson expressed it: "With two James Bonds, Batman, Captain Kirk and MacGyver on the board we are invincible."[2]

In Vermont on this warm midsummer evening, Watson was the host of Sea Shepherd's first global conference. The 250 guests, the majority dressed in black, were blessed by local Mohawk Indians. Seminars were held on the slaughter of dolphins in Japan, sharks in China, meditation and veganism – and demonstrations of drones. Captain Peter Hammarstedt gave a lecture on the whaling campaign in the Southern Ocean.

The whale defence movement constituted Sea Shepherd's history and was its signature cause. After having left Greenpeace because he felt the organization was not sufficiently militant, Paul Watson purchased a 20-year-old trawler, christened it the *Sea Shepherd* and set out to hunt for the whaling vessel the *Sierra*. The *Sierra* was an uncannily effective hunter, said to be behind the slaughter of as many as 25,000 whales. When Watson found the ship in the waters between Spain and Morocco, he gouged a three-metre large hole in the hull of the whaling ship with his own bow.

It was a foretaste of what was to come.

In 1992 Watson and his fiancée, the former Playboy model Lisa Distefano, tried to sink the whaling ship *Nybræna* while it was docked alongside the quay in Lofoten. The sabotage earned Watson a sentence of 120 days in jail, but he was released when the Dutch authorities refused to extradite him to Norway.

In an open letter to the Norwegian people Paul Watson claimed that he had sunk eight ships and damaged eight more. In the letter he also gave an account of the movement's ideology: Sea Shepherd did not submit to anything but what Watson called the laws of nature.

"The Sea Shepherd Conservation Society is a law-abiding organization. We rigidly adhere to and respect the laws of nature or *lex natura*. We hold the position that the laws of ecology take precedence over the laws designed by nation states to protect corporate interests ... The smell of guilt is already a stench in the nostrils of God," he wrote.[3]

For Watson there was no point in sinking a ship unless you could show the world what you had done. In response to the reality series *Whale Wars*, which depicted Sea Shepherd's fight against Japanese whalers in the Southern Ocean, the influx of funds and volunteers to the organization increased dramatically. Due to the success of the Animal Planet series, the whaling campaign overshadowed everything else Sea Shepherd did.[4]

Now Peter Hammarstedt wanted to do things differently. During the former expeditions to Antarctica, he often saw gillnet floats that fleets of toothfish poachers had left behind, before disappearing into obscure ports in Southeast Asia. Hammarstedt wanted Sea Shepherd to change its profile, abandon the whaling campaigns and become known as a protector of the untouched Antarctic.

In Vermont, in the combined meditation room and library with the high ceiling, Peter Hammarstedt took Paul Watson by the arm and requested a chat. The UN's International Court of Justice in The Hague had ordered Japan to stop its whaling activities in the Southern Ocean and a portion of the Sea Shepherd fleet was standing idle.

"What do you think about our taking on the hunt for illegal fishermen in Antarctica?" Hammarstedt asked.

"Do you think it's possible to find them?" Watson replied.

"I'm sure of it," Hammarstedt said.

"OK," Watson replied.

Four months later, the captains Peter Hammarstedt and Siddharth "Sid" Chakravarty were sitting in a hotel room in Wellington. Operation Icefish had been publicly announced. Down in the harbour the campaign vessel the *Sam Simon* was ready to set sail for the Southern Ocean. For weeks Captain Chakravarty had been travelling around visiting ship grave-yards in Mumbai in search of parts for the powerful winch he must build on the *Sam Simon* to haul up the kilometre-long gillnets he expected to find. The *Bob Barker*, with its large fuel capacity, more powerful engine and a hull reinforced to withstand the ice, would find and pursue the ships.

That was the simple plan.

"For how long will you follow them?" Chakravarty asked.

The question came as a surprise for Hammarstedt. He had no ready answer.

"For however long it takes?" Chakravarty asked.

"Yeah. For however long it takes," Hammarstedt answered.

4

THE OCCUPATION
HOBART/THE
SOUTHERN OCEAN

"Oh, no! Not the Sea Shepherd-crazies."

That was the first thought that flashed through Martin Exel's mind when he heard about Operation Icefish.

As general manager of environment and policy for the fishery giant Austral Fisheries, he had lived and breathed for the Patagonian toothfish for more than 20 years.

Exel had administrated a secret intelligence network to confront and stop the pirates; he now operated a fleet of legal vessels that fished toothfish in the Southern Ocean. At Austral Fisheries, Sea Shepherd was commonly viewed as a gang of crazy, unscrupulous assholes – Paul Watson was a man who made a fool of himself with deranged initiatives and lived in an alternative universe. Martin Exel was convinced that Sea Shepherd would attack the legal tooth-fish ships, spray down the hulls and generally speaking raise hell.

When he asked other environmental organizations for advice, they stared at him in terror and told him to stay away from Sea Shepherd.

The publicized Sea Shepherd expedition could end in a commercial disaster for Austral Fisheries. Sea Shepherd's massive media machinery would frighten luxury hotels and top restaurants all over the world, deterring them from serving Patagonian toothfish. Martin Exel saw no other solution but to meet Sea Shepherd halfway and arrive at a form of collaboration.

"The task of searching for one or two ships in the Southern Ocean is almost impossible. We have been chasing these vessels for 20 years and know how complicated and costly it is," he explained in a meeting with Jeff Hansen, the director of Sea Shepherd Australia.

In the early 1990s, Austral Fisheries sent its flagship, the 85-metre-long *Austral Leader*, on a series of expensive and disastrous expeditions to the Antarctic. The hope had been of finding schools of hake. Every day the company lost large amounts on the search, which did not reward them with anything but empty nets. In their desperation they scrutinized the maps for places where they could commence regulated fishing activity and finally they found their way to Macquarie Island, halfway between Australia and Antarctica. Out of the depths a species emerged that was virtually unknown in Australia, the Patagonian toothfish. But the Australians were too late: the toothfish stock had already been over-fished by Russian vessels.

Austral Fisheries continued its expeditions deeper and deeper into the Southern Ocean, all the way to the volcanic island Heard Island. There, the *Austral Leader* sailed straight into a fleet of Argentinean pirate ships. When the Icelandic shipmaster navigated his way into a confrontation with the Argentinean ships, the battle over the toothfish commenced. After having threatened to arm its own ships, Austral Fisheries initiated a highly unconventional and costly intelligence operation to thoroughly investigate the illegal fleet and its owners. The company hired former elite soldiers to acquire information. In Perth they set up a direct line for anonymous tips, they put up posters in ports and offered a reward of 100,000 dollars for information about the toothfish pirates. Eventually they had a network of secret informants all over the world on their payroll. It was a gamble with high stakes and enormous risk. The cover of one of the secret informants was blown and he was beaten up so badly that he was hospitalized for three months. What they first believed to be a gang of opportunistic amateurs, turned out to be a well-organized and cynical crime syndicate. The pirates hired private security companies which kept every single patrol ship under surveillance. When a French patrol vessel refuelled in Réunion on its way to the Antarctic, the pirates knew that it would take four days before they reached the fishing banks and notified their ships.

The management of Austral Fisheries compared the situation in the Southern Ocean to an invasion that challenged both the nation's sovereignty and its financial interests. Between 40 and 100 pirate vessels were pillaging the region, many with Spanish and Norwegian backers. When the Australian authorities sent ships to Antarctica to hunt for the pirate fleet, it was the country's first armed operation in the region since the Second World War. Operation Dirk took place 4,000 kilometres from the Australian mainland and cost taxpayers millions of dollars. In one of the most peaceful regions of the world something was taking place that resembled a war, even though the Antarctic Treaty prohibited all military activity.

When the patrol ship the *Oceanic Viking*, equipped with two 50 calibre machine guns, arrived at Prydz Bay in December 2006, it ran into the pirate vessel the *Typhoon 1*, the ship that would later come to be known as the *Thunder*.

5

HOT PURSUIT
THE SOUTHERN OCEAN, DECEMBER 2014

"I wanted you to be the first to know."

The *Sam Simon* has just set sail from Wellington to join Operation Icefish when Captain Sid Chakravarty receives a phone call from the Southern Ocean. It is Peter Hammarstedt.

"I have in front of me the *Thunder*, I believe. We got several fishing buoys in the water. We got a visual ID on the vessel. They are 5.7 nautical miles away. Based on its superstructure and its profile it has got to be the *Thunder*," he reports.

After having concluded his conversation with Chakravarty, Hammarstedt quickly climbs down the stairs from the bridge, trots through the messroom and into the lounge. He enthusiastically informs the crew of what lies in front of them.

"We have come across a fishing vessel. There is fishing gear in the water. We do need to get a bit closer to get a 100 per cent confirmation, but it does seem like the vessel we have found is the *Thunder*. On the second day of our search. We got one of them!" he says eagerly.

"This shit is for real," one of the crew shouts amidst the excited uproar, rounds of applause and cheers in the lounge.

On the bridge, Adam Meyerson watches the stern of the *Thunder* as it moves closer and closer. He has set their course to cut off the ship, which is now sailing south-eastward – away from the net floats.

"Nine minutes away. We're reeling them right in. It is a nice feeling to be on the faster ship," he chuckles.

"Let's get the flags up. Uncover the boats!" Hammarstedt says, who has just returned to the bridge.

Soon all the deck hands are wearing survival suits. They pull the tarps off the two dinghies that are installed on the foredeck; a number of the crew hang over the rail to catch a glimpse of the ship that is trying to escape between the icebergs. The Dutch flag is waving above the *Bob Barker* along with Sea Shepherd's own flag – bearing the skull of a pirate, but the standard cross-bones have been replaced by a shepherd's crook and a trident.

"We definitely interrupted them when they were fishing. They saw us, and immediately they started running," Hammarstedt says.

"They know they are up to no good. Criminals run," Meyerson replies.

Soon they can see the name of the vessel; it is attached to the sternpost on a wooden board that can be removed with a simple hand movement. The *Thunder*, Lagos.

"That's too much … They actually have their name on them? It is like finding John Dillinger with a name plate on him," Meyerson laughs.

Hammarstedt lifts the manual control for the VHF-radio and announces:

"*Thunder, Thunder, Thunder.* This is the *Bob Barker.* PC9519. Calling you on Channel 16."

"This is *Thunder* on Channel 16."

"Good afternoon, *Thunder.* This is the *Bob Barker.* You are fishing illegally in a CCAMLR region without a permit to fish."

"Sorry, sorry. No English. Just Spanish."

"That's very lucky because *hablo español también,*" Hammarstedt says and asks the captain of the *Thunder* to wait while he summons the Spanish-speaking photographer Alejandra Gimeno to the bridge.

"You are fishing illegally. Do you have a fishing permit?"

"We have a permit, we have a permit. The ship has a Nigerian flag, and we are sailing in international waters. Over," the *Thunder* replies.

"You are fishing in CCAMLR region 58.4.2, and we have an Interpol wanted notice for you."

"We are en route and not fishing. By the way, what kind of ship is that? I see that you have a pirate flag. What's that?" the shipmaster of the *Thunder* asks.

"Tell him that we are international conservation police and that they're under arrest," Hammarstedt says to Gimeno.

"No, no, no. *Negativo.* You have no authority to arrest this ship. We will keep sailing. Over," is the reply from the *Thunder.*

"We have the authority. We have reported your position to Interpol and the Australian police."

"OK, OK, you may report our position, but you cannot board this ship. Neither can you arrest it. We are sailing in international waters and we will continue."

"We are going to follow you, and you are under arrest. Change your course to Fremantle, Australia. If we see you fishing, we will physically stop you," Hammarstedt threatens.

He can feel the adrenaline racing through his body, and trots down onto deck to take the photograph he has been dreaming about, by the railing with the Interpol wanted notice in his hand and the *Thunder* in the background.

Once back on the bridge, he gives the order to maintain a distance of a half nautical mile from the *Thunder*. He does not want to come too close, but simultaneously be close enough to be able to respond quickly should the ship change its course.

"The hard part is over now," Adam Meyerson says.

Before he goes down into the great cabin, Hammarstedt opens the ship's log, leans over it and writes:

"Hot pursuit begins."[1]

6

OPERATION SPILLWAY
LYON, FRANCE,
DECEMBER 2014

From the office on the bank of the Rhône River, Alistair McDonnell can see the morning mist suspended like gossamer above the flowing water. For almost all of December, a heavy blanket of clouds has hung over Lyon, and the city is now in the process of moving into a silent, chilly Christmas slumber. McDonnell, the leader of Project Scale, Interpol's new division against fisheries crime, is just a few days away from a much longed for Christmas holiday at home in Hastings.[1]

At Interpol's headquarters, the last year can be summed up as a success. The police organization played a part in breaking up a ring that was smuggling uranium from Moldova, and they rounded up the backers of a syndicate smuggling ivory from Tanzania. In Central America, close to 30 tons of narcotics have been confiscated.

For Operation Spillway there is not much to celebrate for the time being. The secret operation's foremost target is the pirate ships the *Thunder* and the *Viking*. For eight months, Alistair McDonnell has been pondering over how he can stop them.

Then, around lunch time on 17 December, Interpol's Command and Coordination Centre receives a call from the Southern Ocean.[2] Over the poor satellite connection they are able to pick up more or less that the caller introduces himself as Peter Hammarstedt. He explains that he is the shipmaster on the *Bob Barker* and that he has just found the vessel wanted by Interpol, the *Thunder*.

When the news reaches McDonnell's office, he punches his fist into the air. This is the opportunity the British investigator has been waiting for. He quickly transforms portions of the office landscape into a "Situation Room" and marks the *Thunder*'s position on the electronic maps. He subsequently cancels the Christmas holiday. Operation Spillway is the result of persistent, long-term lobbying activity on the part of bureaucrats and environmentalists. Fisheries crime had long been brushed aside as a joke and held outside police priority areas, even though it had the characteristics of organized crime. Ship documents and fishing protocols were forged; inspectors and port authorities bribed. The ship crews subsisted on slave contracts and the profits were laundered into impenetrable corporate structures. It was a swindle that generated more than USD 20 billion a year.

In 2012, Norway and the USA took the initiative to appoint a committee designated to combat the illegal conditions at sea – "illegal, unreported and unregulated fishing".[3] The same autumn, Interpol carried out its first covert operation against the poaching of fish. Each of the fisheries officers in the respective Interpol member nations held random pieces of a confusing puzzle. They registered shipping arrivals and catch declarations, pirate ships were observed from the air, in one harbour there was a crew list, in another a fine had been issued. Combined they perhaps had enough information that it could be converted into evidence in criminal cases against the ships' officers and backers.

A group of vessels appeared that was a clear target for Interpol: the fleet of trawlers and longline fishing vessels that were plundering the toothfish stock of the Antarctic. It was probably the most profitable and long-term illegal fisheries offensive in history. It took place in a delimited geographic area, it targeted a single species and it had been documented by hundreds of reports, books, newspaper articles and legal documents. Each ship could earn up to 5 million dollars annually. They posed a threat to the fish stocks and destroyed the economic means of sustenance for ordinary fishermen.[4]

In contrast to cocaine smugglers, who actively hid their illegal wares, the pirate trawlers were easy to follow, they were like "elephants in the snow", Alistair McDonnell thought.[5] Now they could test whether Interpol's databases and communication systems would be effective in the fight against the fishing pirates.

Although the *Thunder* and the *Viking* have left countless clues behind them on land, the vessels are difficult to stop. The crimes are committed in international waters, the profits hidden in tax havens, and it is virtually impossible to induce those who know the operation from the inside to talk. The police's most important "intelligence agents" are usually neighbours who sound the alarm, but at sea most consider themselves to be members of a professional brotherhood and they don't snitch on one another. The pirate ships also operate in an area equivalent to 70 per cent of the earth's surface.

In Operation Spillway McDonnell and his colleagues have carved out a strategy they hope will work. The ships are to be harassed and inspected at every single port of call. Charges are to be brought up and prosecution pursued for every tiny law infraction. He has named the strategy "Death by a thousand cuts".

Now Sea Shepherd has its eyes and cameras glued to the *Thunder* around the clock, but Interpol's notices on Paul Watson make any dialogue difficult. Sea Shepherd is also notorious for its unpredictability and lack of patience with the authorities. When McDonnell receives an email from Sea Shepherd's Asia Director about finding the *Thunder*, he nonetheless spots an opportunity.

"Thank you for the information, we will monitor the position updates and material you release identifying the vessel," McDonnell answers curtly.

He hopes Sea Shepherd will take the hint: Keep us updated at all times. Even if we don't respond, we are paying attention.

7

THE ICE

THE SOUTHERN OCEAN, DECEMBER 2014

Everything is in motion.

The albatrosses, suspended effortlessly on the air current with their three-metre-long wings, now cross upward against the wind. Then they set out in a broad-reaching, leeward arc, plummet towards the surface of the ocean and turn back into the wind to ascend once more.

In the south, out of the Prydz Bay, an eternal, invisibly flowing stream transports ice from inner Antarctica to the coast.[1] The winds rush out from the hinterland. Shaped by dense, cold air from the Antarctic continent, they sweep down the uncompromising polar plateau and inward across the coast.

The wind is blowing from the southwest at four knots; the ocean is flowing silently and calmly around the two ships and the waves swelling to heights of barely more than a metre. The *Thunder* is headed west. Does the pirate already know who his pursuer is? Is that why the mate on the *Thunder* is sailing in the opposite direction of the *Bob Barker*'s home port in Tasmania? Perhaps he wants to test how far Hammarstedt is willing to pursue them?

Suddenly, the *Thunder* changes course, heading in the direction of a belt of pack ice. The mate reduces the speed to two knots, heads northwest and around a square ice sheet. The two ships sail along the northern edge of the drift ice for a long while. When they enter a wide gulf with ice on all sides, the *Thunder* stops. It is as if for a moment the ship becomes aware of the danger that lies ahead.

"There's a lot of pack ice. Let's see what these guys do. They may turn, they might go in," first mate Adam Meyerson says. "It is a waste of their time and ours. They may be testing us. We are faster than they are, so they cannot outrun us. Trying to wear down our jaw. I'm sure they are desperate. They have no other options," he says.

"They are just going to see what we will do, I think. Let's get in right on their stern," Peter Hammarstedt says.

During the brief lull, the *Bob Barker*'s photographer runs up on deck to take photographs of the draft marks, which indicate how high the *Thunder* is sitting in the water. This can give them an idea of the amount of supplies and fuel on board.

Then the *Thunder* doggedly directs its bow towards the pack ice, at first carefully and tentatively, as if the shipmaster wants to test how contact with the ice will affect the ship. Suddenly, it speeds up and the propeller churns open an ice-free channel which allows the *Bob Barker* to follow without having to do any icebreaking of its own. Hammarstedt cannot follow more than 700–800 metres behind the *Thunder*, or the channel that has been cleared ahead of them will close up.

"Who knows what the game is?" asks Simon Ager, the Sea Shepherd's Canadian photographer.

"They may be testing if we will go into the ice. They may try to see if they can go through the ice faster than us," Meyerson says, holding one hand beneath his chin and observing the manoeuvre taking place in front of him with an incredulous gaze.

For a moment, Captain Hammarstedt considers calling up the captain of the *Thunder* and asking if he thinks the manoeuvre into the ice is advisable, but he decides against it. He does not want to reveal his own nervousness.

Hammarstedt's foremost concern is that the ice will oblige him to stop. Then it will close up behind the *Bob Barker* and can force its way in between the hull and the rudder, putting the most exposed part of the ship out of commission. That is a nightmare when you are located two weeks from the closest port and the only ship in the vicinity is fighting to get rid of you. The most dangerous of all is navigating between the ice and the Antarctic continent if the wind should suddenly change direction, sending the ice masses towards the ship while the wind laboriously packs the ice around the hull, shutting it in. Then the steel will begin to give way, the pressure from the ice threatening to tear it open. In such a case, getting into the life boats serves no purpose.

"Right now the *Thunder* is acting erratically. Trying to find something that sticks. We have never been up against these guys before. We are going to wear them down. I don't think they will last that long," Meyerson says on the bridge.

The sound of the ice scraping along the hull is like stone against a grinding wheel. The noise grates its way into the cabins, from time to time an explosion can be heard from the treacherous floes of drift ice. These are "bergy bits": on the surface they are no more than 2–3 metres across, but nothing on the ocean surface reveals the actual depths to which they extend. When they break free from a drifting ice berg and reach the ocean, they roll over, washing off the surface snow and remain floating there with a clear surface of glassy ice that makes them difficult to read on the radar. Weighing up to 500 tons, they can easily sink a ship.

Chief Engineer Ervin Veermuelen is standing with his eyes glued to the *Thunder*'s stern.

"It is a huge risk for the crew, but also for the environment. If these ships break down, they rely on other ships to come to their rescue," he points out.

A few months earlier, the pirate ship the *Tiantai* vanished in the Antarctic polar wasteland. When the Australian chief rescue operations centre received the mayday call, initially they tried to contact the owners. It was futile. The ship was registered in Tanzania, but there was no information about the vessel or about who could be contacted in an emergency. The only reliable information about the ship was that it was blacklisted for illegal fishing in Antarctica.

At the same moment that the *Tiantai*'s emergency radio beacon was triggered, an extensive search operation was underway in the south of the Indian Ocean for a Malaysia Airlines plane that had vanished without a trace with 239 passengers and crew on board.[2] One of the Australian airplanes that had been sent to take part in the search for the missing airplane was redirected to search for the *Tiantai*. An Orion airplane from the Australian Air Force was also sent towards the site of the shipwreck.

When the aircraft arrived at the scene, the *Tiantai*'s emergency radio beacon was still active, the waves were rising to heights of up to 7 metres, and the air temperature was 17 degrees below zero Celsius. There was no sign of the ship, the crew or the life rafts. All they could see from the air were some scattered remains from the wreck. One hundred and eighty kilometres from the site of the accident, the pilots suddenly noticed the well-known pirate ship the *Kunlun*. The shipmaster on the *Kunlun* did not respond to any calls and the longline fishing vessel continued sailing silently on its course headed north.

The conclusion of the medical experts was disheartening. In the cold and in the turbulent ocean nobody could have survived, not even in a lifeboat. The next day the rescue operation was cancelled.[3]

While the news media worldwide was full of stories about the Malaysia Airlines flight's inexplicable disappearance, not a single word was written about the *Tiantai*. Nobody knew what had happened to the ship or the crew, but it also seemed as if there were few who cared. When Hammarstedt travelled around fund raising for the upcoming Operation Icefish, he usually concluded with the story of the *Tiantai*. Chasing pirate fishermen out of the Antarctic was also about protecting and helping the faceless crew members of the battered death traps that were fishing in the Southern Ocean.

Around the *Thunder* and the *Bob Barker* the ice grows thicker and thicker. First it closes in around the *Thunder*, subsequently the *Bob Barker*. The ships are surrounded by ice and they plough slowly forward. Soon Adam Meyerson can make out a clear blue strip of open sea. The *Thunder* moves out of the ice first, increases its speed and sets its course north, away from the ice.

From the bridge they watch as the *Thunder* grows smaller and smaller against the horizon, but they know they will manage to catch up with her as soon as they have broken through the last of the ice floes.

A half hour after midnight, both of the ships are out on open water.

"Come on, guys, let's go to Fremantle and I'll buy you a beer. And then I take you to jail," Adam Meyerson laughs.

8

VESTURVON

ULSTEINVIK AND HULL, 1969–2000

23 March 1969. It was a hopeful spring day in Ulsteinvik on the west coast of Norway.

At the shipment quay of the machine shop Hatlø Mekaniske Verksted was a shiny, stern trawler newbuilding equipped with the latest in filleting machines, skinning machines, a spacious cold storage room and an interior outfitted for a crew of 47. The ship also had air conditioning, which would ensure cool temperatures even in tropical waters.

It was the most advanced factory trawler ever built in the long-established shipyard town. The vessel was destined for the Faroe Islands, where it would lead Faroese fishery into the modern age.

"May she bring good fortune to all who sail on her, I hereby name thee *Vesturvon*," the Godmother read before releasing the champagne bottle with a smash against the side of the ship, which many years later would come to be known as the *Thunder*. The shipyard's general manager subsequently asked the Godmother to be sure to accompany the vessel in her prayers for the remainder of her lifetime.

On the Faroe Islands, the trawler was welcomed by a brass band and a jubilant crowd.[1] The first shipmaster, the silent and authoritative Davor Poulsen, held a devotional meeting in the lounge every Sunday, no matter how good the fishing was. For several years they fished in the banks around Greenland. Twice the ship experienced an engine breakdown and had to be towed south. But the *Vesturvon* was a survivor; although the storm blew the roofs off the houses on the Faroe Islands and the towing line snapped, the trawler miraculously made it to a shipyard in Denmark.

After 17 years of service fishing cod around Greenland and the Faroe Islands, the *Vesturvon* was sold to the long-established English family shipyard Boyd Line. When in 1986 the ship sailed into the English seaport of Hull, it was given the name *Arctic Ranger*.

Hull was once one of the world's largest fishing harbours. In the 1950s, the city was the home port of 350 trawlers. The fishing around Iceland, the Barents Sea, Bear Island and along the coast of Labrador was the most dangerous and rough in the world, but the catches were incredible. The ship owners lived like barons and when the trawler seamen came ashore at St Andrew's Dock, the wealth was often squandered in the course of three days. They were called "the three day millionaires".[2] Many of them never had the chance to enjoy the profits reaped from the ocean. Between 1835 and 1983, 900 of the city's ships disappeared at sea. In addition to this came the many seamen who were washed overboard by a wave to vanish into the darkness. Hull had lost 6,000 men at sea.

In August the *Vesturvon* set out from Hull headed for Newfoundland. Seven of the trawler's former crew from the Faroe Islands were on the voyage. The English crew were trawler seamen who had not had work since the Cod Wars 11 years before. These wars were not mentioned as they sailed north; they talked about the Suez conflict and about the Falklands War two years earlier. Some spoke about their fathers, who had fought at Dunkirk during the Second World War, but the subject of the Cod Wars was off limits. It had torn the heart out of "Trawlertown".

In the autumn of 1975, Norway and Iceland expanded their territorial borders and shut the Hull fleet out from its former fishing banks. Hull slowly deteriorated into ruin, the fish merchants went under, the once so lively St Andrew's Dock was levelled to the ground, the warehouses fell into disrepair, the store windows were sealed up with particle boards and nobody lifted the heavy coils of rope on the harbour any longer. Even the churches went by the wayside. The cheerful Hessle Road turned into one of the most impoverished stretches of road in Great Britain.

The aging shipmaster who guided the old *Vesturvon* towards the coast of Newfoundland had never before been on a factory trawler. He seldom spoke with the crew and on the bridge he wore a suit and freshly shined shoes. The crew from the Faroe Islands noticed that the Englishmen had "another attitude to rank and cleanliness".

At the unsheltered fish bank Flemish Cap things were about to go wrong again for the old *Vesturvon*. As the storm released itself upon the ship, the trawler ran aground on the seabed. The ship was narrow, long and had a low freeboard. Before long the ocean was washing over the deck and filling the trawler with water. The Faroese boatswain was flipped over by the waves pounding across the deck and was on the verge of vanishing into the ocean. But this time too, the ship rode out the storm.

At the start of the new millennium, the *Vesturvon*'s proud history came to an end. The shipping company was not granted a fishing quota in Norway and in a partnership with a Russian shipping company, the trawler was sent out to fish in the Barents Sea, this time under the name of the *Rubin*.

In the Barents Sea, the ship, which would later be known as the *Thunder*, disappeared into a maelstrom of shell corporations, bizarre ships registers and shady expeditions.

9

THE PIRATE CAPITAL
PORT LOUIS, MAURITIUS, 2003

In the winter of 2003 a fishing vessel with a blue hull and Togolese flag sailed into the Port Louis harbour in Mauritius.

"Please be advised that the vessel *Rubin* has changed name to *Typhoon 1*. She called at Port Louis for bunkering purposes and provisions and had cargo in transit … I work in the shipping and fishing sector and am privileged to accurate info," wrote an informant for COLTO, the Coalition of Legal Toothfish Operators.[1] The coalition had offered a reward of 100,000 dollars to anyone who could provide information about the illegal fleet. The informant covertly took photographs of the trawler unloading tons of toothfish.

It was the ship formerly named the *Vesturvon*, which would later be known as the *Thunder*.

A few months later, the informant notified the coalition that the ship was the property of a shipping company in Galicia in Spain. And that it was on its way to Antarctica.[2]

The bustling harbour in Port Louis on the northwest coast of Mauritius was not only an ideal anchoring site sheltered from the westerly winds, but also a perfect hiding place. On the quay, ships' cargoes of sugar, tea, cotton, wheat and rice were unloaded. Within the constant flow of goods and beneath the dance of the cranes against the sky, containers full of Patagonian toothfish were secretly unloaded. In dives all around the harbour, Norwegian, Danish and Spanish seamen boasted of the looting of the Antarctic and argued over who had discovered the valuable commodity first. An illegal Norwegian fleet of 12 large vessels was among the most advanced and well-equipped. With its longline fishing system from Mustad they could search for the largest toothfish at depths of 2,500 metres. The Spanish ships were older, scrapped vessels that were forced to fish closer to land. There was therefore a far greater risk of their being discovered.

Half of all the toothfish brought to the market in the West passed for a period of time through the island in the southwest of the Indian Ocean. The logistics surrounding the illegal trading activities were sophisticated. At the harbour, the ship owners could purchase false import and export documents and the catches were often sold to nominee companies that falsified documents for resale on the lucrative US market. Attempts to trace the fish back to the source came to an end at a post office box, or on the doorstep of a company that turned out to be non-existent.

In the New Year of 2006, the research ship *Aurora Australis* set out from Fremantle with 2.2 million litres of fuel and 53 research scientists on board. The destination was the two Australian research stations Mawson and Dawis on the edge of the Antarctic plateau. During the 70-day voyage, the crew and the scientists would collect data for a number of different research programmes. The ships had also received orders to inform the Australian authorities of any whalers and fishing vessels they encountered in the Southern Ocean. All observations were to be called in immediately, regardless of the time of day. As the *Aurora Australis* approached the ice edge north of the Banzare Bank and the Prydz Bay, they saw a storm moving towards them. Despite the poor visibility, they could just make out a blue and white trawler with its deck full of net floats. On the stern was the name *Typhoon 1*, Lome.

The third mate of the *Aurora Australis* feared that the fishing gear could become entangled in the propellers, putting the research ship out of commission. That could lead to a catastrophe. When he called up the trawler, he received the answer that they were longline fishing. The chance meeting in the Southern Ocean was reported to the Australian authorities. The ship that would later be known as the *Thunder* was then blacklisted for the first time.[3]

Every year the *Thunder* set out on two toothfish expeditions in the Southern Ocean. A catch of 80 tons per trip was sufficient to cover the costs of fuel, wages, fishing gear and supplies. In 2010, after having been blacklisted for four years, they fished a total of 700 tons of toothfish. It was a goldmine for all concerned.

After the authorities of Mauritius started becoming aggressive, the *Thunder* found a new hiding place, Penang in

Malaysia, an island in the Strait of Malacca which was once known as the Pearl of the Orient. In Penang, the Chinese millionaires built their mansions on Guernye Road. In the evenings they met in the bar of the Oriental Hotel, where the hospitable Armenian owner would stroll into the bar with a whiskey glass balanced on top of his bald head and allow the guests to stay for free, until he died of liver failure and in financial ruin. Penang and the island's largest city, George-town, disappeared into oblivion for a time when the harbour lost its significance as a port of call on world trade routes. After the authorities of Mauritius relented to international pressure and chased the toothfish fleet out to sea, it made its way to Penang.

The *Thunder* would usually sail into Penang on one of the calmer days on the weekend. Then the two regular Chinese buyers would climb on board. In the cold storage room they assessed the quality of the fish before agreeing on a price with the ship owner's right-hand man – a well-dressed Chilean who spoke fluent Mandarin and went by the nickname "Capitán Nemo".

A middle-aged Spaniard with language proficiency also took part in the bartering. He was a wizard at negotiations. He was the one who procured cheap fuel, solved most of the problems and kept the port authorities happy with gifts large and small. And he was the one who could acquire another flag when the ship needed one.

The ship owner's only concern was the constant atten-tion the ship received. It was included on the EU's own black list of pirate vessels. The EU also went after some of the flag states that provided shelter for the pirate fleet. Togo was one of these. The tiny African nation earned far more on the sale of phosphate, cocoa, coffee and nuts to the European market than on selling its national flag to dubious ship owners. The *Typhoon 1* was thrown out of Togo's ships register in 2010. The ship owner solved the problem by securing flags in two nations simultaneously. Sometimes Mongolia's red and white flag waved above the *Thunder*'s stern post, at other times it was the green and white flag of Nigeria.

To confuse the authorities the ship changed names with increasing frequency. The *Thunder, Kuko, Wuhan No. 4, Ming No. 5, Batu 1.* It was only once the name plate had been attached to the stern that the crew knew what the ship would be called on the following day.

In Australia, the investigator Glen Salmon studied the high-resolution surveillance photos of the trawler with the characteristic incinerator at the stern, the tall mast on the quarterdeck and two additional smokestacks, on the port side and starboard side, respectively. And he was not in doubt: the *Thunder, Kuko, Wuhan No. 4* and *Ming No. 5* were all the same ship.[4]

As manager of the Australian Fisheries Management Authority, Salmon was the person coordinating Australia's efforts to prevent illegal vessels in the Southern Ocean. Every year they shelled out millions of dollars on patrolling the Indian Ocean and the Southern Ocean with ships and sophisticated surveillance planes. There were two ships that he saw more often than others: the *Thunder* and the *Viking*.

Ever since the authorities of Penang gave Salmon the first crew list from the *Thunder* in 2010, he had tirelessly gathered information about the ship. In the harbours of Malaysia where the pirate vessels sought shelter, he started his own little intelligence operation. Salmon was formerly a federal police agent and was known to be a capable investigator. He had a friendly, reserved nature and the ability to put people at ease in his company. This also made it possible for him to extract information without disclosing too much about himself.

In Malaysia he distributed a pamphlet containing photos of the six vessels which several years later would adorn Peter Hammarstedt's "The Bandit 6" poster. Then he asked the port inspectors he met if they had seen the ships.[5]

"Yes, yes, they all speak Spanish," was the most common answer he got.

There was little Salmon could do to stop the ships, but he could arrange a minor form of hell for the ship owners. Every time a surveillance plane spotted the ships leaving Antarctica, Salmon and his team notified the authorities in Malaysia: The ships will very likely be in your parts in four or five days.[6]

And Salmon's tactics produced results. In the winter of 2012, the inspectors in Penang started becoming aggressive and inspected the *Thunder* three times. The ship owner and his two assistants went into hiding at one of Penang's hotels. Two weeks passed before they succeeded in bringing the fish to land.

It became more and more difficult for the *Thunder* to find a safe harbour. When the ship sailed into the shallow Benoa

Harbour in Bali, it was boarded by agents from Indonesia and Australia. To the agents' great surprise they found no fishing gear on board. But a quick glance at the rusty incinerator that was lashed securely to the *Thunder*'s quarterdeck disclosed that the nets had been burned. The ships' documents on the bridge stated that the vessel was flagged in Nigeria, but the ship agent had a ship's certificate from Mongolia on which the same ship was named the *Wuhan No. 4*. The ship was then chased out of Bali as well.

The *Thunder* had been observed by surveillance planes, patrol vessels and research ships and inspected by fisheries officers more than 20 times since the ship was blacklisted. The old trawler was now a repeat offender, whom the authorities in Australia, New Zealand and Norway decided to stop.

On Thursday 5 December 2013, at 8 PM, Interpol issued a Purple Notice on the *Thunder* to its 190 member nations. It was the second time in history that a notice on a fishing vessel was issued by Interpol.

After the Purple Notice was issued, the *Thunder* roamed about to such an extent that there were few on board who had any idea of where they were or where they were headed. From the bridge they seldom received information; those wanting to know something had to purchase it from one of the ship owner's trusted officers. The currency was in beer and cigarettes.

In April 2014, the ship dropped anchor southeast of Teluk Ramunia, an old mining district on the south-eastern tip of Malaysia. These were troubled waters and a well-known smugglers route for oil, refugees and exotic animals. The name of the ship was now the *Ming No. 5*.

But the authorities here had also been tipped off about her. The Russian captain and chief engineer were placed under arrest, on charges of illegal anchoring. The involuntary stay cost the *Thunder*'s owner a lucrative expedition in the Antarctic.

10

THE STORM
THE SOUTHERN OCEAN, DECEMBER 2014

A storm is on its way in from the northeast.

The *Thunder* sets its course out of the 60th parallel south and into the 50th parallel south – "the Furious Fifties".

Straight into the storm.

On the bridge of the *Bob Barker*, Adam Meyerson glances at the weather radar. The yellowish-orange colour codes he sees indicate winds up to 40 knots. The reddish-black field further northwest tells of a full-scale storm – winds reaching up to 60 knots and waves over 7–8 metres tall.

"It is OK if they take us to the mustard. But not the ketchup," Meyerson says.

This is the only place on earth where the movements of the wind, current and waves are wholly unimpeded. Here the low pressure systems race around the continent in an eternal storm. South of the 50th parallel, one storm a week can build up, and the stable summer months of January and February are like mid-winter in the North Atlantic. At "the Roaring Forties", the region between the 40th and 50th parallels, the warm air from tropical waters meets the cold air mass from the Antarctic. The collision whips up the most powerful waves on the surface of the earth, and nothing stands in their way. The velocity and force of a wave depends on its length and the distance between the crests of the waves. There is nothing to stop them here and the longer the wave is, the harder it will topple into the hull of a ship.

Matthew Fontaine Maury, the father of modern day ocean-ography, described the weather at the bottom of the world as "a reservoir of dynamic force for the winds – a regulator in the grand meteorological machinery of the earth".[1] The crew on the full-rigged ships called the wind belt "Dead Man's Road" and knew that it was down here the devil began dancing between the masts.

The Eye of Sauron, Peter Hammarstedt thinks. The image depicted on the weather radar resembles the eye of the evil Sauron in *Lord of the Rings*. First, the reddish-black iris, then – in the middle – the vertical, reddish-yellow pupil.

The storm centre.

It is the seventh day of the chase; the ships have sailed 1,500 nautical miles. The media's interest of the initial days has subsided, but the Dutch authorities are asking for an update on the *Thunder*'s position. At the daily morning meeting in the messroom, Hammarstedt explains that some "pretty nasty weather" is on the way and that the *Sam Simon* is approaching the Antarctic convergence zone.[2] The ship is now three days from the gillnets from which the *Thunder* was fleeing.

Captain Sid Chakravarty on the *Sam Simon* is prepar-ing for an aggressive meeting with the fish poachers. The toothfish that are probably now caught in the gillnets left behind by the *Thunder* is worth so much that they might return to try and retrieve their catch. If that happens, Chakravarty will give them a fight. What if they have weapons on board and threaten to use them?

But the *Thunder* is clearly choosing the same strategy as the Japanese whalers did when they were chased by Sea Shepherd's fleet: escape into the storm. When the whalers encountered stormy weather, they sailed the ship across the storm to make life unbearable for the far smaller *Bob Barker*.

Peter Hammarstedt gives the order to batten down the hatches and secure everything on the vessel. During a storm on a previous expedition he was thrown out of his berth and woke up on the floor to catch a fleeting glimpse of a refrigerator that had been torn off its wall-hinges soaring through his cabin. Before it crashed into the bulkhead, it whizzed past just a few centimetres from his head.

"I am going to assume that the *Thunder* have weather and ice charts and stuff like that," says the Chief Engineer Erwin Vermeulen, who has come to the bridge.

The winds have begun blowing the foam off the crests of the waves; they are beating upon the port side of the ship. The contents of drawers and cupboards spill out across the floor, the lifeboats rock and bang against the cradles. Finally, the lock mechanism on one of them breaks, and it is now held on board only by a thin strap. Then one of the large Yokohama fenders under the wheelhouse is torn loose, the one that is meant to protect the ship when it docks or comes up alongside another vessel. It weighs more than a ton and is dancing back and forth across the foredeck like a wrecking ball.

Hammarstedt must send two of the crew out into the Armageddon taking place on the foredeck before the fender crushes the motors on the dinghies. In this weather he would prefer not to send anyone out on deck; a man overboard has no chance. In 7-metre waves the *Bob Barker* cannot turn around.

The Australian boatswain Alistar Allan and engineer Pablo Watson volunteer to go on deck to secure the dancing fender. The majority of the crew are knocked out by the weather. Only a handful show up for meals; the few crew members who have staggered down to the messroom discuss which of the two ships are having the most hellish time of it.

Hammarstedt knows which stage of seasickness is the worst. He has navigated a ship through 15-metre high waves on the coast of Labrador all the while vomiting into a bucket. But that isn't the worst stage; neither is it when the seasickness has drained you of all your strength and you are just tired, worn down and have the cold sweats. The worst moment is when you feel you are going to die, the moment you really believe that it's all over, but then you realize that it isn't over after all, that liberation will not be forthcoming. Then you start sliding in and out of your dreams, you imagine that you see family and friends, but they too are tottering around seasick in your delusions.

Throughout the entire night the wind hammers away at the two ships and the hull becomes an echo chamber of disturbing noises. Fifty litres of cooking oil spill through the galley of the *Bob Barker*. It leaks down over the decks and gets mixed in with the oil and diesel. Throughout the entire ship, the pounding of the fuel being thrown back and forth in the fuel tanks can be heard. It's as if somebody is trapped inside and desperately trying to break their way out.

When the bow plunges down into the trough between the waves and sends the propeller whirring out of the water, the air bubbles meet the end of the rotating propeller blade with a high-pitched whine, sending vibrations through the body of the ship. With less resistance to the propeller, the sturdy banging from the engine room suddenly changes its rhythm and frequency. The heart of the ship trembles.

From the bridge it is impossible to distinguish the white crests of foam from ice. Hammarstedt has posted a watch-stander at the clear view screen, the window that steadily rotates to throw off ocean spray, sleet and snow, and which is heated to prevent condensation and icing. He constantly monitors the autopilot to ensure that it is navigating correctly, and now and then he sees the *Thunder* like a dim shadow in front of him. You are doing this to frighten us, but now we are in the storm together, Hammarstedt thinks.

Now Hammarstedt is trying to understand the captain of the *Thunder*. He navigated into the ice, but kept their speed down, did not sail at full throttle and he was not there for long. Now he is sailing straight into the storm. Even though the waves are up to 7 metres high, he is navigating with assur-ance and calculation and without being foolhardy or reckless, Hammarstedt thinks.

On the *Bob Barker* all the lights on the bridge are turned off to enhance visibility; only a faint red light filters in from the media room behind the wheelhouse. In front of them, the *Thunder* changes its course by five degrees.

"Was it a big wave or is it course change?" Hammarstedt asks.

The gusts of wind are now blowing at up to 60 knots. The change in course will lead them to the French territories on the Crozet or Kerguelen Islands, and it will soon be morning, with a grey and lifeless light. Adam Meyerson glances down at the map.

"There is not much of anything here ..."

"We're still with the *Thunder*," Hammarstedt says.

11

THE SECRET CHANNEL
LYON AND BERGEN,
DECEMBER 2014

As the *Thunder* and the *Bob Barker* are fighting their way through the storm in the Southern Ocean, Interpol's Alistair McDonnell and his second in command, the agent with the nickname "Super-Mario", are forming a plan.[1]

"Super-Mario" is an expert on fishing vessels, fishnets and fish poachers, but is feeling the absence of the Glock pistol the police organization does not permit him to carry. The husky Portuguese man with a well-groomed bush of black hair is the low-key and correct McDonnell's clear opposite. "Super-Mario" is happiest out in the field and in dark interrogation rooms. In Lyon he likes to end the work day with a good evening meal at one of the restaurants in the Cité Internationale.

This year it looks like it will be an austere Christmas. Mario settles in on the couch in McDonnell's flat. In the evenings he must make do with a hamburger for dinner and on the weekends the two of them work from a café on the Croix Rousse plateau. Every evening they have conversations over the phone with a number of Interpol's member nations, the sole topic of which is the search for the *Thunder*.[2]

When the *Thunder* is finally forced into a port, an Investigative Support Team from Interpol will turn out to assist the local police force.[3] In Lyon the Operation Spillway team is working out a detailed formula for how to handle the vessel as a crime scene. Documents, computer equipment, telephones, maritime maps, nets, floats, cabins and cold storage rooms are to be turned upside down and catalogued in the search for evidence. The catch is to be subjected to DNA testing, and computers and all digital equipment handed over to experts in the Royal Canadian Mounted Police.[4] If they are to succeed in bringing the owner of the *Thunder* to court, there must be no gaps in the chain of evidence. For the time being, the only evidence they have indicating that the *Thunder* has been fishing illegally are statements from Peter Hammarstedt on the *Bob Barker*. The nets and floats that were found beside the *Thunder* will not be sufficient. They are but strong circumstantial evidence.

From the Southern Ocean they now receive daily emails from Peter Hammarstedt reporting the position and speed of the two ships. But the investigators still have questions they can't ask the Sea Shepherd captain directly. The solution is to treat Sea Shepherd like any other police informant within a criminal network, but then they must find a back channel: a person they can trust and who can communicate the questions to Hammarstedt.

They find the secret channel in an office at the Directorate of Fisheries in Bergen. The Norwegian fisheries officer and former homicide investigator Tor Glistrup is head of intelligence for the Fisheries Crime Working Group.[5] Glistrup is assigned the job of maintaining regular contact with Hammarstedt. Telling the world that they are in direct contact with Sea Shepherd is too incriminating, also for the Norwegian fisheries authorities. The head of intelligence's communication with Hammarstedt is kept secret.

In his emails Glistrup asks Hammarstedt detailed questions. He requests photographs of the *Thunder*'s antennas to find out the type of radar the ship has, he asks about the kind of gear found on deck, he wants photos of the hull from every conceivable angle and of every single officer who is imprudent enough to stick his head out of the *Thunder*'s wheelhouse.[6]

Peter Hammarstedt answers the questions by navigating the *Bob Barker* closer to the *Thunder*. Then he sends the ship's photographer Simon Ager out on deck. He sends the photographs from the Southern Ocean to Bergen. From there, unbeknownst to Hammarstedt, they find their way to the Interpol headquarters in Lyon.

Every day the Operation Spillway team tracks the ships' journey by plotting coordinates on a digital map. They analyse oceanographic data and current conditions to see whether this will affect the *Thunder*'s fuel consumption – and thereby its endurance.

Once a day they check the shipping lane and the areas lying ahead of the two ships. A foreign, unidentified ship on the radar image can be an ally of the *Thunder*, who will confront the *Bob Barker* and perhaps attempt to sink the campaign vessel. If they see suspicious vessels, they check their identities and whether they have any connection with the pirate fleet. Hammarstedt can then receive a warning. And time to prepare for an impending altercation.

12

THE LONGEST DAY

THE SOUTHERN OCEAN, DECEMBER 2014

24 December.

It is one of the longest days in the southern hemisphere. On the northern side of the continent of Antarctica there are only a few hours of dusk following sunset before the sun appears again and paints the first faint strokes of blue shadow across the sky.

In gentle swells the two ships move on their course headed northwest. Inside the *Bob Barker* it is still damp and chaotic after the storm. In the evening, oven-baked vegetables, roast potatoes and tofu turkey – a roast turkey substitute consisting of tofu, vegetable broth and bread, herbs and spices – are served. Almost the entire crew of the *Bob Barker* are vegan. For the members of Sea Shepherd, saving one species while simultaneously eating another is considered to be less than consistent.

For the early explorers, Christmas in the Antarctic was a highly treasured period, offering a break from the toil, uncertainty and usual diet of penguin and seal. On board James Cook's the *Resolution*, Christmas was celebrated with "drunkenness and boxing". Roald Amundsen and his crew celebrated Christmas south of the Kerguelen Islands, just a few nautical miles away from where the *Thunder* and the *Bob Barker* are now located. On Christmas Eve, he shut down the engine on the *Fram*. When the crew came down to the lounge which was decorated with coloured lights and a Christmas tree, they were so clean shaven and well-groomed that he barely recognized them. "We had all received something to help sustain us when the requirements of daily life imposed themselves once again," Amundsen wrote.[1]

In the evening, the crew members of the *Bob Barker* are granted a five minute conversation with their families. For a brief moment, Captain Hammarstedt thinks of the famous football match between German and British soldiers who laid down their arms for a few hours on Christmas in 1914.[2] He considers calling the *Thunder* and wishing them a Happy Christmas, but he does not act on the thought. Instead, he has a short conversation over the phone with his family. They are gathered in the small Swedish town of Sigtuna. They are also eating a vegetarian Christmas dinner, his mother tells him.

The first clear memory he has of his mother is in front of a window in Beijing. He was four years old and he watched in amazement as the tanks rolled down towards Tiananmen Square.[3] Then his mother came and lifted him away. She subsequently packed all the family possessions into four suit-cases and hurried to the airport.

Hammarstedt's father worked for the Swedish industrial group ABB, living an increasingly nomadic existence at the company's foreign offices. When Peter Hammarstedt was seven years old, the family moved to the sleepy town of New Hope in Pennsylvania. It would turn out to be years of personal hardship. He was short, frail and wore eyeglasses that covered half his face. He bought the right clothes at the wrong time, and his boyish voice whined and slid all over the place. He also became a vegetarian after a classmate told him about how hens and chickens were bred in narrow cages. He was friendless and was tormented by his classmates. At home he tried to hide the bruises from his mother. He soon developed a compulsion to stand up for the defenceless. Once a month his parents took him to a bookstore in New Jersey, where he found his way to the Afro-American section and started reading in depth about the Black Panther movement. He travelled to California to find John Carlos, one of the two track and field athletes who had done the Black Power salute during the medal ceremony at the summer Olympics in 1968. Hammarstedt wanted to know why Carlos had chosen to utilize the moment in a way that would change his life and make him a traitor in the eyes of many Americans.[4]

When the young Christian boy Hammarstedt as a 14 year old received 200 dollars from his father, he decided to donate it to a charitable cause. Through an Internet search he found the civil rights movements the American Civil Liberties Union and Free Tibet, and the special interest lobby group the National Rifle Association. While he was searching online for worthy recipients of his dollars, he came across a film showing a group of Greenpeace activists in a rubber dinghy. They were trying to stop the Japanese factory ship the *Nisshin Maru* from hauling a whale on board.

That was when he made up his mind. He wanted to be one of them, like the activists in the dinghy who risked their lives in the fight for what they believed in.

At the age of 17 Hammarstedt moved back to Stockholm. The first thing he did was to seek out the team that carried out direct actions in Greenpeace. In 2003, immediately after Iceland had resumed whaling operations, the Greenpeace ship the *Arctic Sunrise* was in Stockholm. While Hammarstedt was on night duty on the ship, he overheard everyone on board discussing what the competing organization Sea Shepherd would do with the Icelanders. Sea Shepherd was a small and scruffy organization: unpredictable, controversial and militant. This was where Hammarstedt wanted to be. He sent in an application, but never received any reply. For a month he called Sea Shepherd every day. Then Hammarstedt suddenly received word that he should come to Seattle to report for duty on the campaign ship the *Farley Mowat* as a seaman. He is now celebrating his tenth Christmas in a row in the Antarctic.

In the messroom on the *Thunder*, Christmas dinner is served at noon. The crew and the officers who are not on duty eat their meal together. On the menu is split cod, prepared in a stew with cabbage and potatoes. A roast turkey is also put out and a few bottles of red wine. But what could appear to be a low-key holiday mood, is in reality an uneasy uncertainty about what will take place in the upcoming days or weeks. Some are discussing how the evening will unfold for those who are at home. Nobody sings, nobody exchanges gifts and nobody says out loud what most of them are thinking: What is going to happen now?

Now there is only one man who can decide the fate of the 40 men who on this Christmas Eve are sitting and daydreaming about a life far away from the dark wood panelling of the messroom on the *Thunder*. The ship owner. *El Armador*. Not everyone on the *Thunder* knows who he is, not by a long shot; some members of the crew had caught a glimpse of him and his business partners when they unloaded their illegal catch in a disreputable harbour in Malaysia or Indonesia.

Those of the crew on the *Thunder* who are closest to him know that he is firm in his faith and that it is very likely that on this particular evening he will light the traditional oil lamps in his home and prepare a holiday meal of shellfish and ham. Later he will put his arm around his wife and lead her up the stairs of the local church. There the prosperous and respected businessman will be greeted with nods of recognition and soft-spoken good wishes. He will then allow himself to sink into the midnight mass as if nothing has happened.

13

THE SHIPMASTER
CHIMBOTE, PERU,
NOVEMBER 2014

As the *Thunder* sailed toward the Antarctic in November, a stocky 47-year-old with a broad, thickset face and a wild, mane of black hair boarded the bus that would carry him from his home city of Chimbote to Lima, the capital of Peru. There was nothing to disclose his identity as a ship's officer on a vessel that for years had been fishing in secret in the Antarctic. In his breast pocket he had a plane ticket and a reference from the ship agent in Malaysia.

"It is hereby confirmed that Mr. Alberto Zavaleta Salas is employed by F.C.S. Trading & Fishery. He will travel to Hang Nadim, Batam to sign on with the vessel MV *Kunlun*."

When the bus started moving and turned out onto the barren desert plains encircling the Pan American Highway, Alberto Zavaleta Salas left one catastrophe behind to travel into another.[1]

Chimbote was once a sleepy fishing village with an inviting harbour and a good selection of hotels for seaside holiday-makers. At dusk the fleet of brightly coloured fishing boats sailed out into one of the world's most productive banks to fish the Peruvian anchovy. On one of these ships, Alberto Zavaleta Salas used to accompany his grandfather and later his father, both captains. He was born into the world's largest fishery enterprise, the Peruvian "anchovy boom", which would transform the slumbering Chimbote into Peru's most powerful fishing port. When the fishing was industrialized and the news spread of the enormous fortunes that accompanied the catches, droves of restless men found their way to the city. They came from the slum districts of Lima and the impoverished villages at the foot of the Andes mountains in search of a wage and a new life in the protein bonanza.

The whores and fortune hunters followed and the slum districts grew on the mountainsides and the perimeters of the desert. In the city, which formerly was blessed with a single traffic light and only one paved street, lorries now thundered past loaded down with anchovies on the way to the more than 50 factories where the fish was boiled down into fishmeal. At its peak the anchovy was "the most heavily exploited fish in world history".[2]

A penetrating stench of rotten fish hung over the city. It came seeping out along with the greyish-black smoke from the smokestacks of the fishmeal factories, and forced its way into every corner of Chimbote. It was said that even the steaks there smelled and tasted of fish.

Wastewater and fish blood were pumped straight into the ocean. Allergies and skin diseases spread through the neighbourhoods closest to the factories, protests were countered with imprisonments and some of the more prominent environmentalists were even accused of belonging to terrorist organizations.

One tragedy would follow on the heels the other. When El Niño came barrelling in across the coast of Peru, the current of warm, oligotrophic water led to the collapse of the already severely decimated anchovy stock. One after another the fishmeal factories shut down. In the end the destitution and unemployment was so extensive that assistance organizations had to distribute food to thousands of fishermen and port and factory workers in Chimbote.[3] Alberto Zavaleta Salas continued sailing ships that fished close to his home city. There was fish to be found, but the largest ship owners were awarded the quotas and Zavaleta Salas would sometimes be out at sea for a week and then remain inactive on land for a month. Although he was a shipmaster, in the end it was not even possible to be hired as part of the ordinary crew.

It is difficult to say whether what happened next was a blessing or a curse for Alberto Zavaleta Salas. After having subsisted on random odd jobs, he was hired as a captain on the Kenyan-flagged fishing vessel the *Sakoba*, which operated off the coast of East Africa. When he was home on shore leave in Peru, the *Sakoba* was boarded by Somali pirates and sailed towards Harardhere, 300 kilometres northeast of Mogdadishu – the dusty fishing village that had been given the nickname "the piracy capital of the world".

At a loss, out of work and with unending money disputes with his ex-wife, Zavaleta Salas once again found himself wandering around Chimbote. In the spring of 2012 he came across an advert from the Panama registered company Red

Line Ventures, which needed crew for a fishing vessel. When he contacted the ship agent, he learned that the ship the *Huang He 22* was going to the Antarctic. That was an opportunity he did not want to miss out on.

The *Huang He 22* would later be known as the pirate ship *Kunlun* wanted by Interpol – one of "The Bandit 6", a ship observed several times in the vicinity of the *Thunder*.

Alberto Zavaleta Salas is one of the few pirate captains ever who have dared to come forward with their story.

Late in the evening on one of the last days of November in 2014, Alberto Zavaleta Salas lands at the airport in Batam. A dinghy takes him out to the *Kunlun*'s anchoring site, a one-and-a-half-hour journey from the coast. As he climbs up the ladder, he notices that the name of the ship is no longer the *Kunlun*, but instead the *Taishan*.

Although on paper he is a shipmaster, he is assigned an ordinary cabin that he must share with a taciturn and melancholy chief engineer from Ribeira, Spain.

It is Zavaleta Sala's fifth expedition to the Antarctic, and this time he notices that there is an uneasy atmosphere on the ship. They have problems procuring enough fuel, there is a mix-up in the order for provisions and just hours before they are about to set sail to the south, one of the other Peruvian officers decides to sign off.

"Either things have already gone to hell or they are going to hell. I would rather wait for four months on land than go along," he says to Zavaleta Salas before disappearing in the dinghy.

Serafín Vidal, the shipping company employee with responsibility for crew recruitment, wants people who don't ask too many questions, who are not plagued by problems from the past and who can collaborate and keep their mouths shut. The Spanish officers on the *Kunlun* are paid between 6,000 and 8,000 dollars a month plus a share of the catch. As a shipmaster, Alberto Zavaleta Salas' salary is 2,700 dollars a month. He sends 2,000 of this home to his wife and spends the rest on cigarettes and telephone costs. On a cargo ship he could have earned far more and without risk. In addition to feeling irritated about the pay, he has constant confrontations with the fishing captain José Regueiro Sevilla, the ship owner family's most trusted man on the *Kunlun*.

Alberto Zavaleta Salas fears that it is he who will be sacrificed should the ship be arrested, that it is he who will have to rot in jail in an unknown port, while the Spanish officers will go free. He therefore carries a mobile phone in the pocket of his trousers at all times. He secretly records fragments of conversations on the bridge. When he is instructed to tear up pieces of paper, he gathers them and hides them in his cabin. When he is asked to delete emails, he saves them. He secures pictures of the officers who do not want to be photographed and he films the *Kunlun*'s fish factory, the effective assembly line that sends millions of dollars straight into the pockets of the ship owner's family. One day he may find use for the recordings.

On the voyage out of the Riau Archipelago the *Kunlun* maintains a good distance away from Singapore, where there may be coast guard vessels. Then they set their course for the Cocos Islands – the atoll located between Australia and Sri Lanka. Zavaleta Salas knows the sailing route well; it is the same every time.

In 28 days they will reach the ice edge by the Banzare Bank.

On the evening of 19 December, 300 nautical miles off the Cocos Islands, they change the name from the *Taishan* to the *Kunlun*. The ship is equipped with two sets of documents; one of these is hidden behind a trap door in the cabin of one of the Indonesian crew members. On board there are also stamped and signed ship's documents that the officers can fill out themselves if they should need a new identity quickly. They have a miniature printing press in the form of a simple set of stamps and a cardboard box full of flags from countries such as Equatorial Guinea, Mauritania and Panama.

Sensitive information from computers on the bridge is stored on mobile hard drives that can be easily hidden or thrown into the ocean and everything in the way of receipts from the ship agent in Batam is shredded and thrown overboard. Should the information fall into the wrong hands, it could lead to disclosing the identity of the ship's true owner.

In the course of the past ten years, the ship has been assigned at least ten names and been flagged in at least five countries. The *Kunlun* is a floating and inveterately persistent offender, a pioneer in what would become the world's most lucrative poaching of fish. The ship was fined in South Africa for illegal shark cargo; it was blacklisted and denied access by ports all over the world. Finally, the *Kunlun* was so open and shameless in its devastating activities that the trawler was debated in the Australian parliament.[4]

The ship now also has the eyes of the Australian authorities on it. An Orion plane from Australia's Air Force sees three ships pass the Cocos Islands on the way into the Antarctic.[5] Along with the *Kunlun* the flight crew also sees the ship that was once painted white, the *Songhua*.

The true commander on the *Songhua* is the aging and legendary fishing captain "El Diablo" from Ribeira in Spain, a hardy veteran of the Antarctic. He has received the nickname for his ruthless treatment of his crew. But "The Devil" also has his more light-hearted qualities. He is the only one of the fishing captains who regularly invites his crew out on the town when they put in at port. The *Songhua* is also the youngest of the three vessels, and for the insurance agents on land who receive detailed reports on how much fish is hauled on board, the *Songhua* is the hardest worker.

The captain of the third ship, the *Yongding*, is the 40-something Juan Manuel Núñez Robles, a man with a fondness for whisky and the good life. He will later claim that the expedition destroyed both his life and his marriage.[6]

The *Perlon* is already at Banzare Bank, where the fishing captain has started what will be one of his better seasons.

The *Viking*, the first ship to be wanted by Interpol, is also out on a mission. Few know where the vessel is located, but on board a wild Christmas party is being planned at which cold beer, sparkling wine, barbecued meat and ice cream will be served and they will dance the *jenka*, a Finnish folk dance.[7]

Soon Alberto Zavaleta Salas will sail into the largest ship search in the history of the Antarctic, a handful of ships caught up in a game of cat and mouse at the bottom of the world.

The pursuit of the *Thunder* has already been underway for one week.

14

DESOLATION ISLAND
KERGUELEN ISLANDS, FRENCH SOUTHERN TERRITORIES, DECEMBER 2014

During the week between Christmas and New Year the *Thunder* sets its course to the north and sails down the middle of the strait running through the French controlled outposts of the Crozet and Kerguelen Islands. The ocean is glassy and still, and the ships move steadily through the water.

Peter Hammarstedt calls their course "fraudulent", contacts Sea Shepherd's office in France and instructs them to forward an email to the French government.

"As a member of CCAMLR, responsible for protecting the untouched marine ecosystem of Antarctica, we implore the French government to send a naval vessel to escort the *Thunder* back to a port where the ship can be inspected and the pirates held accountable," Hammarstedt writes from the bridge of the *Bob Barker*.[1]

He also informs the French research station on the Kerguelen Islands of the ships' position. His hope is that France will send out one of the naval vessels that the nation has stationed on the island of Réunion.

What Hammarstedt doesn't know is that the French authorities have already been alerted. As the ships approached the French islands, a message was immediately sent from Interpol. "You have a bad guy in your waters soon. Get ready for it."[2]

There are 500 nautical miles between the Crozet Islands and Kerguelen Islands, and the *Thunder* is sailing down the middle in between them. As long as the ships remain in international waters, the French naval vessels stay put.

The Kerguelen Islands lie 3,000 kilometres from the closest populated area, silently tortured by the winds from the west. The brutal storms constantly thrashing upon the landscape do not relent even during the night. The islands' bald mountains loom out of the sea where the polar air meets the warmer water from the Indian Ocean – the Antarctic convergence. The confrontation can whisk the waves up to heights of 15 metres and produce winds blowing with a force of more than 100 kilometres an hour.

The French Baron Yves-Joseph de Kerguelen had led an expedition to the coast of Iceland and was accustomed to navigating ice-cold seas. Under orders from King Ludvig XV, in February 1772 his mission was to find the undiscovered continent that had to lie somewhere in the south.

Based on the accounts of the explorer Paulmier de Gonneville, the French believed that there was an enormous southern land mass that balanced the globe. Only a decade after Columbus' return to Europe, Gonneville sailed from France to find a route to India. When he came home, he reported that for six months he had lived in a country far to the south that was flowing with milk and honey and which France should not hesitate to colonize. (Gonneville had probably been in Brazil.)[3]

Kerguelen's commission was to find this unknown continent and establish friendly relations with its inhabitants. After 12 days of heavy sailing through hail, dense snowfall and a cold that Kerguelen described as the most bitter he had ever experienced, he glimpsed a lofty and vast tongue of land emerging out of the fog. They waited two days for the winds to calm before the expedition attempted to send a dinghy ashore, but it was seized by a current, beaten against the cliffs and thrown back to the companion vessel the *Gros Ventre*, the mast of which was broken in the collision.

When they finally came ashore, there was no sign of human life or land animals between the steep mountains, only colonies of penguins.

After 15 minutes the procession buried a bottle containing documents which, on behalf of the French crown, made a claim for the land they called "La France Australe".

Kerguelen claimed to have discovered a fifth continent with soil that could be compared to that of southern France. All manner of vegetables and grains could be cultivated there, along with lumbering activity and the extraction of salt. Kerguelen described the temperate climate; he told of the forests and green valleys, which could only mean that the land was inhabited and cultivated by a primitive people.

He claimed that in the course of six years he would succeed in building a metropolis on the Antarctic continent he had discovered.

Although rumours were in circulation about how Kerguelen's celebrated discovery was a flight of fancy, the French government bestowed the Order Chevalier de Saint Louis upon him and decided that he was to be quickly sent back to colonize the continent in the south. It was to be the proudest French scientific expedition in history, involving three ships and a total of 700 men. This time Kerguelen would continue east and sail around the whole continent. In the overloaded and damp holds below deck, worms and rot got into the supplies and on the voyage south he lost two of the topsails. When they reached the Southern Ocean, the crew was so devastated by scurvy and the meagre rations that several of them fainted on deck from the cold.

Kerguelen's only pleasure was his 16-year-old mistress whom he had smuggled on board and who would probably be the first woman to sail into the Southern Ocean.

When Kerguelen once again reached the snow-covered island that was to bear his name, on 6 September 1773, he personally refused to go ashore, but instead sent one of his officers, who noted that there were some harbours there fit for use.

The great French expedition turned into a fiasco. Thirty-four of the crew had died, and they had not found anything but a godforsaken island which was mockingly referred to as the "Penguins Republic". The humiliation led to the formation of a commission that concluded Kerguelen was a fraud. Initially he was condemned to 20 years in prison, a sentence that was later changed to six years.

When Captain James Cook laid anchor by the Kerguelen Islands in 1778, he elected to name it "Desolation Island". But despite the dismal barrenness of the islands, its seal population was abundant. Then Norwegian, American and British sealers descended upon the islands and did their best to wipe out the population.

In 1996 the toothfish pirates sailed into the waters around the Kerguelen Islands. The ships were outfitted with advanced radar systems to ensure early warning of any patrol ships and during the night they loaded the illegal catch onto a cargo ship. When the French authorities understood the scope of the poaching operations, they sent down a battleship and invested in new surveillance systems on the Kerguelen and Crozet Islands.[4]

It was in the waters around the Kerguelen Islands that the Spanish family that would become the most notorious of all the toothfish pirates, the clan of Vidal Armadores, got its first taste of the white gold.[5] On the ships that plundered the marine regions near the Kerguelen Islands, a striking number of the shipmasters and officers were from the Spanish province of Galicia.

On the bridge of the *Thunder* lies a map that testifies to the fact that also the old Norwegian-built trawler had fished by the French outpost on former expeditions. On the map, which is labelled "Kapp Norvegia to Iles Kerguelen", the fishing grounds around the Kerguelen Islands are marked in yellow ink.

15

THE PHANTOM SHIP
THE INDIAN OCEAN, DECEMBER 2014

Like a phantom ship, the *Thunder* continues north. Nobody moves on deck, but now and then the officers on the *Bob Barker* see a shadow, catch a glimpse of a face glancing quickly down at them from the bridge. When the ship starts constantly changing its course or strategy, it is right after lunch. Is it because somebody has just woken up in Europe and is now sending orders to the Southern Ocean? Lloyds List, the company with the largest database of shipping traffic in the world has no information about where the *Thunder* has been since 2010.[1]

From his hiding place on land, Sea Shepherd's founder Paul Watson is increasingly frustrated over how the international community fails to come to the *Bob Barker*'s aid.

"Interpol states that the nations have united to identify this poacher, yet none of these nations seem to be interested that Sea Shepherd has not only identified the poacher but also escorted the vessel from the CCAMLR region and has seized the net. Instead of supporting this effort by Sea Shepherd, the

Australian government is condemning Sea Shepherd's inter-vention," he writes on social media.[2]

Paul Watson's theory is that the *Thunder* and the five other ships being searched for in the Southern Ocean are connected to Vidal Armadores – the most powerful clan of what is called *la mafia gallega* – the Galician mafia. Watson also implies that there is "somebody" who is not interested in stopping the *Thunder*.

"Sea Shepherd believes that despite all the talk of appre-hending the *Thunder* there is very little enthusiasm to actually stop the ship from operating. Why? Well, first the ship has reportedly earned more than USD 60 million on illegal fishing since 2006. That kind of money buys influence. In addition, organized crime syndicates in Galicia, Spain involving Antonio and Toño Vidal and others, own and operate many of these illegal poachers and may actually control the operations of the *Thunder*," he writes on one of the last days of December 2014.

In the 1990s, Watson wreaked havoc in Norwegian waters. He crashed the ship *Whales Forever* into the Norwegian coast guard vessel the KV *Andenæs* and was charged with negli-gent navigation, a fraudulent distress call and for entering Norwegian territorial waters without permission. Now the bureaucrats at the Ministry of Trade and Fisheries are satisfied that Sea Shepherd is occupied with something more useful than actions targeting Norwegian whaling. A Norwegian local politician goes so far as to claim that Watson and Sea Shepherd should be treated as an international terrorist organization, along the lines of Baader-Meinhof, Al-Qaida and IS.[3]

On the same day that the *Bob Barker* set sail for the Southern Ocean, Sea Shepherd was warned by research scientists that boarding an illegal fishing vessel could constitute grounds for criminal prosecution for piracy and vandalism of private property. Sea Shepherd had no authority and the organization's "citizen's arrest" was not recognized by international law. In addition, they could be charged with illegal fishing themselves for hauling in the nets of others, the scientists warned.[4]

The nations of Operation Spillway cannot accept an environmental organization assuming a role as enforcer of the law. Sea Shepherd can never step in for the police. And it is more than legal arguments and general hostility towards Sea Shepherd that causes Australia, New Zealand, Norway and the USA to hesitate about sending ships to compel the *Thunder* to put into a port. In the country that has the world's largest fleet of battleships, they have no faith in such a mission. It will be a "complicated mess", the USA's man at Operation Spillway, Stuart Cory argues. What will they do with the crew? Put them in jail? They haven't committed any crime in the USA. And what will they do with the ship? Nobody wants a rusty old hulk full of asbestos and other environmental toxins sitting in their harbour. It is not the crew and the ship they are after, it is the owners.

"You don't arrest the car of the bank robber, you arrest the robber," Cory argues.[5]

It is New Year's Eve and the *Thunder* appears to be completely dark.

"Let's have a look at them," Peter Hammarstedt says and orders the crew below deck and two photographers on deck.

Then the *Bob Barker* moves into action and puts in close to the *Thunder*'s starboard side. The photographers succeed in capturing the face of a 50–60 year old man. When the officers later move outdoors, their faces are hidden behind ski masks. The captain on the *Thunder* speaks Spanish, but with an accent. On the net floats they'd left behind when they fled, a Spanish name was engraved: A Poutada, a fishing gear company in Ribeira, Spain.

Where do they come from? Who is controlling the operation? And who is giving the orders?

16

THE WALL OF DEATH
BATAM, INDONESIA,
OCTOBER 2014

At one o'clock in the morning on 21 October 2014, the *Thunder* set out on its final voyage. For weeks the ship had been docked at an anchorage site outside Batam, a restless, free trade zone just south of Singapore. To prevent disclosure of the vessel's true identity, its name was now the *Batu 1*.

A half year earlier, the ship had been put under arrest in Malaysia. The crew had sat in their cabins for months, smoking, playing cards, trading films and trying to keep the heat at bay while waiting for word regarding their fate. Finally, the ship was released upon payment of a fine of USD 60,000.

After the problems with Interpol, the blacklists and the arrests the ship owner had tried to sell the *Thunder*. A European couple had inspected the ship in Singapore and expressed a willingness to purchase it, but the deal was never closed. Now it was as if the ship owner had given up on maintenance of the *Thunder*. Even the Internet connection on board had been removed.[1]

A bunkering vessel had supplied the *Thunder* with almost 600 tons of diesel. The officers were flown in via Istanbul and transported out in groups on the ship agent's dinghies. They were the same as always, hard-working and persevering men from Spain, Chile and Portugal. Men who didn't ask questions and who followed orders.

The majority of them had lived most of their lives at sea, and either could not or were not willing to do anything else. In the Spanish region of Galicia it had become difficult to find young fishermen willing to sacrifice months at sea on a dangerous and complicated fishing operation on board a vessel that was ill-equipped for the uncompromising Southern Ocean. For those who signed on, the pay was generous. On the *Thunder* the Latin American officers earned between 2,000 and 3,000 dollars a month; the Spaniards double that amount. Many received a bonus for every ton of toothfish. The ship owner also treated each of the officers to five trays of Coca-Cola and six cases of beer.

The deck crew was from Indonesia, where the workforce was cheap and reliable. But not indomitable: after the last voyage several of the Indonesian crew had rebelled and physically attacked one of the officers. Now only three of the 30 Indonesians on board had previously sailed with the *Thunder*.

Although the *Thunder*'s hull was bleeding rust, the bridge was clean and recently washed. The dark woodwork around the instrument panel was still shiny. Next to the instrument switches, instructions in Spanish had been printed out using an old-fashioned Dymo label maker. On a shelf on the port side there was tea, coffee, clean cups and a kettle. There was also a mini-fridge and an ergometric bicycle. Oil-filled radiators that had not been used for a long time were bound securely to the bridge on either side. Only the mate's chair testified to the *Thunder*'s age and the ravages of time; the blue synthetic material was cracked and provisionally patched up.

The fishing captain Juan Manuel Patiño Lampon moved into the largest cabin. It had a small library, a separate telephone for the bridge, toilet, shower, dining area, a small office, a TV and a bed all of 150 centimetres wide. No frivolous luxury on board the *Thunder*. The captain, the 47-year-old Chilean Luis Alfonso Rubio Cataldo, had to make do with a smaller cabin afore. Behind his back the crew called him a lunatic due to his fiery temperament. The Spanish first mate Juan Antonio Olveira Brion, also trained as a shipmaster, had sailed with the *Thunder* for only one year. The Chief Engineer Agustín Dosil Rey was respected for his proficiency and was one of the few who knew how to enjoy the life on shore when the *Thunder* was docked. The quiet First Engineer Luis Miguel Pérez Fernández had said farewell to his two young daughters at home in Spain a few days before. Two years would pass before he would have the chance to see them again.

After having struggled for hours at trying to disengage and raise the anchor, the ship finally set its course north. Instead of sailing through the narrow Sunda Strait, they sailed the long way round, north through Malacca and around the northern tip of Sumatra before continuing south in the vast and less trafficked Indian Ocean.[2] When they reached the latitude of Jakarta, the Portuguese deck officer Manuel Agonia Dias Marques received the order to bring up one of the name plates stowed away in the room where work clothes and boots were stored. The *Batu 1* became the *Thunder*.

The voyage down to the Southern Ocean was routine in nature and uneventful. The shifts ran from eight until lunch was served in the messroom at half past eleven. Then a new shift began, lasting from two until seven, then a shower and dinner. An officer passed the time with beer, hard liquor and action films in his cabin, while most of the others were busy preparing the nets. They were custom-made and had been loaded on board in unassembled parts at the harbour in Batam – more than 60 kilometres of synthetic nets and 10 kilometres of mainlines. The total length of the net was seven times the height of Mount Everest. In its entirety, the gear weighed more than 70 tons.

In the course of the voyage, the net was assembled according to the fishing captain's instructions. Every fishing captain has his own way of constructing the gillnets, his own signature technique for the splices, knots and components. The net is his masterpiece.

The fishing captain Lampon used 50-metre chains of nets that were spliced together until they were 15–20 kilometres long. At each end the 7-metre high net was anchored using heavy steel shackles. The mainline, which would descend to depths of almost 2,000 metres, was made of spliced ropework that grew thinner and thinner towards the bottom, so the net did not become too heavy and difficult to handle. The final gillnet would be so effective that it captured everything that came swimming its way. That is why it was called "the wall of death".

When the *Thunder* reached the Banzare Bank, they dropped the first four chains of nets. The catch of a mere four tons of toothfish made Lampon uneasy and despondent. He walked back and forth across deck without telling anyone what he was thinking. He knew that the *Perlon*, another pirate vessel, was located six nautical miles away, but decided against calling her up. Lampon did not want other fishing captains to know where he was fishing.

Then he put the *Thunder* in motion.

Slowly, it glided across the Banzare Bank and Lampon's gaze remained glued to the sonar until he found a new deep hollow where there could be toothfish at the edges. His subsequent attempts struck gold. The cold storage room was filled with 30 tons of first-class fish. On the black market, the fish was worth half a million dollars. Nonetheless, it was still far from enough.

, As they were in the process of putting out another net, Lampon noticed a dot on the radar moving quickly towards them. Was it the *Perlon*?

"It looks like we've got company," he said. He left the bridge, hurried down the stairs from the wheelhouse and knocked on the sleeping captain's door.

At first they thought it was a patrol ship. Then one of the workers on the production line of the *Thunder*'s fish factory recognized the ship, its rectangular blue, black and grey camouflage paint and the predatory shark-jaws on the hull. He had been watching the Sea Shepherd series *Whale Wars* on Animal Planet, and on the bridge he explained about Sea Shepherd's perseverance and fierce confrontations with the Japanese whalers. When the captain shut himself into the navigation room to consult with the ship owner over the phone, Lampon gave the order for the crew to get to work. The factory was to be washed down, fish heads, entrails and waste were to be thrown overboard. Any fish on board was to be put into cold storage immediately.

"*Pica!* Cut the nets," Lampon ordered.

The Portuguese boatswain found a knife and started sawing at the thick ropes. In a rush and on turbulent seas it was a perilous job. Should a foot or arm become tangled up in the ropes, the next stop would be in the 2,000-metre depths.

A flock of shrieking gadfly petrels soon gathered above the *Thunder*.

One of the lowest ranking officers in the ship's hierarchy thought they should give in and follow Peter Hammarstedt's order to sail with the *Bob Barker* to Australia. Among the Indonesians a confused atmosphere reigned. They knew they were fishing illegally and for a long time believed they were being chased by a battleship.

In the navigation room, four of the Spanish-speaking officers convened in front of a half-metre tall red and gold Madonna figure hanging on the wall behind the map table. None of them were counting on much help from the other side. They knew the ship chasing them was much faster than their own, so they would try and enlist the assistance of the elements to give their pursuers the slip. Following a brief consultation, Lampon took the wheel and set their course for a belt of floating drift ice. But the sight of the first floes of pack ice before the bow gave them pause. Should they venture through the ice? Shipmaster Cataldo opposed the manoeuvre. With a "do whatever the hell you want with the ship," he escaped into the messroom.

As he was eating his evening meal, he felt the collisions with the ice shudder through the vessel. Still, the *Bob Barker* didn't get stuck as they had hoped. After two hours in the ice the ship owner called and ordered them to set their course for open waters. Then their pursuer would give up.

A storm front coming in from the north could be seen on the radar. It could be their salvation. A ship of the *Thunder*'s size and stability could manage the storm better than the smaller *Bob Barker*. When they finally reached the storm, they could see their pursuer struggling out of the swells as if gasping for breath, before descending once more into the troughs between the waves. The white shark jaw, however, popped up again. The *Thunder*'s helmsman said he wanted to continue regardless of what happened to the *Bob Barker* in the storm.

But the *Bob Barker* attached itself to the *Thunder*'s stern and held its own.

17

THE WORLD RECORD

THE INDIAN OCEAN,
JANUARY 2015

"We have broken the world record for chasing a poacher!"

In the lounge of the *Bob Barker* applause breaks out when Peter Hammarstedt gathers the crew for the morning meeting on 8 January. When there was no news to report, Hammarstedt turned the mission into a story unrelated to the daily routines, a story in which he can personally control the dramaturgy and create a feeling of moving forward also when things are at a standstill. In the past few days the *Thunder* has been lying virtually dead in the water.

The lounge is the ship's clubhouse and museum, not unlike a common room in a student dormitory. A flat screen television hangs above a shelf containing a clutter of worn out DVDs, and a battered acoustic guitar rests in a corner. Along the bulkheads hang portraits of all the activists who have served on board, beside a bamboo cane thrown by a Japanese whaler. The shabby, shapeless couches invite sinking into and the shelves overhead are full of reading materials. The book many of the crew want to read is the documentary about the search for the fishing vessel the *Viarsa 1*, the story of the last world record.[1]

In 2003 a patrol vessel from Australia chased the ship out of Australian waters in the southern part of the Indian Ocean and all the way to the southern tip of Africa. The chase, which went on for 21 days, has since been referred to as the world's longest pursuit at sea. Hammarstedt has studied the history of the *Viarsa 1* in detail,[2] and he has no intention of repeating the mistakes of that episode. The *Viarsa 1* was taken carrying 97 tons of toothfish. The vessel was observed within Australian waters, but after criminal procedures lasting several years in Australia, the ship's officers were acquitted. The prosecuting authorities did not have the floats and fishing gear and could not prove that the fish was poached in their waters.

That is why Operation Icefish now consists of two vessels: one to resume the chase and one to haul in the nets and secure evidence.

For Hammarstedt it has virtually been an obsession that the chase after the *Thunder* would go on for longer than the *Viarsa 1* chase. He has Sea Shepherd's press division send an email to the Guinness Book of World Records.[3] He now hopes that the chase is moving towards an imminent conclusion and that the authorities of the African nations located to the north will find the courage to force the *Thunder* in to land. Hammarstedt wants to return to the Banzare Bank to find more members of "The Bandit 6".

To the north lies the Mozambique Channel, the strait between Mozambique and Madagascar which is so narrow that it is impossible to navigate without moving into one country's exclusive economic zones. If the *Thunder* decides to sail there, not only Mozambique and Madagascar, but also France, which controls several of the islands in the channel, will have the hunter and its prey in their national waters.

From Interpol's headquarters in Lyon an alert has been issued informing of the approach of the *Thunder* and the *Bob Barker* and in Mozambique the Director General of Fisheries is putting all ports from Maputo in the south to Pemba in the north in a state of preparedness. The patrol vessel the *Antillas Reefer*, a former pirate craft rebuilt using Norwegian and Icelandic development aid funds, is being prepared to receive the *Thunder*.[4]

"Mozambique leads the charge against the *Thunder*," Peter Hammarstedt writes in an article on Sea Shepherd's website.[5] He has a number of ulterior motives for the article. He wants to goad the rich, Western nations, who he feels should have forced the *Thunder* into shore a long time ago. And he wants the captain of the *Thunder* to know that sailing north towards East Africa will serve no purpose.

A certain fear also reigns amongst the crew of the *Bob Barker* that the *Thunder* will set its course for the coast of Somalia. A ship named after an American multimillionaire can easily attract undesired attention.[6] East African pirates will probably be far more interested in the *Bob Barker* than in the *Thunder*.

On the *Thunder* several of the officers are starting to lose faith in the shipmaster's strategy. So far he has lost every duel. Now the two ships are slowly circling each other in the southern part of the Indian Ocean, like two boxers trying to find their opponent's weak spot.

18

"THE ONLY SHERIFF IN TOWN"
THE INDIAN OCEAN, JANUARY 2015

The *Thunder* is performing strange manoeuvres. The ship moves in circles, directing a searchlight on the *Bob Barker*, then suddenly stops and drifts for a few hours. Then the mate puts the ship in motion again, heading for a point in the middle of nowhere.

Every day the *Thunder*'s captain receives an update from his wife, who is sitting home in the couple's luxury apartment in Viña del Mar in Chile and following the chase on the Internet. Now he knows Hammarstedt by name and from his photograph and he knows that the *Thunder* – the ship that as few people as possible were supposed to know about – is currently one of the world's most photographed vessels.

He is desperate, he drinks and he is beginning to come apart at the seams, Hammarstedt thinks, after having called up the *Thunder* to receive an explanation for the confusing light signals. The *Thunder*'s captain is clearly drunk and as usual he refuses to give his name. Before hanging up he calls

Hammarstedt an idiot and says that he doesn't have the authority to pursue him.

What worries Hammarstedt more than any of Cataldo's excesses is the photograph he sees on "Marine Traffic". A China flagged ship has sets its course in their direction. It can be on the way to a research base in Antarctica, or it can be on the way to help the *Thunder*. Hammarstedt calls an extraordinary crew meeting in the lounge.

"Last night we saw a Chinese vessel heading in our direction. That brought to mind the possibility that the *Thunder* may try to offload their catch at sea. Alternatively they get fuel or water or other supplies from another vessel. If they do refuel at sea, we must assume that they might outlast us. That is a situation we can't allow to occur. In the same regard, we can't have them offloading to another vessel, then the physical evidence of the crime is gone. I won't let them take off with this fish. And I won't allow them to refuel," Hammarstedt says.

If a ship were to come to the *Thunder*'s aid, Hammarstedt would launch the dinghies and cut the fenders off the supply ship so the two could not position themselves side by side. His final recourse will be to put the *Bob Barker* between the ships.

"But there is a possibility that they will strike our ship, and there is a possibility of a collision. They are unpredictable. It is important for me to know where the whole crew is at all times. Is anybody uncomfortable with this plan?"

Nobody answers Hammarstedt's question.

"Any likelihood of the *Thunder* tossing anything overboard?" one of the crew asks.

"We know that after the fishing season they have millions of dollars' worth of catch in their hold, and that is not something they will give up lightly," Hammarstedt replies.

There are quotes hanging on the walls of the great cabin from classical authors which Hammarstedt now and then will recite for the crew at the morning meetings. But more than anything else he loves his police metaphors.

"If a drug dealer has a lot of cocaine on him he only flushes it down the toilet when the police are right at the door," he says as he returns to the bridge.

There he learns that the New Zealand Navy is now searching for three members of "The Bandit 6".

For the *Kunlun* the first days of fishing have been wonderful. The fog snatches at the peaks of the ice bergs around the ship, the air temperature is a comfortable five below zero Celsius and the waves are not rising to more than 2 or 3 metres. It is 12 January, and before the day comes to an end, they will haul on board another four chains of nets. In the relatively calm weather, this will take eight hours.

Alberto Zavaleta Salas is distressed about bad news from home. In Peru his son has been born prematurely. Nonetheless, he tries to enjoy the clear air and the translucent night that never really becomes dark.

Down in the fish factory, the movement of the cutting blades glitters from early in the morning. The washing tanks are dark red from fish blood and in silent concentration the Indonesian crew sends ton after ton of the fatty toothfish meat into the flash-freezers. In contrast to the ship's miserable exterior, the fish factory is clean and free of rust. It could have been the kitchen of a first class restaurant. It has capacity for 220 tons of fish and they will not leave Antarctica until the cold storage room is full – or the fuel tanks empty. No other reason is acceptable to the ship owner.

Suddenly, Alberto Zavaleta Salas sees a grey-painted bow cutting through the ocean mist. It is the battleship the HMNZS *Wellington*, which has been hidden behind the icebergs to avoid detection by the pirate's radar. Now the crew are lowering the dinghies and sending them on their way towards the *Kunlun*.

For the first time a country's armed forces are to be used to challenge a pirate ship in the Antarctic. That means 2,000 tons of high technology, brute force and superior speed against a rusty and dodgy slaughterhouse. Two 50-millimetre machine guns against a terrified crew from the third world. The 35-year-old Lt. Commander Graham MacLean against the despondent officers from Peru and Spain. The *Wellington* commander's orders are to document the illegal fishing operation, procure evidence and board the vessel. The *Kunlun*'s officers' orders are to refuse to allow the Navy to come on board, pull up the nets and flee to the north.

If one can say that a criminal is as cold as ice in action when faced with a hostile naval battleship on the outskirts of the Antarctic – if outskirts of the Antarctic even exist – that is an apt description of the *Kunlun*'s fishing boat captain José Regueiro Sevilla.

The moment he sees the *Wellington* emerge from the mist, he calls the ship owner in Galicia and is instructed to pull in the nets and deny the Navy permission to board the ship, but to give them the papers they ask for.

The *Kunlun* is sailing under Equatorial Guinea's flag and is in international waters. In order to be allowed to send his men on board the longline fishing vessel, Commander MacLean must have permission from the closed dictatorship in Africa. Because of the time difference, José Regueiro Sevilla hopes that it will take at least 12 hours before Equatorial Guinea answers the phone.

In front of the *Wellington*'s cameras, the *Kunlun*'s Indonesian crew begins pulling up the gillnets, but the ocean is becoming rough, and they cut the nets, leaving half of them behind. At any moment the *Wellington* can receive a phone call informing them that the papers from Equatorial Guinea are false. Then they can board the *Kunlun* without asking permission first.

Alberto Zavaleta Salas therefore sails the *Kunlun* at full throttle to the north. If they can manage to outmanoeuvre the battleship, the two vessels with which the *Kunlun* is collaborating, the *Yongding* or the *Songhua*, will return to pull up the four nets left behind.

After six days, Captain Zavaleta Salas sees the *Wellington* come about and change course. MacLean has observed the *Yongding* fishing in the midst of a sheet of pack ice. The *Wellington* commanding officer has finally received an answer: Equatorial Guinea can find none of the ships in its register and grants permission to board. MacLean calls up the *Yongding* and asks for permission to enter the ship, but the response is to stay away.

Due to the fog and the 2–3-metre waves, MacLean decides it is too risky to board by force. He has too little fuel to chase the *Yongding* and decides to return to New Zealand.

MacLean has filmed and documented the illegal fishing activity. Interpol will be notified and can now circulate wanted notices on the three vessels.

On board the *Bob Barker* the news of the *Wellington*'s retreat is received with disbelief. The most pessimistic among them imagine that the Sea Shepherd crew are the only ones who will end up in prison after the chase is over.

At first, Sea Shepherd decides not to criticize Graham MacLean, but when the *Wellington*'s chief commanding officer implies in an interview that he does not have much respect for Sea Shepherd, Paul Watson decides to strike back.[1]

"Commander MacLean proceeded to lament to media about the rough sea conditions, cold weather and potential dangers. Maybe he is trying to convince the public that it was a resounding success, but the reality is that it was a pathetic and cowardly failed intervention," Watson writes in a press release.[2]

Watson also asks the question of why the *Wellington* does not fill up its fuel tanks and return to the Southern Ocean.

"My bet is that the New Zealand government and Navy will do nothing, that they will allow volunteers – including Sea Shepherd's Kiwi volunteers on the Sea Shepherd ships – to take the risks that they will not and to undertake the responsibility from which they have walked away," a frustrated Watson writes.

For New Zealand's government, the incident in the Southern Ocean resembles more a PR disaster. In the end, Minister of Defence Gerry Brownlee must defend the failed operation against the pirate fisherman in the Senate: "Look, remember that we're talking about illegal fishing, we're not talking about starting a war …"[3]

Peter Hammarstedt and Sid Chakravarty decides that the sister vessel, the *Sam Simon*, will commence the search for the three pirates who escaped. Simultaneously, he also directs a jab at the Australian government.

"New Zealand was left to single-handedly tackle the poachers – one vessel up against three. With the New Zealand Navy ship en route back to Wellington, and the Australian government nowhere to be seen, Sea Shepherd is now the only sheriff in town."[4]

19

THE FLYING MARINER

THE INDIAN OCEAN/
LAGOS, JANUARY 2015

The *Thunder* slowly circles its way northwest. Three knots, then a stop. Two knots, and then an about face. Four knots, then a bit to the east, before turning the ship around again. In Norway and at Interpol's headquarters in Lyon, the investigators continue to plot coordinates into a digital map and as the days and weeks pass, the maps resemble more a child's connect-the-dots drawing than a shipmaster's carefully considered route. It is a waltz without rhythm or precision and the pattern does not offer any warning of where the *Thunder*'s captain may be headed.

On 27 January, the *Thunder* speeds up its pace. The two ships are located in the Indian Ocean, a mere day's sail from South African waters. The closest major ports are Durban and Cape Town. On the bridge of the *Bob Barker* the speculations start up again. If they follow the same course, they will cross the Atlantic Ocean and end up in Montevideo in Uruguay, a city several of the Spanish pirate syndicates previously used as a home port. But it's a long trip. Hammarstedt believes that the *Thunder* will sail around the Cape of Good Hope and there the ship will meet another vessel to unload the illegal catch.

On the *Thunder* Captain Luis Alfonso Rubio Cataldo tells the crew that they will perhaps sail to Nigeria, because it's possible the difficulties they have run into can be resolved there. The countries Gabon and Papua New Guinea are also mentioned. The latter is located an ocean away and in the opposite direction of the ship's course. The information produces more confusion than clarity, but Nigeria at least makes sense. Everyone knows that the name Lagos is on the stern of the ship.

So, after a day and a half of something resembling a properly considered course, Cataldo suddenly stops the ship again. Perhaps he fears what he will find if he were to sail around the Cape of Good Hope.

On the same day, Captain Warredi Enisuoh of NIMASA, the Nigerian coast guard in Lagos, receives an unusual request. Over the telephone he is encouraged to join a secret intelligence group with a connection to Interpol. The group's primary mission is to stop a fishing vessel.

The name the *Thunder* sounds familiar to Warredi Enisuoh. He remembers a letter he received from Australia's High Commissioner in Nigeria expressing a wish for information about the old trawler that was registered in the ships register in Lagos and sailing under the Nigerian flag.

Warredi Enisuoh will now become critical to the future fate of the *Thunder*. The same evening he takes part in a telephone conference with the Interpol group.[1]

The Gulf of Guinea is Africa's most violent fairway, and seamen, ship owners and the authorities all over the world expect the Nigerian coast guard to bring the brutal kidnappings, random killings and the thefts of valuable oil cargo to an end. In the recently opened surveillance centre in Lagos, Enisuoh and his team study satellite images every day and have complete oversight of all the ships moving in and out of Nigerian ports. He can requisition battleships and aircraft immediately if he receives notification of a hijacking.

Enisuoh was born in the eternally conflict-ridden Niger Delta in the mid-1960s and in his youth he signed on with a shipping company in Singapore, where he climbed through the ranks to mate and captain. His boyhood dream came true when he became a pilot on the svelte jet aircraft Embraer E-190 for the company Virgin Nigeria. Privately he began calling himself "the flying mariner". Now he was back on the ground once more.

When he starts digging into the *Thunder*'s secrets in Nigeria, what he discloses is a story he has difficulties believing.

Four years earlier, the ships register had received a letter from the ship agent Maritime Consultants Limited, under the address of a bankrupt amusement park in Lagos. Maritime Consultants Limited wanted to register a new vessel: FV *Thunder* – formerly MS *Typhoon*. Enclosed in the letter was a sales agreement stating that the Lagos-based company Royal Marine & Spares had bought the ship for 140,000 dollars. The seller was a company in Panama.[2]

The Lagos company that supposedly purchased the *Thunder* is owned by two of West Africa's wealthiest businessmen. The youngest, Henry Macauley, had long been Sierra Leone's High Commissioner in Nigeria and is now the Minister of Energy in his native country. The eldest, Dew Mayson, has been a powerful man in his homeland of Liberia for almost 40 years – a freedom fighter, ambassador, peace mediator, professor and Liberia's first multimillionaire.

In the early 1980s, the freedom fighter Dew Mayson was rescued from death row by the coup leader Samuel Doe, who in 1980 led a group of drunken and disillusioned soldiers towards the presidential palace in Liberia's capital Monrovia. Doe killed the president and made himself a general and head of state. After his assumption of power, Doe's soldiers threw themselves into an orgy of violence in which ministers and supporters of the former regime were paraded around the capital naked before being massacred on the beach by Doe's inebriated executioners.

Doe appointed Dew Mayson leader of Liberia's national investment commission and later the country's ambassador in Paris. In 1985, Mayson stepped down, according to his own account, in protest against Doe's brutal regime. When Charles Taylor overthrew Doe in 1989, Mayson took his family with him and moved to the neighbouring nation of Nigeria. As his homeland descended into full-scale civil war, he worked his way up in the oil industry and had soon gone from being a refugee to a flamboyant millionaire.

Dew Mayson later ran for president in Liberia, but received only one-half a per cent of the votes. The country's truth commission labelled him a dubious ally of Liberia's dictators and questions were asked about where his sudden wealth and fortune had come from.[3]

One of the companies that were important in the building up of Mayson's fortune was Royal Marine & Spares. According to the documents, the company now owned the *Thunder*.

In October 2013 the ships register had received another letter from Royal Marine & Spares. The owners of the *Thunder* wanted to change the ship's name to the *Raz* – to "reflect the management's new visions" as the letter signed by Dew Mayson read. But the address the company gave for its headquarters in Lagos did not exist.

"A careful assessment of your documents has revealed a number of inconsistencies. Your presence is therefore requested," the Nigerian ships register replied.

Then everything related to the *Thunder* fell silent in Nigeria.

Warredi Enisuoh begins digging into the roles of the alleged owners. Royal Marine & Spares has a well-known history as an oil service company in Lagos, but he can't find any connection to fishing vessels or fishing licences, other than in the *Thunder*'s documents. Do Mayson and Macauley really own the *Thunder*? Or have their names and signatures been stolen to hide the identities of the true owners?

The Interpol group wants the Nigerian authorities to ask South Africa for help in arresting the *Thunder*. South Africa has ships and resources to stop the trawler, but as a flag state, it is Nigeria that rules over the *Thunder*'s fate, at least in a legal sense.

Enisuoh is uncertain. There is nothing in the country's laws stating that it is a criminal offence for Europeans, Indonesians and Latin Americans to fish in international waters. The *Thunder* will very likely just be forced ashore in a large-scale and costly operation only to be released again. It will be embarrassing for everyone involved, Enisuoh thinks.

There is also another obstacle. In order to ask South Africa for help he must go via the Nigerian foreign affairs authorities, a virtually impenetrable bureaucracy. Enisuoh is also worried that an untrustworthy servant within the bureaucracy might leak the entire plan, warning the owners. If the captain on the *Thunder* is alerted, the battle can be lost before it has begun.

Warredi Enisuoh begins discretely investigating whether it is really the multimillionaire Mayson and Minister Macauley who own the *Thunder*.

When he one day marches up to the powerful Coast Guard Director Patrick Akpobolokemi's office on the eighth floor of the yellowish-brown office building a few blocks from the harbour in Lagos, he notices a book lying on one of the tables. On the cover there is a photograph of Dew Mayson, the suspected owner of the *Thunder*.

Is it a coincidence that a book about Mayson is lying on the table? Has there been a leak? Has somebody in the Interpol group unexpectedly blabbed to someone, who then sold the information to someone else? Has Mayson gone to the head of the coast guard to have the investigation stopped? If so, his career is very likely over. At worst, his life can be in danger, Warredi Enisuoh thinks.

Before he hurries out of the director's office, Enisuoh asks questions about a subject completely unrelated to the search for the *Thunder*'s owners. Out in the corridor he fishes out his telephone and calls one of the Norwegian members of the Interpol group. No, nobody in the group has mentioned his investigations to anyone else, he is told.

Now there is no turning back. Enisuoh must meet with the powerful Mayson in person. He summons his courage and returns to Akpobolokemi and asks him how he knows Mayson. The head of NIMASA tells him that he has recently had a meeting with Mayson and a man from the oil industry. They wanted to discuss business prospects.

When Enisuoh and Dew Mayson finally meet, the powerful millionaire states that he has never heard of the *Thunder*. If that is true, someone must have used Mayson's company to hide the true owners of the *Thunder*.[4]

Enisuoh contacts the shipping authorities in ports the *Thunder* has visited previously and soon receives ship's documents that were supposedly issued in Nigeria. The *Thunder*'s registration certificate states that Nigeria has given the vessel permission to fish in foreign waters. That is not the case. And how can the Nigerian authorities have issued detailed safety and pollution certificates to a vessel that has never been inspected in Nigeria? The documents must be forgeries. The bureaucrat, who has allegedly signed the documents on behalf of NIMASA, denies having any knowledge of them whatsoever.

If Mayson and Macauley have nothing to do with the *Thunder*, where then do the signed company documents come from? Is there a spider operating on the inside of the Nigerian company register that has copied company documents and records of proceedings from meetings of the board of directors of Royal Marine & Spares and then sold them?

The American authorities have called Lagos an epicentre for identity theft and financial crime.[5] By using post office boxes, the kidnappers can ensure that the correspondence of a given company never ends up in the hands of its actual owners. In the same way that somebody acquires a fake driver's licence by using the identity of a deceased person, someone could have used the identity of the dormant company Royal Marine & Spares to procure ship's documents for the *Thunder*. That must be how it was done, Enisuoh thinks.

He tries to track down the two consultants who procured the ship's registration in Nigeria. He has names and photographs, but the bankrupt amusement park which they gave as their address was recently raided by the police and environmental protection authorities armed with guns and bulldozers. The once so popular amusement park was inhabited by petty criminals and vagrants and in one corner somebody had established a makeshift cemetery.

It's as if the *Thunder*'s consultants in Lagos have vanished off the face of the earth.[6]

Enisuoh encourages the Nigerian federal police and the national Interpol office in the capital Abuja to react. Nigeria perhaps doesn't have good fishery laws that give the country the possibility to punish pirate fishermen, but document forgery is definitely a criminal offence. Enisuoh asks the Nigerian Interpol director to alert all nations in the region that Nigeria would like assistance in arresting the *Thunder*. He also requests that a Nigerian team be put together that can go along and board the *Thunder*.

Enisuoh has done what he can. The decision must be made at the office of the cabinet minister in Abuja.

At sea, nobody knows about the plans being made on land. While the authorities of six nations are trying to build an alliance to stop the chase, a new ship search is underway near the ice edge in Antarctica.

20

A BLOODY NIGHTMARE
THE STOREGG BANK,
FEBRUARY 2015

596 metres. 445 metres. 262 metres. On the echo sounder, the Sea Shepherd Captain Sid Chakravarty can see the Storegg Bank rising up steeply beneath him. The *Sam Simon* is located less than 50 nautical miles from the mainland of Antarctica, the cloud cover is light and the visibility unusually clear. The remote Storegg Bank is the ideal location for fishing vessels seeking to avoid detection, Chakravarty thinks.

The stinking evidence from the *Thunder* lies on deck. Six weeks earlier, the *Sam Simon* came sailing into the Banzare Bank to haul up the gillnets from which the *Thunder* had fled. After the first 30 consecutive hours of work on rough seas and amidst dense snowfall, Chakravarty had to divide the bone-tired crew up into four-hour shifts to ensure that nobody collapsed. It was a bloody nightmare. There was no end to the nets. After three weeks of toil, more than 70 kilometres of nets lay in huge coils on the deck of the *Sam Simon*. Along with skates, jellyfish and crabs, they pulled out 1,400 toothfish in different stages of decomposition. It was a catch that would have brought in millions of dollars in profits for the *Thunder*'s owner. Operation Spillway wanted the nets as evidence against officers and ship owners.[1] After all the hard work, the *Sam Simon* continued west in search of the five members of "The Bandit 6" who were still on the run.

Now Chakravarty is hoping to search the Storegg Bank before the wind shifts to the north bringing with it new snow squalls and fog.[2] The sunrise is glimmering an almost gaudy bright red.[3] Chakravarty is standing with his cup of morning coffee in his hand and his eyes on the radar when he sees what he is looking for: A signal that can be two unknown ships.

Then he grabs the telephone, calls Peter Hammarstedt and tells him that he will reach the targets in the course of 15 minutes. He then gives the order that all the portholes are to be sealed in case of a collision. Slowly it comes into view, the rusty bow that had once been white. It is the *Yongding*.

"Ask everybody to stand by if these guys don't move. We're not going to be scared by these guys for sure," Chakravarty orders, before calling up the *Yongding* and asking the ship to leave the area.

The pirate vessel does not respond, but suddenly veers, pointing its bow straight at the *Sam Simon*. It looks as if it is going to attack. If the *Yongding* wants to put the *Sam Simon* out of commission, the mate will have to ram it amidships – by the engine room.

But the *Yongding* speeds past the *Sam Simon* on its port side, clearing it by a scant 10 metres.

"He steered away, that fucking chicken," Sid Chakravarty bursts out, before he sees the *Yongding* disappear to the east and out of the Storegg Bank. Instead of starting a chase he decides to find and confront the *Kunlun*, which is also located in the area.

When Shipmaster Alberto Zavaleta Salas catches sight of the pirate flag on the bow of the *Sam Simon* and hears the call on the radio, he does not respond. In the past few days, the *Kunlun* has only put out short chains of nets in case they have to flee the area. Now they draw the curtains in the wheelhouse shut to prevent being photographed and sail straight into the pack ice.

After having been chased for six days, the *Kunlun* changes its course for the northwest. For the *Sam Simon*, the change in course is the worst imaginable. It brings her away from land in a situation in which the ship already has too little fuel. After consulting with the crew, Captain Chakravarty decides to terminate the pursuit of the *Kunlun*. He sets their new course for a point located 750 nautical miles southeast of South Africa.

There the *Thunder* and the *Bob Barker* are adrift on the whims of the wind and the weather.

Every day at noon, Chief Engineer Ervin Vermeulen comes up onto the bridge of the *Bob Barker* with an overview of how much fuel is left in the tanks. On some days, Peter Hammarstedt does a detailed calculation to determine for how long they can continue the chase. The answer depends upon their speed, the weather and the wind. But as long as the two ships are operating without using the engines, it is only the generators that are consuming fuel. If it continues like this, they can be at sea for two years, is what he figures out.

The result of the calculation causes Hammarstedt to leave the bridge; he clambers through the galley and into the dry storage room, where the buckets of rice and beans are stacked up against the bulkheads.

"Do we have enough food to last for two years?" he asks.

"We have enough rice and beans to *survive* for two years," the Chief Cook Priya Cooper replies.

The answer is clear enough. He leaves the galley, continues through the narrow, oblong messroom and into the lounge. There he gathers the crew for a meeting. The proposition he now wants to make can have consequences he would prefer to avoid.

"Worst case scenario we will be at sea for two years. The food is going to decline and we really don't know how this is going to end," he says.

Then he gives the crew a choice. They can stay on, continuing the chase and be stuck at sea for several months, in the worst case, for years.

"The *Sam Simon* will be here in two weeks. Those who want, can sail with her to Mauritius and travel home from there," he says.

When he leaves the lounge, Hammarstedt prays a silent prayer that the chief engineer will not abandon the ship.

Erwin Vermeulen is his most trusted man and probably the only ship's engineer in the world who is a vegan. He is also a dedicated and loyal activist who spent 64 days in custody in a Japanese remand prison for an altercation with a dolphin trainer.

Peter Hammarstedt gives the crew 24 hours to decide whether they want to continue on the chase or leave the *Bob Barker*.

21

LA MAFIA GALLEGA
BARCELONA AND RIBEIRA, FEBRUARY 2015

He is quiet-mannered in a way that awakens suspicions of his knowing far more than he is willing to tell.

It is early in the morning. We meet him at a nondescript office in an office complex on the outskirts of Barcelona. The private eye of some 50 years does not want to be identified by name. We can call him Luis. All his activities involve his being anonymous and faceless, and that is how he wants it to stay. He hangs up his brown leather jacket; it is shapeless and worn. Then he gets some coffee from the coffee machine, the only fixture in the otherwise empty office premises, with the exception of the photocopier, which appears extravagant.

Out at sea, infinitely far from the enterprising Barcelona morning, the chase is in its second month. The *Thunder* and the *Bob Barker* have switched off the engines and are circling one another in a calm dance.

"The owners of all the pirate vessels are Spanish. And they are from Galicia. But it is almost impossible to get to the bottom of the ownership structure," Luis says.[1]

For many years he has been investigating narcotics smugglers and pirate ship owners in the Spanish province.

"Everyone in Galicia knows what is going on in Ribeira, but nobody says anything. It is like the *omertà* code of honour in Italy," he says.

"A Corleone near the ocean?"

"The Corleone gang are like young children compared to the people in Galicia. Galicia is a region run by criminals. Before they lived off fishing. Now it's narcotics and tobacco," Luis the Catalonian says.

"Is there anyone who can talk?"

"Travelling to Ribeira and asking about pirate fishermen is like going to Naples and asking who stole a lorry. Everyone knows, but nobody says anything. Even for our local contacts it is almost impossible to acquire information. We have tried, but those who talk risk ending up in serious trouble."

"How dangerous are they?"

For a moment he doesn't speak, and then places the palms of his hands on the table.

"Some of the pirate fishermen use the same channels as the narcotics smugglers. They can be extremely dangerous. But if you go to a tapas bar in Ribeira, stand beers and a dinner with prostitutes, it could be that you will learn who is in business or not," Luis says.

"I don't know much about the *Thunder*. But I have heard that the ship is owned from Galicia," he continues.

In the course of the chase, a number of the well-known pirate ship owners in Galicia have been designated as the owner of the *Thunder*. Vidal Armadores in Ribeira is a candidate. The Panama-registered company Trancoeiro Fishing is as well. According to the company documents from Panama, Trancoeiro Fishing is run by the Spanish citizens Manuel Martínez Martínez and the brothers Juan Antonio and José Manuel Argibay Pérez, all of whom are from Galicia. And each of them has a criminal record from the poaching of toothfish.

When we call Martínez, we receive the following answer:

"The *Thunder*? Then you must go to Ribeira to speak with Vidal Armadores."

Another Panama company – Estelares – could also be the owner of the wanted ship. Estelares appeared for the first time in the *Thunder* saga when the ship was registered in Togo in 2006. Estelares was also registered as owner of the ship on an insurance policy and when the vessel changed flags in 2010. On paper, the company's management consists of two lawyers in Panama, but they deny having anything to do with the operations of Estelares.[2]

"The real owner of Estelares is Florindo González from Galicia," the private eye Luis says as if it were the most obvious thing in the world.

"I don't have any documents that prove it, but I am 100 per cent sure that he owns Estelares. He is a powerful figure in Galicia," he adds, before planting the palms of his hands on the table as if to signal that the conversation is over.

"There's one more problem," Luis says before we go our separate ways.

"And that is?"

"In Galicia it is difficult to get people to talk but finding them is worse. The addresses are a nightmare. Like this one: 'The square up in the mountains, right before you reach the ocean, house number 3.'"

You have arrived when the dust from the dry, red soil of Castilla y León lies behind you and you can smell the scent of the ocean, wet moss and eucalyptus. Galicia is perhaps the least described and most slandered of Spain's provinces, an illegitimate child one does not want on display. A number of Spain's powerful noble families come from here. They received their titles as a reward for their battles against the Moors, but then they disappeared from the province and into oblivion. Only the fishermen and the farmers remained.

Much like Andalusia, the region is accused of being a wilful laggard, but without the mitigating climate of the south. Galicia is damp, green and hilly, a Spanish Scotland with a rugged and isolated rocky coastline – a landscape that is especially attractive if you are a cocaine smuggler.

A significant portion of the cocaine that comes to Europe is brought to land by boats along the coast of Galicia. But although the cocaine gangs in Galicia are notorious for their efficiency and brutality, the term *mafia gallega* is reserved for the fishermen.

And if there is a godfather to be found among the "mafia fishermen", it is "Tucho" – Antonio Vidal Suárez, head of the family and majority shareholder of both the shipping company Vidal Armadores and a conglomerate of companies. In Ribeira he is a legend. The only thing he has ever said to the press is: "Go to hell."

Ribeira is located on the western side of the Barbanza peninsula, below a heather-covered hill and facing the Atlantic Ocean. The city lacks the charm of a Spanish small town, and the hotels are few and inhospitable. But there is plenty of available parking.

"Fuck."

That is all that is written on the facade of the dive closest to the harbour. Inside, beneath the faded pin-up photographs, the fishermen, the buyers and the pensioners gather to hear the news about the fishing.

"We always get the blame. The entire world points their finger at us. We are proper seamen and run an organized and legal fishing enterprise. Look at those bloody Chinese. Nobody cares about the unpainted hulks they poach from," says one of the fish merchants in the bar without a name.

A middle aged man, he says he is a retired pizza baker, asks us to go outside the bar with him to talk.

"The network of ship owners is so strong and tight-knit that nobody dares tell the truth. Whoever gabs about pirate fishing will be unemployed forever. Or beaten up," he explains.

He lights a cigarette and pulls us even further away from the entrance to be sure that nobody can hear him.

"There are also those who dislike that the pirate ship owners have given Ribeira a bad reputation, but for many people they are role models. They are admired for being brave, wealthy, not paying taxes and always getting away," he continues.

Then the silence of the evening in Ribeira is broken by a high-pitched alarm. As it blasts through the moisture-corroded walls of the stone buildings, the men abandon their half-empty glasses, rush out of the dives around the harbour into the darkness and down to the fish market. It is the signal that a ship has arrived at the quay and the catch will be auctioned off.

Three different ship owners are identified as possible owners of the *Thunder*. Many point the finger at the notorious pirate shipping company Vidal Armadores. At the company's main office in Ribeira, an unassuming concrete building a few streets up from the harbour, the receptionist denies knowing anything at all about the company. Or the management.

More than 20 years have passed since the Vidal family first heard the rumours of the fortune hidden in the depths off the coast of Antarctica. Since then the family's ships have been fined, seized and chased without this bringing their appetite for toothfish to an end.

When the American authorities issued a wanted notice through Interpol for the family's oldest son and sharpest business mind, Manuel Antonio Vidal Pego, for the import of 26 tons of poached toothfish, he appeared in a court in Miami and accepted a fine of USD 400,000 to avoid imprisonment. He also made a solemn vow to stay away from illegal fishing in the future. It was a promise he would never keep. Instead he moved the pirate fleet to countries like Equatorial Guinea, North Korea and Sierra Leone – states that have not adopted the international conventions regulating fishing in the oceans of the world. The ships were owned by companies in tax havens such as Panama, while the profits were funnelled back to Galicia, where the family invested in a fish oil factory, real estate and windmills. From Brussels, Madrid and the provincial government of Santiago de Compostela, the family received EUR 10 million in subsidies – to the accompaniment of loud complaints from the green movement.[3]

The family itself holds a low profile. In 2011, Manuel Antonio Vidal Pego gave his first interview and started by pointing out that he had neither a wooden leg nor a parrot on his shoulder, and that he was out of the toothfish business.[4] At that time the family business had already been linked to 40 cases of illegal fishing.

At the Vidal family's luxury villa, which is situated on a well-groomed and securely fenced-in property on a hill over-looking Ribeira, neither is there anyone who opens the door.

We return to the harbour. It is midday and there is little activity. An Indonesian crew is playing football at the far end of one of the jetties. The only sign of Vidal in the harbour is a small fish-landing facility and a trawler bearing the logo of the company Hijos de Vidal Bandín, which in 2012 was sentenced to pay a fine of GBP 1.6 million due to overfishing that a British judge referred to as "systematic", "repeated" and "cynical".[5]

A middle-aged man is carrying crates of fish from the vessel. It is José Vidal Suárez, brother of the powerful "Tucho".

"I'm not going to say anything I shouldn't say. Everyone has problems and each of us must sweep before our own door. I don't meddle in other people's lives," he says curtly.

"Where can I find your brother?"

"I don't know anything," he answers and disappears inside the fish market.

The bar Doble SS situated by the harbour is full of hollering, cheering and, here and there, despairing men. On the flat screen television just below the ceiling in the tiny bar, the football teams Real Madrid and Sevilla are battling it out. As we take our places at the bar and order a beer, the room falls silent.

It's as if all the sounds in the premises cease; there are no hospitable gestures offering a vacant seat in the almost full bar, only uninterested gazes, some scrutinizing and others hostile. We empty our glasses and leave. The rumours about how two *periodistas* were in town asking questions had stolen the march on us. The story about what happens immediately afterwards reaches us later.

Right after we leave the bar, an elderly gentleman gets to his feet. He has greying hair and a prominent jaw. He settles his bill, leaves the bar and departs in a car. It is "Tucho" – Antonio Vidal Suárez, the patriarch who, according to the authorities and environmentalists, has built up one of the world's most profitable illegal fishing operations. The pensioner has left responsibility for a good portion of the operations in the hands of his sons Manuel Antonio and Angel, but always has the final word when the family meets to make important decisions. And he is now under suspicion of being the owner of the *Thunder*, the *Kunlun* and several of the other ships that have come to be known as "The Bandit 6".

It is starting to get dark. We are on our way from Ribeira. Above the gently sloping mountain pass between Galicia and Castilla y León, there are light snow flurries in the air. Then a peep can be heard from the mobile phone. It is an email from Captain Peter Hammarstedt on the *Bob Barker*.

"Dear Kjetil & Eskil. Please find attached a composite of photographs of the FV *Thunder* crew. Perhaps they can aid you in the search for the owner?"

There are four photographs. Four men who can be seen scowling on the *Thunder*. A rough and blurry photograph of a giant dressed in coveralls. Another cautiously slouches his way forward from the bridge and looks toward the photographer in the same way one looks into a dark and unfamiliar room for the first time. The chap wearing the full-face sunglasses and with Latin American features must be the captain. The clearest photograph shows a partially bald man in his early 60s. He wears eyeglasses with steel frames. A determined and unwavering, almost obstinate gaze can be seen behind his glasses.

We turn the car around and drive back to Ribeira. To show people the photographs.

22

GOD'S FINGERPRINT
RIBEIRA, FEBRUARY 2015

He is thirsty, tipsy and the stories are probably exaggerated.

In Ribeira, a retired fisherman is willing to speak about the illegal toothfish expeditions in which he had personally participated. He tells us about 16-hour shifts on old, rusty hulks, crew members who are washed overboard, illness and injuries that are never treated by a physician, fleeing from coast guard ships and flag changes at sea to conceal the ship's identity. For a five-month-long expedition he was paid around 60,000 euros.

When we show him the recent Sea Shepherd photographs of the officers on the *Thunder*, he recognizes several of them, among them the fishing captain Juan Manuel Patiño Lampon. But he doesn't know who his employer is.

The women of Ribeira are also silent. The spouse of one of the *Thunder* officers refuses to open her door; on the phone she says that she does not have permission to speak. Another confirms that her husband is on the *Thunder*, that there are problems on board and that it is the last time he will travel with the ship. She tells us that she doesn't know what problems he is referring to, but that her husband calls home every Saturday.

The home of Lampon the fishing captain is a presentable villa, situated on a site secluded from the coast road and a few kilometres away from the fish market in the centre of Ribeira. According to the Spanish register of companies, up until 2010 he ran the company Ivopesca together with another ship owner from the region. The company sold fish products and owned the vessel the *Banzare*, which fished toothfish from Uruguay. The environmental organization Oceana accused the company's primary owner José Nogueira García of extensive poaching of fish and for being a member of *la mafia gallega*. But it was not just the environmentalists who were following the activities of Lampon's partner. In 2008 Nogueira García was arrested for smuggling more than two tons of cocaine from Uruguay to Spain. The cocaine, at a market value of EUR 70 million, was hidden in containers of frozen fish. The case proved what the police commissioners in Madrid had long suspected: the fish and shellfish industry was being used both as a distribution channel for narcotics and to launder the profits.

Nogueira Garcia was sentenced to nine years in prison and lost all his holdings. Lampon was never a part of the case.

"He's at sea," the fishing captain's wife says when we call her in Ribeira.

"Is he on the *Thunder*?"

"I don't know the name of the vessel. I don't know how long he has been at sea nor when he is coming back," she says.

Then she hangs up.

We drive once again out of Ribeira, over the silently flowing Ría de Arousa, one of the river mouths teeming with shellfish in Galicia, full of *bateas*, square floating piers of eucalyptus wood that have made the fish farmers Spain's largest producers of mussels, scallops and oysters. According to the legend, the five river mouths in the Spanish province are God's fingerprint. On the seventh day God had to rest and then he put his hand down upon Galicia. But if it is true that God blessed Galicia with abundant shellfish harvests, he must have simultaneously have forgotten the numerous and often devoutly pious deep sea fishermen in the province. They have little in the way of fishing quotas. That is why the fishermen from Galicia have for decades sought out increasingly dangerous waters in search of a livelihood. And along the way they have made many enemies.

There is a strange and invisible connecting line running between Ría de Arousa, the search for the *Thunder* and Norway – a line of connection that perhaps more than anything else was the beginning of the end for the *Thunder* and "The Bandit 6".

In the 1990s, an armada of fishing vessels popped up in the Barents Sea bearing flags from nations such as Belize, the Dominican Republic, Togo and Cambodia. During the worst years they fished 150,000 tons illegally. The Norwegian authorities and the environmental activists declared war on the fleet. They began recording the ships' movements, owners and harbours where the illegal fish were unloaded. For a period of time, every single fishing vessel that travelled from the Barents Sea with fish to harbours in Germany and the Netherlands was monitored and dozens of cases were tried in courts in Russia and Norway.

One of the ships, fisheries control agencies in Europe noticed, was the reefer ship the *Sunny Jane*, which accepted on board illegal fish from a group of blacklisted trawlers known as "The Rostock Five". "The Rostock Five" were controlled from the Russian enclave of Kaliningrad and had their winter base in the north German harbour town from which they had received their nickname.

"The fish you receive are not to be landed in Norway, the oil you use is not to come from Norwegian vessels and our harbours are closed," the Norwegian Minister of Fisheries and Coastal Affairs Helga Pedersen warned them.

After having been turned away from a number of harbours in Europe and Africa, the *Sunny Jane* finally set its course for Galicia. One summer day the ship laid anchor in the Ría de Arousa carrying 600 tons of frozen tuna fish, an abandoned Russian crew, empty fuel tanks and a freezer that was threatening to break down. The *Sunny Jane* had run out of safe harbours to turn to, the crew had not been paid in months, and now 13 men were sitting at the mouth of Ría de Arousa, clinging tightly to their catch, the only thing of value on board that could be traded in for plane tickets home to Russia.

The *Sunny Jane* became the symbol for a successful fight to shut fish poachers out of harbours in Europe. But the majority of the ships sailed on to new harbours and fish banks, often in West Africa, where there were fewer coast guard vessels, surveillance planes and inspectors.

After they had chased the pirate fleet out of the Barents Sea, the Norwegian fishery authorities and environmentalists had amassed an extensive card file of pirate crafts, shady ship owners and dubious flag states. They had also recognized something new. Fish poaching was controlled by organized crime and could only be countered through international cooperation. In Norway a special criminal investigation group was appointed which was named the Norwegian National Advisory Group against Organized IUU-fishing, in common vernacular called "the fish crime investigation squad".

Norwegian bureaucrats travelled around the world spreading their message of how fisheries crime was just as serious, cynical and cunning as human trafficking, narcotics and arms smuggling. The backers forged ships' documents and catch protocols, laundered money, bribed port authorities and hired crews on slave contracts.

It was this recognition that induced the Norwegian authorities to finance Interpol's intelligence operation targeting illegal fishing.

The Norwegian environmentalist Gunnar Album was probably the person who worked the most systematically. For many years he had been charting the activities of fishing vessels, shipping companies, flag states, call signals, owners, tonnage and port calls all over the world. Every single suspicious fishing vessel was given its own profile in his card file, a unique database Album shared with the authorities of many countries and which would turn out to be a goldmine in the search for the pirates. Two of the ships in Album's file stood out as being the most active: the *Thunder* and the *Viking*. The first two fishing vessels in history to be wanted by Interpol.

In an ironic twist of fate, the evidence against the *Thunder*'s officers and backers led to the small town in Galicia where the *Sunny Jane* ended its days.

Before it was sold for parts, the unhappy ship with the jolly name lay for three years in the harbour in Ribeira.

2 3

BUENAS TARDES, BOB BARKER
THE MELVILLE BANK, FEBRUARY 2015

After sailing for a short while towards the Cape of Good Hope, the *Thunder* does a complete about-face and continues east at half throttle. The *Bob Barker*'s first mate Adam Meyerson hopes the pirate vessel is on its way to Malaysia, the country where the trawler has gone into hiding previously.

"We could be there at the end of February eating insects on a stick and drinking Singapore Slings."

"Is it vegan to eat insects?" he wonders.

For the crew of the *Bob Barker*, one day blurs into the next. They are north of "the Roaring Forties", where the cold winds from the west never relent, but although the weather and temperature are agreeable, the horizon is still just as never-ending. Only five of the crew decided to sign off when Captain Hammarstedt gave them the option.

The crew manning the *Bob Barker*'s dinghies the *Gemini* and the *Hunter* are longing to feel the adrenaline that will be triggered when they are skimming across the waves in the quick, light vessels. Jeremy Tonkin, the man who was in the crow's nest when they found the *Thunder*, draws lines above his berth to keep track of the days he has been at sea, like a prison inmate. He started doing this when he was lying there wracked by seasickness. He now has 60 lines. The ship photographer Simon Ager is extremely satisfied with the cabin which was renovated before departure – under the linoleum flooring they discovered a beautiful wood floor that his cabin mate polished and restored. All the same, he is now far more concerned about there being a proper showdown with the captain of the *Thunder*.

"Give me somebody who is going to put some boxing gloves on and bring it to us. That's a personal message to the Spanish family who is running this organization. Give us some captains with attitude!" Ager says to a chuckling group of men and women on the bridge.

It's almost as if the captain of the *Thunder* can hear him.

After a few days' listless sailing to the east, the *Thunder* suddenly turns its bow north. They are on the underwater plateau called the Melville Bank, as the crow flies, directly south of Madagascar. On the bridge of the *Bob Barker* they are now wondering whether the captain of the *Thunder* is planning to sail there or perhaps to Mauritius?

But the *Thunder* begins sailing in circles around the Melville Bank, where the ocean is no more than a mere hundred metres deep.[1] Are they using the sonar to find a suitable place to put out the nets? Or is this just another move in a psychological game?

"They could just be bored and playing with the fish finder. Maybe they are just taking advantage of being in the area to survey it. Hard to say," Meyerson says.

Just before midnight, a searchlight is lit on the stern of the *Thunder*. Then two more lights are switched on, a red one above a white, the light signal communicating that the crew on the *Thunder* is planning to start fishing.

"They have not had a light on the stern before. They could go for squid, get them to come to the light. Maybe they want to change their diet," Meyerson suggests.

Captain Hammarstedt is called up to the bridge. He goes to the radio and tries to make contact with the *Thunder*.

Nobody responds, but the hatch on the stern opens. The *Thunder* was built as a trawler, but was later converted into a longline fishing vessel. When the crew fishes with nets, the system is deployed from the back and hauled in from the front through the trawl door. In the darkness, Hammarstedt can see shadows moving about on the quarterdeck and that something flies out resembling a marker line. Then Hammarstedt sees net floats and marker lights in the water. He immediately asks Meyerson to steer clear of the *Thunder*'s stern and back wash, so as to prevent the nets and ropes from getting tangled up in the propeller.

There is no doubt. The crew of the *Thunder* have decided to fish, but the Melville Bank is located too far north for there to be toothfish.

"Maybe they are fishing for tuna," Chief Engineer Erwin Vermeulen suggests.

"Get closer on their quarter, just don't cross the stern," Hammarstedt says to Meyerson.

He has promised the crew that they will try to stop the *Thunder* if they are fishing, but it is difficult without putting the crew and the ship in danger: it is pitch dark, and the wind is whipping the waves up to heights of three metres.

"They could be fishing for supplies. We can't do anything while it is dark and they know that. Fifty days and it had to be in the fourth quarter of the Super Bowl," Hammarstedt says.

All day long the crew has been looking forward to watching the recording of the Super Bowl final between the New England Patriots and the Seattle Seahawks which was played a few days earlier in Arizona, but now they are preparing to spring into action. The crew manning the dinghies finally see an opportunity to release some of the tension in their bodies, but Hammarstedt holds them back. He fears that this is exactly what the captain of the *Thunder* wants. In this weather there is a lot that can go wrong when the time comes to hoist a dinghy on board again, and the *Thunder* can then exploit the situation to take off.

"We have to choose our battles here. It will not be tonight," he says.

He stands in the darkness on the bridge and sees that the stern hatch of the *Thunder* is shut before the ship slowly moves away from the net.

"It is a very short net they have put out. About half a mile. They haven't done it to get a big catch. I think it is a test," he says.

It is raining and windy. The bad weather is supposed to last for at least another 12 hours, but Hammarstedt knows he cannot permit the *Thunder* to do any fishing. The crew expects him to do something.

"The most important thing is to stay with the *Thunder*, but we have to make a statement," he says to his colleagues on the bridge.

The next morning the officers meet on the *Bob Barker* to devise a plan. They do not have the equipment required to haul up the net, but can't they pretend that they do? Both the ships are now located more than 10 kilometres from the net floats. If the *Thunder* follows when the *Bob Barker* sets its course for the buoys, it means that they want the fish now caught in the net. If the *Thunder* puts about, it means that they deployed the net in an attempt to outmanoeuvre Sea Shepherd so they can take off.

"We could go there as fast as we can. They won't be able to get there before we cut the buoys," Meyerson suggests.

"We could put the small boats in the water and let *Bob Barker* stay with the *Thunder*," Vermeulen says.

"It is too rough to launch the small boats and if they are going to hit us it is better that they do it in calm seas," says Hammarstedt, who has long been prepared for the possibility that the chase could end with a collision between the two ships.

The fishing captain on the *Thunder* could also deploy another net if the *Bob Barker* sets its course for the net floats. Then Hammarstedt will have two nets to deal with.

Throughout the entire day the two ships act out a drama on the turbulent seas. They turn towards each other and turn around again. Accelerate their speed and then slow down. All is quiet on the radio, but they have not been this close to one another since they were in the ice a month and a half ago. Hammarstedt has given an order that the distance is not to be more than two cable lengths – 370 metres – but nobody takes the initiative to put an end to the charade.

Meyerson and Ager make a discovery that means they have lost one of the elements of surprise they have been discussing.

"The *Thunder* knows that we can't haul nets. Our specs are on our website," Ager says.

On board the *Bob Barker* there are containers of expanding foam insulation. What if they were to open four or five of the containers and throw them towards the trawl door? Then hauling in the nets from on board the *Thunder* will be hell for the crew.

Had the *Sam Simon* been accompanying them now, they would have had more options. Then they could have launched the dinghies.

"We have never gone up against this kind of an adversary before. They feel backed into a corner and could potentially be quite dangerous," Hammarstedt says to Erwin Vermeulen.

"They could be going another month at this speed. It's not going to change anything for them. We can speculate but we have been doing that for 50 days, we might be doing it for another 50 days," Vermeulen says.

He is convinced that the *Thunder*'s fishing captain is an experienced and skilled fisherman, so there must be a reason why they are at the Melville Bank. But he is unable to understand what he is thinking.

"It doesn't make sense. The gillnets need to go on flat land and this is like a volcano," he says.

Just before dusk begins falling, the *Thunder* glides past the *Bob Barker*. One of Sea Shepherd's officers sees the silhouette of a man on the bridge who is raising a clenched fist at the *Bob Barker*.

"Something will kick off tonight. Our nights of peaceful sleep are over," Adam Meyerson predicts.

The captain of the *Thunder* calls up the *Bob Barker* again and again, but this time it is Hammarstedt who neglects to answer.

"They have ignored our calls before. I think now we can ignore them," he says.

The *Thunder* draws closer. Hammarstedt presses the alarm that is a signal to the crew that everyone who is not busy doing something is to meet in the messroom. All the bulkheads are now to be secured. He wants to know where each and every member of the crew is to be found, in the event of a collision and if the *Thunder* breaks open a hole in the *Bob Barker's* hull, they must ensure that the water cannot spread throughout the ship. He sees that the bow of the *Thunder* is headed for the helicopter deck astern on the *Bob Barker*. Then the captain of the *Thunder* calls him up again on the radio. It's a sign of weakness, Hammarstedt thinks.

"They don't seem that confident in close quarters," he says.

Hammarstedt has been in many close-range battles at sea and is certain that he has more experience in manoeuvring in such duels than the *Thunder*'s captain.

"We can do this little rodeo thing," he says to Meyerson, who has come up onto the bridge again.

"The *Thunder* has tried to back into us, turn into us and run us down. I hope they have learned not to be aggressive towards us. Do the right thing. Go into port and face the music," Meyerson says.

The *Thunder* is now perilously close to the quarterdeck of the *Bob Barker*, but all of a sudden, the trawler changes course and avoids a collision. Then the *Thunder* stops moving. It is almost as if the captain has decided that the vessel needs to rest. All night long the two ships pitch beside one another, like an old married couple that have argued themselves to sleep.

The next morning, the *Thunder* begins moving slowly in the direction of the net. The Norwegian fisheries officer Tor Glistrup has asked Hammarstedt to try to get hold of one of the net floats. If it is from the same brand and the same series as the floats the *Sam Simon* picked up where Hammarstedt found the *Thunder*, it is evidence that it was the *Thunder* that left behind the illegal gillnet at the Banzare Bank. Hammarstedt gathers the crew in the messroom. If the weather is good enough, he wants to try to navigate the *Bob Barker* between the *Thunder* and the net floats.

"We will do what we can to make it difficult for them, but there are different factors that may make it too dangerous for us to intervene. If we have a collision situation, we lose them. If we have a crane going bad, we lose them. I just don't want you to see it as a failure if they manage to get the gillnet up," he says to the crew.

They approach the net floats and the two vessels move into close quarters once again. Hammarstedt positions the *Bob Barker* between the fish net and the *Thunder*, but now the captain of the *Thunder* is navigating more aggressively. The trawler cuts in towards the starboard side of the *Bob Barker*, and it appears as if the captain has planned to pass right in front of the bow of the Sea Shepherd ship. It is a fatally dangerous manoeuvre. He calls up Hammarstedt again and again, says that he isn't afraid and that "Peter" is a terrible captain. For a few short minutes he is suddenly on a first name basis with Hammarstedt, who responds with a long blast of the ship's horn. Then Hammarstedt presses the ship's alarm again, so the crew of the *Bob Barker* runs to the messroom.

The ships are so close together that Hammarstedt can make out the faces of the deck crew on the *Thunder* who are now standing lined up along the railing. It is clear that they have prepared themselves for fishing. Is it a coincidence that at least a dozen Indonesians are now standing in the exact spot where the *Bob Barker* will hit the *Thunder* if they collide? Or has a cynical devil ordered them to stand there?

Two officers exit the bridge of the *Thunder* and are both holding something in their hands that resembles a compact camera. One of them is dressed in black trousers and a brown jacket, and he is wearing a black cap pulled down to the frames of his oblong glasses. He leans down behind one of the white containers that protect the life rafts from the wind and weather. Now they are protecting the officers from the tele-photo lens of Simon Ager. The officer wearing a dark purple jacket with washed-out patterns, camouflage trousers and a ski mask makes no attempt to hide. He positions himself straddle-legged and almost demonstratively in Hammarstedt's field of vision and looks toward the bridge. The two ships pitch slowly up and down on the swells that the bad weather left in its wake. If neither ship backs down, they are going to collide.

"That's going to be close … Zero pitch. Zero pitch. Let's go ten astern. Twenty astern!" Hammarstedt calls.

He guns the engine astern, and when the *Thunder* passes in front of the *Bob Barker* headed for the net floats, there is barely half a metre between the two steel giants. At all times the man behind the ski mask is looking in the direction of his opponent on the *Bob Barker*. It is as if he wants to demonstrate that he will win this battle.

Hammarstedt knows that he has lost the opportunity to prevent the *Thunder* from hauling up the nets. Soon the crew of the *Bob Barker* will be obliged to observe the sight of wriggling marine life dangling along the hull of the pirate trawler. The first thing Hammarstedt does is to beg his officers' pardon. He backed down; that is unusual for a Sea Shepherd captain.

"As long as there are crew hanging out on the deck on the *Thunder*, there is little I can do," he says.

The catch was not much to speak of. A few small cod, some crab and lobster and a small shark or two that was thrown back in. The lobster goes straight to the cook who that same evening prepares a feast.

The fishing captain Juan Manuel Patiño Lampon is in a better mood than he has been for a long time. He has been fed up with the standstill and the monotonous diet of split cod, frozen chicken and rice. He wants to work, he wants to eat fresh seafood and he wants to test how far Hammarstedt is willing to go to prevent him from fishing. And if Sea Shepherd should attempt to pull up the nets that could give them a chance to take off. The officers on the *Thunder* saw that Sea Shepherd filmed everything they did. They heard the young captain repeating over and over again on the radio that they were fishing illegally and that they were going to stop them but he failed to do so. It was Sea Shepherd's captain who backed down.

After the net had been hauled up out of the ocean, a lengthy outburst of expletives poured over the radio. Captain Luis Alfonso Rubio Cataldo told Hammarstedt that they had been given a green light from the ship owner to fish and that they had a permit, but Hammarstedt did not want to listen.

The next day the *Thunder* once again begins gliding slowly towards the Melville Bank. The Sea Shepherd crew prepares itself for another confrontation and now they know how the captain navigates the *Thunder* when they are fishing. The weather is also better. On the foredeck, the tarp is removed from the largest dinghy, the *Gemini*. While the dirt and salt are being washed off the outboard motors, the third mate Anteo

Broadfield navigates the *Bob Barker* closer to the *Thunder*. He sounds a blast on the ship's horn to get the *Thunder*'s captain's attention; he wants to show him that the dinghy is ready for launching.

Then the *Thunder* stops. The captain calls up the bridge of the *Bob Barker*.

"Buenas tardes, Bob Barker."

Cataldo says that he has received permission from the government of Nigeria to fish, a lie that will be quickly communicated to Interpol's headquarters in Lyon.

"We don't believe you. If you start fishing, we are going to cut the nets," Hammarstedt replies.

"If you cut the nets, you will be destroying private property. I will take photographs and video everything you do," Cataldo threatens.

"Tell him that he can take as many photos and videos as he likes. He can get some great shots of us cutting his nets," Hammarstedt says.

The *Thunder*'s captain does not back down. They have received orders and if Sea Shepherd behaves aggressively towards them, they will behave aggressively in return.

"OK. Tell him that we are ready," Hammarstedt says.

Now the crew prepares the ship for action. They are going to carry out what they failed to accomplish the day before. If they can manage to fish up one of the net floats with an iron hook, they can cut the net. Hammarstedt takes the helm while Meyerson regulates their speed.

The *Bob Barker* glides slowly in the wake of the *Thunder* with its course set for the closest net float, which has just been expelled from the hatch on the *Thunder*'s stern. On the *Bob Barker*'s starboard side the crew stands at ready on deck to throw out iron hooks attached to long ropes to capture the floats.

"Grab it when you can," Hammarstedt calls over the walkie-talkie to the long-haired, strapping boatswain Alistair Alan.

The entire net is now in the water, and they both see that the trawler is about to turn around.

"Hurry up. The *Thunder* is coming back at us," Hammarstedt says.

The first attempt to throw out an iron hook falls short. On deck, Alan urges the deck crew to throw it out again and the next throw is perfect. The hook attaches itself to the ropes, and powerful arms hoist net floats and marker lines up on the broadside of the *Bob Barker*.

"Tell us as soon as we are free from the line," Hammarstedt shouts.

If they fail to cut the floats away quickly, it could all be dragged backwards and into the propeller. And now the *Thunder* is headed straight towards them. The marker line is cut with a sharp knife and the net slips out of the danger zone. On the bridge, Hammarstedt and Meyerson clap their hands together in a high five.

Then they hear the voice of the *Thunder*'s captain over the radio. He is furious and says that they are coming to save the net floats.

"I will get it back the good way or the bad way," Cataldo says.

"We have to pick up speed. He might hit us," Hammarstedt says to his officers.

Anteo Broadfield can hardly believe his eyes.

"The chase is reversed," he says.

On the radio, the *Thunder*'s captain continues his tirade.

"This is theft and we want the nets back."

"We are collecting evidence for your prosecution," Hammarstedt answers.

"We are going to follow you. You were the ones who started this war. I have received an order to retrieve the floats."

"Tell him that they can follow us to Mauritius," Hammarstedt says.

The captain of the *Thunder* makes a few desperate attempts to psyche out his opponent. He says that "Peter" can't navigate, but they both know that it would take an engine breakdown on the *Bob Barker* for the *Thunder* to manage to catch up with the Sea Shepherd vessel.

"So he said that we started this war?" Hammarstedt asks.

"Yup. Wars to save the planet and the fisheries," Adam Meyerson replies, who decides to tease the *Thunder*'s captain. "Let's keep the speed just a little bit faster so they will continue to chase us and spend as much fuel as possible. They can chase us all day long," he chuckles.

Hammarstedt is ecstatic. Can he get the *Thunder* to chase them all the way to Mauritius?

The *Bob Barker* is now doing 10.8 knots and creeps slowly away from the *Thunder*.

"So now we know that they can do 10 knots if they want," Chief Engineer Erwin Vermeulen says.

"The engine is fine, Erwin?" Hammarstedt asks.

"Yes."

On the *Thunder*, the delicious lobster meal of the night before is now a distant memory. The first thing Captain Cataldo did when Sea Shepherd hoisted the floats on board and cut the net was to call the ship owner in Galicia in Spain. The order was clear: Follow the *Bob Barker*, we want the floats back. But they knew that it was futile. Cataldo continues sputtering. He repeats that he didn't believe that this would happen. Calls Hammarstedt a punk. The fishing captain Lampon is also angry, but is not as communicative as the captain. They can push the engine all they want, but it won't do any good.

After a couple of hours they give up the chase.

24

MESSAGE IN A BOTTLE
THE INDIAN OCEAN,
FEBRUARY 2015

Although they are trapped in the same hopeless situation, the Spanish-speaking and Asian crews on the *Thunder* live in two different worlds.

During the first month of the chase, the Indonesian crew was told to stay below deck. They hung out smoking in the narrow hallways outside the crew cabins. In the evenings they played poker in the messroom or watched motocross videos, action films and recordings of the most recent World Cup football matches. When they finally received permission to move about on deck, they made a football out of a knotted tangle of rags. There was a small library on board with a shelf of books by Isabel Allende and a handful of other Spanish-speaking authors, but nothing in Indonesian.

For most of the Indonesians, it was their first voyage on the *Thunder*. Half of them came from the city Tegal in the Central Java province, a traditional fishing community where sailing on a foreign trawler could at best reward them with adventure, a proper income and a higher status than that of the coastal fishermen in their home town. But it could also mean gruelling labour, sudden accidents and racial conflicts. They earned one-tenth of what the Europeans did and were at the bottom of the ladder in the ship's rigid hierarchy.

When the *Thunder* was arrested in Malaysia in 2014, the Indonesians rebelled. They complained about the fishing gear and about racism, and the confrontation culminated in a fist fight and mutiny. After the rebellion, the *Thunder* sailed out with an entirely new Indonesian crew. Only the Indonesian cook and two deckhands went along on the final voyage. The entire crew was now on one-year contracts and received 350 dollars a month – four times more than they would earn for unskilled work at home.

Few of the Indonesian crew now dare ask why they are being chased; they speak seldom or never with anyone but each other. Only a minority know the names of the officers on the bridge of the *Thunder*. The eldest of the Indonesians, a man in his late 40s named Edy, assumes the role of leader. He is the one they gather around now with the question that is weighing on them the most: will they ever be paid their wages?

The *Thunder* maintains a speed of four knots northward, very likely to make its way out of "the Furious Forties", where the weather is a constant threat.

Every morning Hammarstedt sends a news update to Interpol. He also updates the Dutch and British authorities, but he seldom or never receives a reply. The lack of response bothers him. Had the *Thunder* been loaded with cocaine or weapons instead of toothfish, the ship would have long since been boarded.

But if he can add some information about slave labour and human trafficking to the *Thunder*'s criminal record, Interpol can be forced to become involved.

In the great cabin, Peter Hammarstedt sits down at the little writing desk and writes a letter to the Indonesian crew. He explains who Sea Shepherd is and that the *Thunder* is blacklisted, wanted and being monitored by international authorities.

"We mean no harm and you should not worry, as we are compassionate people who follow the law. We really appreciate it if you can trust us. If you need help we will help you. If you have any problems about pay and your treatment we will fight for your rights under international law. Please tell us how we can help you? Do you need any food, or medical help, or other help?" Hammarstedt writes in the letter.

He continues with an invitation to join forces in a joint venture.

"When you see our small boat in the water, you can throw us messages in a plastic bottle, especially messages for your families. We will pass your messages to your families and their replies to you. We understand you are just workers and only do everything according to the orders of your superiors. You may not even know that the company you work for was illegally fishing. Our target is not you and we have no intention of causing you any trouble, that's why we should work together.

"As your captain and officers are criminals according to the law, we want to see them prosecuted. We have more fuel and more food than *Thunder* and will stay with the ship until the *Thunder* goes into port. The captain and the owner must be brought to court to answer for their illegal fishing but you have done nothing wrong. Any information about the names of the officers and owner of the ship, including their nationalities will greatly help us."

Through a contact in Australia he has the letter translated into Indonesian, prints out numerous copies, and inserts the messages into plastic bottles containing rice to give them ballast.

Then they lower the dinghy from the *Sam Simon*, which has come from the Southern Ocean to join the *Bob Barker* for a few days. The dinghy first sails in along the starboard side of the *Thunder*, and as soon as they see somebody from the Indonesian crew, they fling the messages on board.

The sight of the plastic bottles pelting down upon the *Thunder*'s deck is like a spark for Juan Manuel Patiño Lampon's easily ignited fuse.

"Bloody punks," he shouts.

He grabs one of the black ski-masks on the bridge and pulls it down over his head. Then he runs off the bridge and down the ladder to the deck, where he orders the crew to collect the bottles and deposit them on the bridge. He walks toward the quarterdeck, picks up a bottle, opens it and sits down on a crate under the wheelhouse to read the message. He promptly gets to his feet, tears it up and throws it into the ocean. For a while he remains there, walking back and forth on the deck looking for more messages, until he bends down, picks up a short length of chain and walks towards the railing.

Peter Hammarstedt has navigated the *Bob Barker* as close to the *Thunder* as he can get to gain a clear view of what is now taking place on deck.

"The Balaclava Man has got something to throw," Hammarstedt warns on the radio as Lampon moves toward the stern of the *Thunder*.

He hurls the chain towards the dinghy with all his might. The Sea Shepherd photographer Simon Ager sees it coming through the camera's viewfinder. As he ducks to the right, it grazes against his helmet. Then a short metal pipe flies through the air and hits the photographer on the inside of his thigh.

"Are you all right, Simon ... What was it?" asks the boatswain Giacomo Giorgi, also in the dinghy.

"A bolt ... It was a good shot," Ager answers.

Simon Ager is uninjured and Peter Hammarstedt has a good story to sell. The episode reinforces the image of the *Thunder* as a bandit ship on which officers wearing balaclava helmets refuse to allow the crew to communicate with the surrounding world, something which strengthens Hammarstedt's theory about their being held on board the ship against their will.

"The metal implements were thrown with the intent to cause injury or death. The deck officer wore a balaclava to conceal his identity. One RHIB crewman was struck but sustained no serious injuries," Peter Hammarstedt writes in the report he sends to Interpol.

The police and authorities following the ship's progress from land are gravely concerned that the chase will end with a loss of human lives.

25

RAID ON THE HIGH SEAS
THE INDIAN OCEAN,
FEBRUARY 2015

The operation was planned in detail and cleared all the way up to the minister level. For the first time the Australian authorities would board one of "The Bandit 6" vessels in international waters.

On the morning of 27 February, the group of silent, armed agents dressed in black climb on board the *Kunlun*.

The Peruvian captain Alberto Zavaleta Salas is asleep while the plans are being made. When he is awakened and learns what is about to happen, he trots up to the bridge. There, right beside the *Kunlun*, he sees a strange and awkward military-grey ship with three hulls and the word "CUSTOMS" painted in clear letters on the side.

A feeling of invincibility had spread on board the *Kunlun* after they had outmanoeuvred the battleship from New Zealand. During the last weeks of January they filled the cold storage room with 181 tons of toothfish worth in excess of 3 million dollars, but then Sea Shepherd showed up and chased them away from the fish bank. Now their course was set for Sri Lanka.

On the bridge the fishing captain Sevilla is working frenetically to ward off the pending catastrophe. Over the radio he tells the captain of the Australian patrol ship ACV *Triton* that they are in international waters and that the agents are not authorized to board. But his words fall on deaf ears.

It is the first time the *Kunlun* is boarded on the high seas. On the bridge there are documents lying about the authorities must not see.

The first thing the agents ask for is the captain. Sevilla indicates the shipmaster Zavaleta Salas, who points back at the fishing captain Sevilla. But the Spanish fishing captain speaks English and he has the crew list, which states that Zavaleta Salas is the *Kunlun*'s captain – and on paper, responsible for the ship. When the agents ask Zavaleta Salas for his name, address and telephone number, he reluctantly obeys. What he has feared throughout the entire voyage is now in the process of happening. Everything is rigged to make him the scapegoat, the one to be sacrificed so the fishing captain Sevilla and the others will be spared taking responsibility for the ship's catalogue of sins.

On the mere suspicion of pirate activity, slave traffic, illegal broadcasting, statelessness or that the ship is from their own country, the Australian agents could force their way on board.[1] Now they finally had a pretext. The authorities of Equatorial Guinea have confirmed that the *Kunlun* is not flagged in the country. The *Kunlun* is probably sailing under a false flag. In order to check whether or not the ship is stateless, they must inspect all the papers and find the owner.

Arresting the ship and forcing it to land in Australia is not an option, since the *Kunlun* has not been fishing in Australian waters and there are no Australian citizens on the ship.

The customs agents have been instructed to document the cargo, acquire the ship's documents and search for emails, telephone numbers and scraps of paper with names and addresses. On the bridge they find the telephone numbers of several members of the Vidal syndicate in Galicia, emails containing messages from the ship owner, receipts, illegal gillnets and data documenting the catch and where it was from.

They also make another surprising find. The *Kunlun* has been monitoring the movements of Australia's large research ship, the *Aurora Australis*. The only thing they can't find is the documents proving that the ship has two identities.

After the raid the *Kunlun* is permitted to sail on. For the bird of ill omen, Alberto Zavaleta Salas, the adversity feels endless. When he receives the order to set his course for Phuket in Thailand, he has the feeling that he is headed for his own downfall.

For almost 20 years the Australian authorities have been trying to stop the pirate fleet, but that it was the pirates' arrogance that would prove to be their greatest vulnerability was something Glen Salmon, the man in charge of the work, had not anticipated. Formerly the pirate fleet sailed under real flags and with genuine documents. Now they evidently used their imagination and forged documents to pretend they had all the formalities in order. They believed they were untouchable, Salmon thinks.

When Salmon starts going through the materials confiscated on board, he is able to piece together large segments of the mission the *Kunlun* has been on, as well as who has been giving the ship its orders.

He burns the evidence onto 17 DVDs and sends them to the authorities in Spain and to "Operation Spillway".

On the *Bob Barker* Peter Hammarstedt starts the day by describing the drama that took place west of the Cocos Islands.

"No word yet as to whether there will be an arrest. The *Kunlun* must have headed home after the *Sam Simon* left them. Must have been a very bad season for them," he says to applause from the crew.

When he comes up onto the bridge and studies the *Thunder* through his binoculars, he becomes convinced that the news about the boarding has reached the ship. All the fishing gear has been removed from the deck.

"I wouldn't be surprised if they are destroying evidence and that it is an indication of their being ready to head home," he says on the bridge.

The jubilation of the morning meeting evaporates when the crew hears that the *Kunlun* has been allowed to continue sailing. First mate Adam Meyerson leans over the map table and shakes his head in despair over the Australian authorities.

"Wow! Those guys are pretty weak."[2]

26

OPERATION SPARROW
RIBEIRA, MARCH 2015

They react with the speed of lightning. First they lock the door. Then they turn off the light. Subsequently they start up the paper shredder.

Three fisheries officers are standing beneath the colonnade by Vidal Armadore's offices in Ribeira. They have in their hands a search warrant, but nonetheless announce their arrival by ringing the doorbell. The moment that environmentalists and the authorities of several countries have for years been waiting for is about to culminate in a clumsy anti-climax. Operation Sparrow, named after Johnny Depp's unpredictable character in *Pirates of the Caribbean*, was supposed to be a unique operation in a European context. For the first time, the secret owners of "The Bandit 6" were to be flushed out into the light of day.

Now the officers are standing and staring irresolutely at a closed door. Then they call the local police station and request assistance. Fifteen minutes after ringing the bell, they are finally inside the room where the paper shredder is in the process of cutting to ribbons the evidence of 20 years of illegal fishing in Antarctica. The first thing the fisheries officers do is to turn off the shredder. Amongst the strips of paper, they see the remains of documents from 2012. In a tiny storeroom deep inside the premises, they find several boxes of documents that somebody has obviously attempted to hide.

One of the three individuals frantically at work inside the shipping company premises is Serafín Vidal, the man who hired Alberto Zavaleta Salas as captain of the *Kunlun* and who is responsible for recruiting crew members for the fleet that has been plundering toothfish stocks in the Southern Ocean. Soon Manuel Antonio "Toño" Vidal Pego also come rushing in. "Toño", the family's business mind, who has a predilection for luxury apartments, expensive restaurants and fast cars, sits down and writes 50 pages of comments on the documents that are confiscated. But it is too late.

For decades the Spanish authorities have been accused of protecting the fishing mafia. Now there is another tone. The new law that gives the authorities the right to fine any Spaniard who has demonstrably had dealings with a vessel that is fishing illegally is brought to "Toño's" attention.

When the officers leave Vidal Armadores' head office on the afternoon of 11 March 2015, they are carrying more than 3,000 documents. The contents of the cardboard boxes will prove disastrous for the Vidal family.

At his spacious office in Madrid, Assistant Director Héctor Villa González is anxiously waiting in the inspection department of the Spanish Ministry of Agriculture, Food and the Environment for the results of the raid in Ribeira.

He has already learned one thing: the next time they are going to raid a shipping company under suspicion for poaching fish, they will be accompanied by policemen who can break down the door. But the take is nonetheless formidable. Based on the confiscated documents, the 17 DVDs of data the Australian authorities confiscated on the *Kunlun* and information from Interpol, New Zealand and Belize, they can reconstruct a number of the missions of the Vidal ships in the Antarctic. The documents also provide unique insight on how the ship owners have organized their business.[1]

The toothfish expeditions to the Antarctic have been led from the office in Ribeira. From there the shipping company has planned the expeditions, recruited crew, bought equipment and supplies and paid for fuel and insurance. To cover up the tracks of the illegal fishing activities, the family has constructed a conglomerate of companies in Europe and Latin America. The owners of the four ships that can be connected to the Vidal family's Antarctic expeditions, the *Kunlun*, *Songhua*, *Yongding* and *Tiantai*, have been companies in the tax havens of Panama and Belize. It is also through these companies that the Vidal family has hired crew for the missions. But what has happened to all the money?

Only the name of one company could be seen on the facade of the Vidal office in Ribeira: Proyectos y Desarrollos Renovables – renewable projects and development.

In recent years the Vidal family has invested heavily in the local community – and they have invested for the future. In the neighbouring municipality, Manual Antonio Vidal Pego opened a windmill park in 2013. Leaders of the province and local mayors attended the formal inauguration ceremony. In another neighbouring municipality, the family has established a large fish oil factory that has received EUR 6.6 million in subsidies from the EU, the Spanish government and local authorities in Galicia. After having ruined the city's reputation, the Vidal family would rise again as environmentally conscious and innovative investors in the local community. They would create jobs and be applauded by the authorities.

In Madrid Villa González studies the confusing company chart the officers have drawn. Towards the bottom of the pyramid he finds something strange – a company in the tax haven of Switzerland. Manuel Antonio Vidal Pego, his brother Angel "Naño" Vidal Pego and an experienced Swiss investment manager have seats on the board. The company from the mountainous country without a coastline is listed as being a specialty wholesaler of fish, crawfish and molluscs. Has the Vidal family brought money back to Spain via Switzerland, for subsequent investment in renewable energy and the fish oil industry? Villa González wonders. It can appear so.

Villa González sits down at the desk and takes out a calculator. Based on the appraisals, they know too little about the total sales volume of the Vidal family's Antarctic fleet over the course of 20 years, but estimate that the family in a two-year period has sold illegally caught toothfish for at least EUR 17 million.

As he is trying to figure out a suitable punishment, Villa González has already started planning the next raid. Against the ship owner he suspects of owning the *Thunder*.

27

EXERCISE GOOD HOPE
OSLO/LAGOS/CAPE TOWN,
MARCH 2015

"I think they're going to round the Cape," an elated Peter Hammarstedt says on the bridge of the *Bob Barker*.

The two ships are 400 nautical miles south of the African continent. After having drifted for weeks, suddenly the *Thunder* picks up speed heading west. Is this the end game? Hammarstedt wonders.

"Should we get our hopes up this early, Peter?" the third mate Anteo Broadfield asks.

"What's the point in having hopes if you're not going to get them up once in a while," Hammarstedt replies.

He feels certain the *Thunder* does not have enough fuel to make it back to a harbour in Southeast Asia. It is likely that the chase will end somewhere or other along the west coast of Africa, perhaps in Namibia or Angola. Spanish ship owners have virtually taken over the city and the harbour in Walvis Bay in Namibia. There are processing factories there and a good motorway running down to Cape Town, where poached Patagonian toothfish have been shipped out in containers previously, often facilitated by bribes and creative customs declarations.

And then there is Angola, the dictatorship with many small harbours and few customs inspectors. It is difficult to predict what awaits them if the chase ends there. The worst part is perhaps the constantly gnawing uneasiness that the *Thunder* will receive help from another vessel at sea, and when they see a ship appear on the radar with its course set in their direction, the speculations start up again.

"It is not on Marine Traffic," the communications officer Stefan Ehmann says, who is monitoring the enormous database providing an overview of the locations of more than a half-million vessels.

"Very strange to see traffic this far south and because they're coming so close to us that gives us cause for alarm," Hammarstedt says, who can now see the lights from the ship through his binoculars.

Should he call them up on the radio or should he wait to see whether the *Thunder* adjusts its course or speed to meet the mysterious ship? What if the vessel is something else entirely, something he hasn't considered before?

"Could it be a navy ship?"

In an old villa beside a frozen apple orchard in a small town outside Oslo, the Norwegian lawyer Eve de Coning is sitting and pondering. She is a member of the intelligence group that is trying to stop the *Thunder*; night and day for more than two months she has been thinking about the chase that is now taking place in the Indian Ocean. No sooner has she changed out of her pyjamas than the two vessels have again forced their way into her consciousness.[1] Now she has a plan. Off the coast of Cape Town, a mere day's sail from the two ships is a fleet of German and South African battleships that can stop the *Thunder*.

The boarding and arrest of pirate trawlers has been done on the high seas previously and has in many cases ended with the crew and ship owners going free. International waters are a wet Wild West where nobody actually has any authority. If the *Thunder* enters the economic zone of a coastal state, it is simpler, but the *Thunder*'s captain has consistently stayed in international waters. He knows what is at stake, de Coning thinks. If they are going to succeed with an operation at sea, Nigeria and South Africa must collaborate. Nigeria is a flag state and South Africa has modern vessels and experience with boarding on the open ocean.

There are countless opportunities for things to go wrong, but they have a concrete plan. De Coning believes they can succeed.

On Monday 9 March, a powerful armada sets out from the naval base in Simon's Town on the eastern side of the Cape Peninsula. The first vessel out is the South African submarine the *SAS Manthatisi*. Following it are the three frigates the *SAS Spioenkop*, *FSG Hessen* and *FSG Karlsruhe*. Once they have sailed out of the lively waters of False Bay, the huge, cauldron-shaped bay that received its name from seamen who believed they were on their way in to Cape Town, a large Super Lynx helicopter lands on the deck of one of the frigates. For the many observers watching the battleships from land, it is a dramatic sight.[2]

At the same time, the worst forest fire in living memory is raging on the craggy mountainsides surrounding the bay. Smoke and flames are whisked up along the rocks by the intractable wind that will soon create difficulties for the military operation "Exercise Good Hope".

Every other year the South African and German Navies train together in the maritime regions off the coast of the southern part of the African continent, a series of windblown cliffs that for seamen mark the end of one ocean and the beginning of another. Along this strip of coastline the warm Agulhas stream, which flows south-westward at speeds of up to six knots, meets strong and unpredictable winds from Antarctica and the South Atlantic. The collision can produce monstrous waves more than 20 metres high. As many as 3,000 ships may have gone down along South Africa's savage coastline.

The modern German and South African battleships have no difficulties manoeuvring their way out of False Bay and past the Cape of Good Hope. On board are soldiers trained in boarding ships on turbulent seas. In Nigeria, Captain Warredi Enisuoh has asked the country's Interpol office to send in a request to South Africa for assistance in arresting the *Thunder*. All that is missing is for the authorities in Nigeria to send a formal legal request to South Africa for help. Then they can stop the

Thunder and simultaneously demonstrate to Sea Shepherd that the authorities are not helpless. This is the best opportunity the Interpol group will receive, Eve de Coning thinks.

But why is Nigeria waiting?

In Lagos Captain Warredi Enisuoh has received a disturbing letter. The sender is the Special Services Office from the office of the president of Nigeria and the letter is addressed to the Minister of Agriculture in Nigeria. Next to the threatening title of the letter – "United States Government Indicts Nigeria over Illegal Fishing", the minister has written the word "Urgent" in red ink. The USA is threatening to impose sanctions on Nigeria because despite the fact that the country has two vessels on its ships register that have been fishing illegally in the Antarctic year after year, the authorities' have failed to take any action. One of them is the *Thunder*. "I thought that actions were taken?" the Minister of Agriculture has written on the letter in the same red ink.

This turns the situation upside down for Enisuoh. Becoming involved in a dangerous, uncertain and expensive operation at sea with South Africa is no longer the best alternative for the Nigerian authorities. There is a much simpler solution for Nigeria, a solution nobody can blame them for and which will fix relations with the USA. Instead of asking South Africa to send out battleships, the Nigerian coast guard decides to throw the *Thunder* out of the ships register. With a stroke of the pen, the *Thunder* is made a stateless vessel. Now, in principle, anyone at all can go out and arrest the vessel without Nigeria's help. At the same time, the country need not fear sanctions from the USA.

Enisuoh knows that Eve de Coning and others in the intelligence group will be disappointed. Everyone has produced strong arguments in favour of Nigeria's taking responsibility and now they will probably think that he has found a simple solution to a difficult problem. But they don't know Nigeria like he does, Enisuoh thinks. The worst that can happen is that the Nigerian prosecuting authority initiates criminal proceedings against the officers. The country is in the midst of a turbulent presidential election campaign, and the laws regarding the alleged infringements are too weak. The best and simplest solution is thus to remove the *Thunder* from the Nigerian registers, Enisuoh thinks. Nigeria failed to take action. And the members of the Interpol group think that's worth weeping over.

Now there is only one remaining option. Take the *Thunder* when the ship puts in at port.

The *Bob Barker* and the *Thunder* have long since rounded the Cape of Good Hope and are at the latitude of the harbour town of Lüderitz in the south of Namibia. The *Thunder* continues north and shows no sign of moving towards land.

"On day 22 of the chase we all speculated what it would be like around day 90. Now you know what it feels like," Hammarstedt says to the crew in the morning meeting.

The unfamiliar vessel they believed to be a battleship turned out to be a commercial ship on its way to Singapore. The captain asked where the *Bob Barker* was headed and Hammarstedt replied:

"We are bound for ports unknown."[3]

28

THE BIRD OF ILL OMEN

THE SOUTH ATLANTIC OCEAN, MARCH 2015

It is a bad omen: an albatross whacks into the foremast of the *Bob Barker*. The powerful bird drops down onto the foredeck, and lies there flapping helplessly.

Peter Hammarstedt carries his superstition like a much older seaman. If he sees somebody spilling salt in the messroom, he gets up immediately and throws a handful of salt over his right shoulder. If he hears somebody whistle, he immediately orders them away from the bridge before they succeed in summoning a storm. To hint that one's own or another ship could ever sink is also taboo. It is therefore one of the possible fates of the *Thunder* that is never discussed on board the *Bob Barker*.

To allow an albatross to die on the foredeck is also a cardinal sin.

For generations, the albatross has lived in the imaginative universes of sailors. For a long time nobody knew exactly where the bird came from or where it was headed. When it soared up along the side of a vessel, it was as if it was only making a brief visit to our world. In mythology, it carried the souls of drowned seamen. In Samuel Taylor Coleridge's poem "The Rime of the Ancient Mariner" a ship is blown off course and finds itself helpless in the Antarctic. An albatross appears and leads it out of the ice and fog, but when one of the crew shoots the albatross, a curse is put on the ship. The cadaver of the albatross is hung around the neck of the shooter as an eternal burden, while the thirsty and helpless crew drifts towards the equator and death.

On board the *Thunder* nobody can afford to believe in the dead albatross' curse. At first the illegal fleet fished toothfish with longlines. The albatrosses that always followed the ship dove for the bait, were dragged down into the depths and drowned. The loyal giant, which can live more than 50 years and remains faithful to one partner throughout an entire lifetime, was almost wiped out. At most, the illegal fleet killed 100,000 albatrosses a year. Of the 22 different species, 19 were on the verge of extinction.

While the *Thunder* was wreaking devastation in the Southern Ocean, Prince Charles, the British heir to the throne, wrote a letter to the Labour Party government's Minister of the Environment to bring the poaching of toothfish to his attention. It was the fate of the albatross that triggered the prince's concern.

"I particularly hope that the illegal fishing of the Patagonian toothfish will be high on your list of priorities because, until that trade is stopped, there is little hope for the poor old albatross, for which I shall continue to campaign," he wrote in a letter in 2004.

The Prince of Wales also suggested that the British Navy should be involved in the search for the illegal toothfish fleet.[1]

To save his own disabled albatross, Hammarstedt slows down the *Bob Barker* and calls the ship's physician and veterinarian Colette Harmsen. Folding its wings together, Harmsen picks up the bird and carries it out onto the quarterdeck. There it has a runway long enough to allow it to take flight.

When the albatross is airborne once more, Hammarstedt returns to the great cabin and closes the door behind him. The cabin is situated directly under the bridge, so he can get there in just a few seconds. The portholes in the cabin face forward, so at all times the shipmaster can see what is happening on the foredeck.

It is the only place where he can remove himself from the questions, speculations and expectations. Some of the crew view him as being private and reserved, bordering on anti-social, but they appreciate his dark, cunning sense of humour. Few have heard him raise his voice.

In the corner of the great cabin there is a small desk and a tiny kitchenette with a freezer that is always filled with blue-berries for Hammarstedt's daily smoothies. The bulkheads are clad with dark, African bamboo and decorated with a replica of a sword bearing the eye of Odin embedded in the haft and a painting of a sperm whale. The berth is luxuriously wide, but runs lengthwise across the cabin so the pitching of the ship is transmitted through its entire breadth. When the *Bob Barker* is plunging in the waves, Hammarstedt lies rolling back and forth like an empty bottle.

When Hammarstedt found the ship it was called the *Polaris* and was abandoned and forgotten in Abidjan, the capital of the Ivory Coast. The *Polaris* was covered with a fine layer of red dust found only in West Africa. Streaks of moisture were running from the bulkheads, and when Hammarstedt swept the beam of his flashlight over the flooring, he saw the cockroaches scurrying into their hiding places. The motor started with a reluctant sigh. Nonetheless, she was the vessel he wanted.

The *Bob Barker* was built as the *Pol XIV* in Fredrikstad, Norway in 1951, and became a part of the fleet that made Norway a whaling superpower. For ten years the ship operated out of Grytviken in South Georgia. By the time it was removed from service, more than 350,000 blue whales had been slaughtered in the Southern Ocean since the beginning of the century. The Norwegian whalers were so effective that they boasted about being able to cut up 50,000 kilos of whale meat in the amount of time it took a housewife to clean a mackerel.

Then the fate of the ship underwent a series of strange reversals. Back in Norway it was converted into the coast guard vessel the *Volstad Jr.* and used to chase Sea Shepherd's *Whales Forever* out of Lofoten during their action targeting Norwegian whalers in 1994. Three years later, the *Volstad Jr.* was rebuilt for the transport of tourists in the waters around Svalbard, but the ship never had any success there. Finally, it ended up in the Gulf of Guinea as a bunkering ship for the fishing fleet.

Sea Shepherd had long been looking for a new campaign vessel. During a meeting with the American television host and multimillionaire Robert William "Bob" Barker, Paul Watson claimed that for 5 million dollars he would manage to stop the Japanese whaling crafts in the Southern Ocean.

"I think you do have the skills to do that. And I have 5 million, so let's get it on," Barker replied.[2]

This saved the vessel from being scrapped. Subsequent to rebuilding in Mauritius, in 2010, painted black and under a false flag, it sailed into the Antarctic as the MY *Bob Barker*. The ship was registered in Togo, but the Norwegian flag fluttered on its bow.

"The Japanese could be forgiven for thinking that the pro-whaling Norwegians had sent a ship to support their illegal whaling activities in the Southern Ocean Whale Sanctuary. But any excitement turned to disappointment quickly as the Norwegian flag was hauled down and the black and white skull with crossed Trident and Shepherd's crook was raised to announce the arrival of the *Bob Barker*," Sea Shepherd bragged after the incident.[3]

She was the most important tool he had in the search for the *Thunder*. The *Bob Barker*'s radar has a range of 20 nautical miles. If the *Bob Barker* were to let him down, the *Thunder* would be out of sight in less than two hours.

29

THE WANDERER
GABON, MARCH 2015

"It is a whole world of crazy," Peter Hammarstedt thinks as he looks at the map lying in front of him on the bridge.

The *Thunder* and the *Bob Barker* are sailing north at the outer edge of the Benguela Current, the cold ocean current carrying nutrient-rich water from the South Atlantic Ocean along the West African coast that has made Namibia and Angola into wealthy fishing nations. The interior is a scorched and ruthless landscape that was desiccated 80 million years ago. When the warm, dry air from the Namib Desert meets the cold, damp ocean air, the coast is enveloped in a thick belt of fog. More than a thousand ships have perished due to the fog, currents, cantankerous winds and waves along Namibia's Skeleton Coast. It could just as well have been named the Dictator Coast, the long strip of land that without warning veers off to the east: Angola, Congo-Kinshasa, Congo-Brazzaville, Gabon, Equatorial Guinea and Cameroon, all brutal, corrupt states disguised as democracies and republics. Pirates are known to wreak havoc in the surrounding seas, so Hammarstedt gives an order that the *Bob Barker* is to be made unassailable. A guard is posted around the clock on the helicopter deck to ensure that they are not boarded from behind, additional locks are welded onto all the hatches and bulkheads, and the jack ladder is covered with aluminium plating. Iron spikes are installed along the railing pointing down towards the water like spears.

On the Angolan coast, a mere two days' sail to the east, there are small port towns scarcely anyone on the ship has heard of before. Namibe, Porto Amboim, Lobito. If the *Thunder* were to make a quick move towards one of these ports, the local authorities and Interpol's emergency response team would have little time to respond.

Peter Hammarstedt needs all the help he can get. The *Sam Simon* has been at Mauritius to deliver the nets the *Thunder* left behind; now he asks Captain Sid Chakravarty to sail towards the *Bob Barker* as quickly as he can. In this area they will be much stronger if there are two ships. To gain some time, the *Sam Simon* will follow close to the coast of Namibia. Then the Benguela Current will provide him with added propulsion.

Hammarstedt must also find an ally on land. In the dim light of the great cabin he sits down to write an email to the only person he believes can help him in this situation: the explorer J. Michael "Mike" Fay. Besides having a doctorate on the western lowland gorilla, he has flown into war zones to protect elephants from guerrilla groups, been shot by poachers and barely escaped with his life when an elephant attacked him, inflicting him with 13 deep stab wounds. Mike Fay has been called "the world's greatest living explorer", and he has powerful friends in the area that can come in handy for Hammarstedt.

"Dear Mr. Fay, for the past 92 days I have been in physical pursuit of the internationally wanted Nigerian-flagged poaching vessel FV *Thunder*," Hammarstedt begins.

"I am currently chasing the FV *Thunder* north along the Namibian coast and believe that the poachers will attempt to offload their illegal catch in a West African port."

When Mike Fay came wandering in onto the coast of Gabon in the late 1990s, it was after 455 days and some 3,500 kilometres on foot. He appeared wearing salt-water sandals, shorts and a thin synthetic T-shirt that could be washed every morning. His entourage consisted of 13 pygmies, serving as pathfinders, baggage carriers and assistants.

Fay had covered the entire Congo Basin, the fertile landscape along the river Congo with the world's second-largest tropical rainforest and its unique animal and plant life. The purpose was to quantify, measure and document the vegetation and ecosystems that were not cultivated or razed by humans in this vast natural landscape.

In Gabon Mike Fay contacted the dictator Omar Bongo and proposed that they must establish national parks to protect the rain forest of the sparsely populated country. President Bongo allocated more than 10 per cent of Gabon's land to 13 national parks.

His explanation for his collaboration with the dictator was simple. It was better to work with him than to watch the final remains of the African rainforest disappear. When he went to work cleaning up the beaches of the country (amongst the piles of garbage he found 100,000 flip-flops and a kilo of cocaine), he became aware that the ocean was also threatened by the insatiable greed of human beings. Along the mouths of the rivers by the Atlantic coast there were fleets of Chinese trawlers sweeping up shoals of fish as "thick as bouillabaisse".[1]

The realization led to Fay's commencing work initiatives geared to protect Gabon's maritime zones.

"I understand that you are a special advisor to the President of Gabon and that you have a passion for combating illegal fishing in Gabonese waters," Hammarstedt continues in his email.

"I would very much like to keep you updated on our movements so that authorities in Gabon can have as much advance notice as possible of any attempt to transship or offload. Thank you for your tireless work in protecting natural areas. I look forward to hearing from you."

The next day Hammarstedt receives a short reply.

"No problem. Keep me informed and I will get proper authorities in action if necessary. I would be surprised if she put into Gabon, more likely her home in Nigeria, but if she does, we will be ready. Mike."

Fay alerts the fisheries authorities and the admiral who has command over Gabon's tiny fleet of small, but robust, French-built patrol boats. He also alerts the fisheries director of the tiny island nation of São Tomé and Príncipe and has his acquaintances in Gabon's Navy warn colleagues in Equatorial Guinea and Cameroon. If the *Thunder* attempts to put into port in Gabon, the ship will be denied entry. Another option is for the Gabonese authorities to lure the vessel in and detain the crew long enough to allow Interpol time to arrive in the country.[2]

At the very least there is one country in the region that has an unpleasant welcome prepared for the *Thunder*, Hammarstedt thinks before curling up in his berth in the great cabin.

3 0

THE MAN IN THE ARENA
THE SOUTH ATLANTIC OCEAN,
MARCH 2015

Every morning at 7:30 Hammarstedt walks up to the white-board at the end of the lounge, wipes it clean and writes a new number. "110 days at sea."

The monotony of the chase has converted his existence into a series of numbers: the number of nautical miles to the closest port, the speed of the ships, the amount of fuel in the tanks, the height of the *Thunder*'s freeboard, the barometer's pressure reading and the height of the waves.

The inactivity takes its toll on the crew. In the morning meetings they sit silently and listen, staring down at the flooring or at one another. Hammarstedt has no clear answer to the question of how long the chase will continue; he has no more theories about what is happening on board the *Thunder*.

The two ships maintain a steady speed of between 6 and 7 knots and cover 200 nautical miles per day. Now it is only the remaining amount of food and fuel that will determine how long the chase can continue. Cataldo's fixed and goal-oriented course makes Hammarstedt believe that he has a plan. He rules out that it involves Great Britain or crossing the Atlantic. The Canary Islands or one of the many ports along the west coast of Africa are possibilities discussed on both the *Bob Barker* and in Interpol's restricted corridors. If so, the chase will be over in the course of three weeks.

"For them it's about finding a port where they will be least likely to go to prison," Hammarstedt tells the crew at the daily morning meeting in the lounge.

Although he is located a few days' sailing east of Angola's capital Luanda, Hammarstedt has a road map of the USA lying on the bridge. When the chase is over, he is going on a road trip in the USA. He will walk through national parks, see bison, climb glaciers, stomp his feet against solid ground. He wants to see trees and forests – and they are to be the thickest and tallest trees in the world.

On the table in the great cabin he measures the distance from Sequoia to Yellowstone, finds the names of motels where he will spend the night, restaurants he will visit, and fantasizes about a world completely different from the empty horizon's imperceptible changes from blue to grey to the black standstill of the night.

Then the *Thunder* stops. Peter Hammarstedt runs quickly up to the bridge and the moment he enters, he asks Adam Meyerson what is happening.

"Great drift part four," Meyerson answers.

"Maybe they have a mechanical issue, but I guess it could be the beginning of another long drift. They're obviously in a very desperate situation," he continues.

Peter Hammarstedt lifts the binoculars. The *Thunder* is now lying to almost motionless on the quiet ocean, drifting slowly upon the current.

Without a word Hammarstedt leaves the bridge, takes a few long steps down the stairs and into the great cabin directly under the wheelhouse. He closes the door behind him, and sits down in the chair by the desk. There he slumps and buries his head in his hands.

They have no plan, he thinks. Or is it yet another attempt to test our stamina? Is it the final attempt to break us? he asks himself.

He tries to collect his thoughts, and is glad nobody can see him, especially not Captain Cataldo. He glances up at the door and the quote he hung up when he signed on as captain. It is the speech Theodore Roosevelt held at the Sorbonne in the spring of 1910, a speech Hammarstedt recites for the crew:

The credit belongs to the man who is actually in the arena, whose face is marred by dust and sweat and blood; who strives valiantly; who errs, who comes short again and again, because there is no effort without error and short-coming; but who does actually strive to do the deeds; who knows great enthusiasms, the great devotions; who spends himself in a worthy cause; who at the best knows in the end the triumph of high achievement, and who at the worst, if he fails, at least fails while daring greatly, so that his place shall never be with those cold and timid souls who neither know victory nor defeat.

At dawn on 25 March he will strike back against Cataldo. He has prepared an unexpected manoeuvre. Not everyone in Sea Shepherd will approve of Peter Hammarstedt's next move.

31

THE THIRD SHIP
THE COAST OF CENTRAL
AFRICA, MARCH 2015

Shipmaster Steve Paku on the *Atlas Cove* worked out that the trip from the shipyard in Raudeberg on the west coast of Norway to Port Louis in Mauritius would take 28 days.

The 68-metre-long *Atlas Cove* was the most recent new acquisition of Austral Fisheries' fleet of toothfish vessels. For four months the ship had undergone extensive rebuilding to equip it fully for the upcoming longline fishing expedition in the Antarctic. When the shiny, freshly painted vessel reaches the coast of Portugal, the shipmaster receives a phone call from Director David Carter of Austral Fisheries.[1]

Carter tells him about the chase currently taking place off the coast of Central Africa. The *Atlas Cove* is already running late for the summer season in the Southern Ocean, and now Carter asks the shipmaster to make a detour to join the chase for the *Thunder*.

"Oh shit," the *Atlas Cove*'s captain Steve Paku replies.

"Sea Shepherd is doing the job that we and the authorities

should have done. But I know what you're thinking," Carter says.

After his initial hesitant objections, Paku goes along with changing course. He has had a run in with the *Thunder* himself in the Southern Ocean.

"And don't do anything stupid," Carter concludes.

Austral Fisheries' Japanese part-owners were shocked and terrified about what would happen if they were to form any kind of collaboration whatsoever with the environmental organization that terrorized the country's own whaling fleet. But Carter stuck to his guns and assured them it would have a positive public relations effect.

Like the majority of the stakeholders in the toothfish industry, Carter also knew that his own shipmasters were sceptical of people who lived on vegetables and soybeans. But now it was about business.

The illegal fishing also gave toothfish a bad name. Buyers long believed the fish to be in danger of extinction. For a period of time in Australia, convincing restaurant patrons to order toothfish was paramount to requesting they consume panda bear cubs.

"What the devil is this?"

As the oceanic space is filled with light, Juan Manuel Patiño Lampon sees a movement on the radar.

It is eight o'clock in the morning on 25 March. The *Thunder*'s fishing captain has just turned up for the morning shift. He is wearing his glasses with the thin steel frames, and around his left wrist hangs a silver chain. As usual, he is wearing his watch on his right wrist.

The ship that has suddenly become visible on the radar is located 3 nautical miles away. It is coming from the north and is on a collision course. On board the *Thunder* the sight of any vessel, either on the radar or visually, provokes a testy uneasiness among the officers.

There have been enough trials in the past 24 hours. The *Sam Simon* arrived from Mauritius; throughout the entire previous day dinghies transported supplies to the *Bob Barker* – the first in 112 days.

Lampon feared that they would also receive more fuel and prepared to navigate the *Thunder* in between to obstruct the operation. But all he saw were crates of fruit and vegetables being winched on board the *Bob Barker*.

Now both the Sea Shepherd ships are behind him. He also sees a third ship on the radar. Juan Manuel Patiño Lampon calms himself by deciding that ship is probably headed for a fishing bank.

"The idea is for the *Atlas Cove* to swing in, take up position on the starboard quarter and then we will have three ships in formation following the *Thunder*."

At the morning meeting on the *Bob Barker* Hammarstedt tells the crew about the fishing boat that is on its way to join the chase. Radio silence between the ships has been ordered so the *Thunder* won't become suspicious about what is about to take place. The *Atlas Cove* is already on the radar and will be with them in half an hour. Then it won't be only two ships, but two worlds that meet. Hammarstedt wants the crew to go on deck and wave the *Atlas Cove* welcome, but he doesn't want to force anyone. A number of the activists on board are against fishing, whether it be illegal or legal.

"We are not out to stop the fishing of toothfish, but the illegal fishing. We have been waiting for the authorities for 100 days without any response. We need all the allies we can find. Now we will have the support of the fishermen. Who are we not to accept that?" Hammarstedt says. Nobody objects.

As the *Atlas Cove* approaches the *Bob Barker*'s stern, the mate veers the ship suddenly up towards the *Thunder*. The entire crew of the *Bob Barker* is lined up on the bridge.

"It's good to be looking at a vessel that isn't the *Thunder*," Hammarstedt says over the radio.

"It's just one mammoth effort there, Peter. I've seen this vessel around Heard Island … Be a good eight years ago," Steve Paku, the shipmaster of the *Atlas Cove*, says.

"We're just hoping to knock them out one by one," Hammarstedt says.

Then he orders the ships into formation and asks them to stay a quarter of a nautical mile behind the *Thunder*. Once again he has raised the Dutch flag.

"It must be a terrible day for them to see you resupplied yesterday and three ships this morning," Siddharth Chakravarty says on the radio from the *Sam Simon*.

On the *Atlas Cove*, the engineer has taken control of the radio and calls up the *Thunder*. In his hand he has a memo written by Steve Paku on the way down from Portugal. He now reads it in Spanish:

"Fishing vessel *Thunder*, good morning. I speak in the name of my captain. This is marine fishing vessel *Atlas Cove*. This ship is a member of COLTO, Coalition of Legal Tooth-fish Operators. We have set position along Sea Shepherd ships *Bob Barker* and *Sam Simon* in support of their actions to stop all illegal fishing operations. Your ship is part of the ones that keeps fishing illegally. Both governments and NGOs are determined to stop this illegal activity. These people behind you won't let you go passively. Their reputation speaks for them, and you, sir, are their target. They won't stop until you stop, so do yourself a favour, go home and stay there. If you want to keep fishing in the Southern Ocean, do it through the right channels like everyone else does, and become a responsible person, a responsible and legal operator. And most important, you help yourself being a responsible person, a responsible human being. We have to take care of the little that is left in the seas, because if we don't there will be nothing left for our children, grandchildren and great-grandchildren. Over."

Captain Cataldo is not in the mood to listen to a cautionary tale about love for nature and children. As the *Atlas Cove* approached, he was summoned up onto the bridge. He is tired and under the weather; the chase has begun to take its toll on his strength. During the past few weeks he has not been especially talkative, but now he picks up the phone and calls Spain. The numbers of the owner and his two closest colleagues are written down on a yellow Post-it hanging on the wall of the navigation room.

"Now there are bloody well three of them!" he shouts over the phone.

According to one of the officers on the bridge, Cataldo then receives an order to run into one of the ships pursuing him. Throughout the entire chase Cataldo has bragged about how he is a better captain and shipmaster than Hammarstedt.

"We're going to put about now," he says after having finished the call to Spain.

Abruptly he puts the vessel hard about starboard and towards the *Atlas Cove*.

"The *Thunder* is turning, just got to get on the helm here, Steve," Hammarstedt warns over the radio.

A black cloud of smoke shoots up out of the *Atlas Cove*'s stack as the ship picks up speed to escape the *Thunder*'s sudden attack. The *Sam Simon* and the *Bob Barker* must also navigate out of the formation to avoid being hit.

"Hey Steve, they are a bit unpredictable. Don't take it personally," Hammarstedt says.

When Cataldo finally speaks up over the radio, he is clearly upset.

"Here *Thunder* is sailing in international waters with the Nigerian flag. What is the problem with the three ships?" he asks.

"Yes, yes, what is the problem? It is three ships already, three ships. The *Sam Simon*, *Bob Barker* and *Atlas Cove*. What is the problem? We are sailing in international waters, in international waters with the Nigerian flag, what is the problem? Over."

"The problem is that you are fishing illegally, like our colleague said, and we are trying to stop you. Over," the *Sam Simon* answers.

"Negative, negative. We are not fishing, we are sailing. You are going to cause an accident and there are people here, and you have people in your ships, too. You have to be careful and keep a safe distance, over."

"If you keep changing course like you are doing, maybe you will cause a collision, otherwise there will not be any accident. Over," the *Sam Simon* replies.

One of Sea Shepherd's dinghies is positioned in front of the bow of the *Thunder*, ready to film the altercation. Hammarstedt does not yet know whether he will publicize the story of the meeting with the three ships, out of fear of the reaction of Sea Shepherd supporters who oppose fishing.

"And your small boat should not cross our bow anymore. That is dangerous. It might make us nervous, and when someone is nervous, he can cause an accident. Over," Cataldo says.

"Don't worry about the small boat, it is not going to cause any accident, it keeps staying away from you. Over."

"Say to the captain of the *Bob Barker*, the captain of the *Sam Simon* and the captain of the *Atlas Cove* that I am not afraid of them. I am not afraid of them. If they want to ram me, ram me. If they want to sink me, sink me. But I will keep on with the orders that I have, to sail in international waters. I am not afraid of you. Over."

"Understood, but while you keep sailing in international waters, since we are not afraid of you either, we will stay with you. Over."

"But don't accuse me and don't bother me. I am not afraid of you. If you want to sink me, sink me, but under your responsibility. Remember that we have people here. There are people on board, we are fulfilling a job, and we are going to stay here until we receive another order. Over."

"It is not our intention to put your ship or your crew or anyone in danger. We only want to make sure that you go to port and stop fishing. But we don't want to put anyone in danger, you or us," the *Sam Simon* answers.

"Then why are you so close, why are you so close, the crew here is getting anxious and nervous, and that is dangerous. If there is an accident or a tragedy, or someone jumps overboard, it's going to be your responsibility. Over."

"OK, we will stay with you trying not to make you nervous and keeping a distance. It is not our intention to put anyone in danger or hurt anyone. Over," the captain of the *Sam Simon* says through his interpreter.

After two hours, with a blast of the ship's horn, the *Atlas Cove* leaves the formation. Several of the crew on the *Sam Simon* choose to stay below deck when the fishing vessel sails towards Mauritius to prepare for the season in Antarctica.

Every time Cataldo has previously called up the *Bob Barker*, Peter Hammarstedt has tried to discern his state of mind. Perhaps this could give him a warning of what the man would get up to later. He has never heard him so upset and stressed out as he is now, and thinks he has achieved what he wanted with the manoeuvre: to demoralize Cataldo. But the last message from the *Thunder* on this day worries Hammarstedt.

"You sent a lot of letters to the ship. You are worried about the Indonesian crew, and now all the Indonesians are nervous. One person attempted to take his life. Over."

32

"YOU ARE NOTHING"
THE COAST OF CENTRAL
AFRICA, MARCH 2015

For breakfast the next morning, Hammarstedt serves up an offer Cataldo will most likely refuse.

"Good morning, is this the captain of the *Thunder*?"

"Yes, how are you, good morning, go ahead, over," Cataldo answers.

"We are concerned with the message yesterday about the self-harm, and we wanted some more information about that," Hammarstedt says through the interpreter.

"That is information from the ship, and everything's fine. The only problem is when you get too close and start to harass us and bother us, that's the problem, over."

"We have doctors on board and we can lend medical assistance."

"Yes, here, too, I have the medical assistance preparation, there is no problem."

"If you are concerned about your Indonesian crew, we wanted to offer you the possibility of transferring them to the *Sam Simon* and pay for their flights to go home," Hammarstedt suggests.

"No, negative, negative. They are fine here working with our contracting agency. They are content with us, they are fine. We have all the food and their salaries, everything's fine. The problem is you. When we get to port we will make everything clear with you and the authorities," Cataldo answers.

The *Thunder*'s captain seems calmer and more collected on the radio than he had the day before, when the fishing vessel the *Atlas Cove* joined the chase for a brief period of time.

"If you are concerned for your Indonesian crew, you should go to port. The only reason why we are here is because we are waiting for you to go to port, and we won't leave you until you do so," Hammarstedt says.

"But you are no one. You are no authority, no army, no one to order me to go to port. I only take orders from my contracting agency and from the country of my flag, Nigeria. Until this point they have said nothing to me, so we will remain here. That is the idea, and that is what we are going to do."

"OK, if you need medical assistance, or medicines, radio us. We will be here on channel 16, thank you."

"OK, OK, thank you. We have everything here on board, medical supplies, food, everything. We have enough to be here nine months without any problem, over."

Nine months! Hammarstedt prays a silent prayer that he's bluffing. Then he gives the order to prepare the dinghies.

"We will launch the boat at 2 o'clock," Hammarstedt says over the ship's internal communication radio.

He wants to try once more to throw bottles containing messages to the Indonesian crew on the *Thunder*.

"Greetings Indonesian crew, we understand that you cannot come and speak freely while your captain is on board but we will always be standing by on VHF 77 and should you have the opportunity, just transmit a message and we'll try and receive it," he writes in the new message.

Hammarstedt sees no activity on the deck of the *Thunder*. He guides the *Bob Barker* in close to the *Thunder*'s starboard side and blasts the ship's whistle for half a minute to provoke a reaction. He also sends one of the two dinghies out in front of the *Thunder*'s bow to distract the officers. Suddenly he sees movements on deck and calls up the dinghy:

"There are three of them out on deck now!"

Perhaps one of them will manage to snatch the message out of the water.

On the *Thunder*, Captain Cataldo has decided to respond to the information siege and calls the Indonesian third engineer up onto the bridge. He sailed on the Spanish trawler the *Pitufo* – "The Smurf" – for several years and speaks a few words of Spanish. Cataldo has written a few sentences down on a piece of paper in advance and asks the third engineer to read them out loud to Hammarstedt. None of the others in the Indonesian crew are informed of what is about to happen when Cataldo calls up the *Bob Barker*.

"We have received the letters that he has sent. And the person in charge of the Indonesian crew is going to talk to you now, so that you will hear from them that they don't want you to bother them again. He is going to tell you now. Over," Cataldo says.

"OK, go ahead," Hammarstedt asks.

Then the microphone changes hands. In faltering Spanish the engineer reads out the message.

"I mariner from Indonesia, please, your small boat, not possible anymore, and um, no throwing cans here, because here mariner no problem, here good. Lot of food, when I call the family, no problem. Captain good, and company much good too, food also a lot, and salary, there is no problem. Everything, everything good."

"I got your message, could you give me your name and talk about the person that attempted to take his life?" Hammarstedt asks.

For a moment everything is silent, and then Hammarstedt once again hears Cataldo's voice.

"No, we can't do that. That stays here. It is this ship's business. That's something personal about the ship. I don't go asking you about your ship's stuff. We talked to the person, he calmed down. It was nerves when he saw three ships that wanted a collision, any person would be nervous with that. Over."

"If he said he can speak to his family, can you give us a contact to their family so we can check with them to make sure this is correct?" Hammarstedt asks.

That is a question that causes Cataldo to lose whatever vestiges of compliance and patience he had at the beginning of the conversation.

"You are nothing, no authority, you are nothing. Why would we have to give personal information to you? He's got his family, his son, his things at home, and you want to bother them! The only one working here is him, no one else, his family is happy where he is working. And he already told you to please don't bother anymore, and that the letters that you are writing are pure lies. Over," Cataldo shouts.

"The police are investigating you for human trafficking and if you can at least give us the name of the crewing agency they used, we can clear everything up with the police," Hammarstedt says.

"Everything that you are saying is false. You never saw us fishing, you never saw us fishing, only sailing. Now, about the Indonesian matter, they're happy here, their families are happy, their welfare is good with us. There is no problem. They are all content here. And the person that talked to you represented the Indonesian crew. What you are doing is taking away their job, you are 'cutting their hands' so that they can't work and maintain their families. Over," Cataldo says.

"On any normal fishing boat we can talk with the crew, we can laugh with the crew, but with your boat, we are not allowed to speak to them, why is that?" Hammarstedt asks.

"You heard the Indonesian mariner say it, they don't want to have any communication with you because you say a lot of lies. You are causing problems for them and their families. And I won't communicate with the captain of the *Bob Barker* by telephone either because everything that I say can be heard by radio, I have nothing to hide. Over."

"We will take what the Indonesian crew said into consideration, is there anything else?" Hammarstedt replies through his interpreter.

"Yes," Cataldo answers. "He wants to say the last words, he wants to say one last thing so that you stay assured and stop bothering the Indonesians, since you won't get anything from us, any information, and that's what he wants to make clear now. He's going to talk to you now, over," Cataldo says before once again handing the microphone to the Indonesian engineer on the *Thunder*.

"Please, no bother anymore because here all mariner Indonesian happy. Everything fine. Captain very, very good, agency also very, very good. Lots of food, lots of medicines, and much fuel, for 10 months more."

"We understand that you are annoyed with us following you, but if you have nothing to hide, why don't we go together to port right now, we can sort this out, and then we won't have to see each other again."

Cataldo is back on the radio.

"I would gladly do that, but I obey orders, you receive orders from your boss Paul Watson, and I receive orders from my contracting agency. I am not the owner of the ship. I have a contract and I have to follow it and accomplish it. I have always accomplished my contracts. I don't see why I wouldn't now. Over."

"Don't you think it's strange that the owner would rather have you stay here in the open sea and not go to port?"

"Look I have a contract, and I earn money for every day, every month and every year. If I am here, we are all winning. We are all winning. And if the contracting agency wants to keep paying me, and feeding me, and keeping me here, we are all very happy here then. Over."

"We have our orders, too, so we will continue to enjoy spending time with one another for a long, long time,"

Hammarstedt answers before the *Thunder*'s captain vows to give him a long and exhausting fight.

"As I told you, we have a lot of fuel, a lot of supplies. We don't have any need for another ship to come and resupply us. We are ready physically and mentally to be here for a long, long time. Over," Cataldo says.

"OK. We will enjoy spending the foreseeable future with you," Hammarstedt replies and glances toward the *Thunder* before turning to face Adam Meyerson. "They're throwing a lot of big numbers out there today," Hammarstedt says.

In the evening, the *Thunder* turns around and sets its course for the southeast.

It is probably just temporary. Just mind games, Hammarstedt thinks.

One hundred days. The chase has travelled across three oceans. It is the longest ship chase in history, it is the longest campaign in Sea Shepherd's history, and it is one of the longest days in Peter Hammarstedt's life. He says it to himself, he says it to Adam Meyerson, he says it to the majority of those who come onto the bridge:

"I wish a Navy ship would come."

But for the time being, nothing appears on the horizon, other than thin shafts of light breaking through the clouds. Nobody offers them assistance or a new supply of provisions.

The morning arrived with some good news. The *Viking* has been arrested in Malaysia and the captain thrown in jail. Hammarstedt believes that the *Thunder* and the *Viking* have the same owner, and hopes the arrest will have an impact: that the owner will take some action with the *Thunder* other than simply allowing the ship to drift for month after month. The *Kunlun* was stopped in Thailand.

"The Thai customs authorities said that the boat will be held until the investigations were concluded and that could take a very long time … Huge," Hammarstedt explains on the bridge.

"It's like half the ships that we're looking for are out of the game now. Fantastic!" Adam Meyerson answers.

"Yeah! Half of them down," Hammarstedt replies.

On social media, Sea Shepherd now calls the *Thunder* a "floating prison".[1] They hire Dr Glenn Simmons, a researcher and specialist in human trafficking, to describe what he thinks is taking place on the *Thunder*. For several years Simmons has been researching the working conditions of Asian fishermen and he maintains that the alleged suicide attempt on the *Thunder* was a desperate act on the part of a man being held on the ship against his will.

"We have reasonable cause to believe that the crew are indeed being held captive and against their will. The worst thing you can do is leave the scene as crew would lose hope," Simmons writes in his statement to Sea Shepherd, which Hammarstedt forwards to Interpol.

That is the story Sea Shepherd wants – and which they quickly distribute to the media.

The news of the duel at sea also reaches the bridge of the *Thunder*. From her exclusive apartment in the luxurious Viña del Mar in Chile, the *Thunder*'s captain's wife sends him regular updates on the chase by telefax. Luis Alfonso Rubio Cataldo therefore knows everything about his opponent Peter Hammarstedt and Sea Shepherd. He also knows that Hammarstedt has not succeeded in establishing the identities of the officers on the *Thunder* and has ordered them to wear ski masks to hide their faces when they are moving around on deck.

In an attempt to refute the accusations that he is sailing a slave ship, Cataldo now orders the entire crew on deck. As the *Bob Barker*'s dinghies approach the side of the *Thunder*, everyone on board is told to pull on their ski masks and bring with them pieces of metal pipe to bang against the railing. In this way Cataldo will demonstrate that everyone on the *Thunder* is united against Sea Shepherd.

"It's strange that the Indonesian crew are now hiding their identities," Hammarstedt says as he sees the procession of balaclava-clad fishermen on the deck of the *Thunder*.

Through the binoculars, Hammarstedt can see the crew members hammering on the railing with the iron pipes as the dinghies pass by. It resembles a bizarre theatrical performance.

In the evening the *Thunder*'s captain changes the ship's course, this time to the northeast. To the other officers on the *Thunder*, Cataldo seems tired and depressed. The story of the suicide attempt on the *Thunder* was a bluff – a morbid attempt to induce Peter Hammarstedt to give up the chase.

Those who know that the *Thunder* has just lost its Nigerian flag also find Cataldo's next move to be strange. All the fishing buoys are to be removed from the quarterdeck. The *Thunder* is to be prepared to put in at port.

At Port Harcourt in Nigeria.

33

THE SNAKE IN PARADISE
PHUKET, MARCH 2015

On the evening of 4 March, the fishing vessel the *Kunlun* is transformed into the freighter the *Taishan*. The operation is done in the twinkling of an eye: using some well-worn cardboard stencils, one of the crew members paints the new name on the wheelhouse and the rust-corroded bow. Then Captain Alberto Zavaleta Salas sails his wanted ship in towards the port of the tourist paradise of Phuket. In the cold storage room there are 181 tons of first class toothfish worth almost 4 million dollars.

They have outmanoeuvred the Navy, been chased by Sea Shepherd and were boarded by the Australian authorities. Now all that remains is to offer the authorities of Thailand a credible story to enable them to get the illegal cargo through customs.

At the port in Phuket, the duty paid on the cargo is for the far less expensive species the seabass. The fishing captain José Regueiro Sevilla explains that it was transshipped from another fishing vessel and that it will now be dispatched by ship to Vietnam. After the port bureaucrats have provided their stamps of approval, six freezer containers are transported by lorry to the deep-sea harbour in Songkhla, 500 kilometres southeast of Phuket.

Then Alberto Zavaleta Salas drops the rusty hulk's anchor off the coast of the luxury holiday destination Sri Panwa – a well-guarded playground for jet-setters and celebrities from the entertainment industry. There the ship remains, bobbing like a rotten branch in an infinity pool.

While the *Taishan* pitches in the clear, turquoise water off the coast of Phuket, one of the officers of the Marine Police in Phuket is made aware of the Interpol notices for the *Kunlun*. The authorities in Australia and New Zealand have not given up on the idea of ending the *Kunlun*'s pillaging missions once and for all.[1] They ask the special investigators of the Thai customs service to inspect the *Taishan* and the cargo the crew brought ashore. When they break into the containers, the fish they find is not the type that was cleared through customs. It is the *Kunlun*'s "white gold".

When a few hours later the maritime police board the ship to put it under arrest, they are met by an appalling sight: the vessel is filthy and the sanitary conditions atrocious. They also notice another detail. There is no fishing gear on board.

On the journey north, somewhere halfway between the Antarctic mainland and the southern tip of South Africa, the crew packed kilometres of gillnets into plastic bags and dumped them over board. In secret, Alberto Zavaleta Salas made a note of the coordinates: 52 06 04 S 40 48 70 E.

The atmosphere on the *Kunlun* is just as oppressive as the tropical night outside. The cargo has been confiscated, nobody is allowed to leave the ship, even the fishing captain has been charged with document forgery. Zavaleta Salas is at risk of being held responsible for having illegally changed the vessel's name and flag – from Equatorial Guinea to Indonesia. The police have also discovered that he is not qualified to sail vessels weighing in excess of 300 tons. The *Kunlun* is more than twice that size. In newspapers all over the world he is identified by name as the pirate captain; some even claim that he is in jail. The only thing Alberto Zavaleta Salas can think about is how he is going to get home.

During the entire voyage he has shared a cabin with the first engineer, a robustly built 57-year-old from Ribeira in Spain. For the past few weeks the Spaniard has been reticent and silent; he keeps to himself, as if he is carrying some enormous sorrow. When he is asked to go into the engine room, sometimes he just shakes his head, crawls into his berth and lies down facing the bulkhead. He is constantly complaining to Alberto Zavaleta Salas about insomnia. One night he tells him that he has money problems at home in Galicia.

Just as Alberto Zavaleta Salas is about to fall asleep he registers that the light in the upper berth is switched on. Then he hears the engineer climbing down from the berth, followed by a dull thump. As he turns over to face the room, he sees the Spaniard collapsing onto the little writing desk and against the wardrobe.

Is he drunk? Zavaleta Salas wonders, but then he catches sight of the blood dripping down onto the floor. He throws himself out of bed and notices that the man is hanging forward, lifeless, his body shaking as if ravaged by shivering contractions. He slaps him on the cheek and shouts his name, but the man doesn't respond.

Then he discovers the deep gashes in both the engineer's wrists. Alberto Zavaleta Salas steps over him, opens the door leading out into the ship's corridor and calls for help.

It takes hours for the water ambulance to arrive. The engineer is already bandaged up and conscious, he begs Zavaleta Salas to accompany him to the hospital in Phuket, and to call his family home in Ribeira.

He has slashed his wrists with a razor blade, but all he says is that he's afraid.

When the police arrive, he refuses to be interrogated.

Sea Shepherd's founder Paul Watson is the first to applaud the arrest and investigation of the *Kunlun* in Thailand. But information has also been leaked from the local investigation indicating that the *Kunlun* will be chased from Thailand without being penalized.

"That's the problem with illegal fishing all over the world. A combination of bribes, corruption, inadequate legislation and a huge demand for fish enables the illegal fishing to continue. There is no excuse for Australia's or New Zealand's failure to seize the ship and cargo when they had the chance. There is no excuse for their not forcing the *Kunlun* into a port the way Sea Shepherd is now doing with the *Thunder*," Paul Watson says.

On social media, Watson also uses the occasion to propose a final option for the captain of the *Thunder*:

> The Captain of the *Thunder* and his officers must be feeling lonely, neglected and very insecure at the moment. No fuel, no provisions, no instructions, no assistance. But there is a way out for them. They need only surrender their vessel to the authorities where they can make a deal to finger their Spanish bosses in return for leniency and a place in a witness protection program. I believe the *Thunder*'s days are almost over.[2]

On one of the last days of March Zavaleta Salas receives permission to sign off from the arrested ship and travel home to Lima. The ship owners no longer have any use for him.

Late in the evening, as he is packing his suitcase, the *Kunlun*'s new shipmaster arrives, a middle-aged Asian-looking man who does not speak Spanish. Zavaleta Salas greets him curtly and watches as the rest of the Indonesian crew crowd around him to tell him of the countless adversities that have plagued the *Kunlun*.

After the engineer's suicide attempt, he has barely eaten or slept and he has been arguing constantly with the fishing captain Sevilla. Even though he is leaving, he can feel panic and paranoia taking hold of him. He imagines that the Spanish ship owner has full control over the authorities and the police and that somebody could easily get rid of him if they were to perceive him as a threat and a snitch.

Before he leaves the *Kunlun* for the last time, Zavaleta Salas runs down to the fish factory and retrieves a fish slicing knife which he hides in the waistband of his trousers.

In the harbour, the agent's car is waiting for Zavaleta Salas. First they drive to the office in Phuket to pick up the airplane tickets, subsequently they continue out towards the airport. He can feel the hard handle of the knife pressing against his abdomen when he is sitting in the back seat of the car; he fantasizes about what he will do if the car drives off onto a byroad. Should he jump out and run? Should he fight back?

Finally he sees the approach to Phuket's international airport. He bids the agent's driver a terse farewell. Once out of the car, he walks around the car park and finds a bin where he gets rid of the knife.

He doesn't feel safe until he feels the landing gear fold up against the body of the plane. In the future it will be money that determines his loyalty. If the ship owner pays him what he owes him and simultaneously gives him a bonus for being loyal, he will not speak to anyone. Home in Chimbote he has something he believes can be extremely valuable. A number of notes he took in secret of positions, dates, times, almost illegible scribblings, filling the margins of tiny scraps of paper. Together they constitute his version of what happened to the *Tiantai* – the black-listed ship that disappeared without a trace and under mysterious circumstances in the Antarctic in March 2014.

34

THE ARMPIT OF AFRICA
GULF OF GUINEA, APRIL 2015

4 April. Operation Icefish is taking place somewhere nobody could have anticipated.

The heat wears down the crew's concentration, energy and desire to work. A faint breeze is blowing from the southeast. A pod of Risso's dolphins break through the surface of the water between the two ships.

A few minutes past half-four in the afternoon, the *Thunder* suddenly makes a 70-degree turn to the east and sails into Equatorial Guinea's economic zone.

"All right, we are going somewhere," Peter Hammarstedt says while keeping an eye on the electronic maps on the bridge.

Never before has the *Thunder* been so close to land. For the first time, the hunter and the hunted are less than 200 nautical miles from the mainland. If they stay the same course and continue at the same speed, they will be able to see the coast of the African continent within three days.

The unexpected change of course triggers new speculations on board the *Bob Barker*. Has the captain of the *Thunder* received new orders from land?

It could all be a diversionary tactic, whereby they will suddenly put about and sail south again – or in towards one of the small islands in the region, so more supplies and fuel can be brought on board. Do they have contacts on land? Will a boat come out and pick up the officers, leaving the *Thunder* and crew to their own devices and the whims of the ocean? Are they making their way to port because it is Easter, a holiday, with a diminished level of activity in the ports?

"They speak Spanish in Equatorial Guinea, don't they?" Hammarstedt asks.

Adam Meyerson has just come up onto the bridge with his usual prediction that the *Thunder* is about to run out of both fuel and options.

"My prediction is that this is very near to being over," he says, and continues: "Equatorial Guinea does have a navy so it's possible they will come out and see what these guys are up to and hopefully arrest them. Equatorial Guinea has been building its naval fleet like mad men over the last two years. It has the biggest navy in Africa."

Hammarstedt too has a sensation that the chase is approaching its end. He decides to alert the media in Equatorial Guinea about how the hunted vessel could be on its way into one of the nation's ports. Media coordinator Michelle Mossfield googles "Equatorial Guinea" and "Media", but the search engine does not give her any answers.

This is because in Equatorial Guinea there are no newspapers. In the capital Malabo, where the decay chews its way up along the walls of the old, pale yellow colonial buildings, giving them the colour of rancid flesh, there is not a single bookstore or newsstand. It is a coastal nation where fish is imported and the farmlands have been invaded by the creeping jungle – a country ravaged by torture, random arrests, ill-fated prisons, isolation, violence, discrimination and mind control. Not a vessel is to be seen in the waters abundant with fish that surround the tiny state.[1]

"What kind of place is this?" Peter Hammarstedt asks himself.

For Equatorial Guinea's ruling family the ocean is a threat and an enemy. In the beginning of the 1970s, the country's dictator, Francisco Macias Nguema, introduced a ban on all fishing. One hundred and forty-five days after he was elected president in the former Spanish colony, Macias appointed himself absolute monarch and called himself "the unique miracle".

"The Miracle" was the son of a witch doctor. He had never passed an exam and was haunted by inferiority complexes, nightmares and delusions. In a state of combined intoxication and an accelerating psychosis, he made decisions inspired by his own nightmares. In a speech he called Adolf Hitler "Africa's saviour". He set the dinner table for dead guests and terrified servants saw Macias having conversations with the ghosts of men he had executed.

All positions in Equatorial Guinea were filled by members of his own clan. Priests were obliged to mention him in their sermons under threat of torture. He reintroduced traditional medicine, closed the hospitals and fired the doctors. He forbade use of the word "intellectual", shut down the schools, burnt the books and fired the teachers.

On Christmas of 1975 he executed 150 of his adversaries in a football stadium in Malabo. The soldiers were dressed like Santa Clauses and shot their victims while an orchestra played the Mary Hopkins song "Those Were the Days". Crucified corpses were hung up along the road to the airport as a terrifying warning to visitors. Macias wiped out families and eradicated villages; of a population of 380,000, 70,000 are believed to have been killed and one-quarter of the country's residents fled the country. Russia, China and Cuba supported the regime of terror, while French diplomats flirted with the dictator to secure the natural resources of that which was called "the most evil place on earth".

Agriculture operations collapsed, the small cities descended into darkness, and the island residents jumped into boats to escape. Then Macias ordered that all boats were to be sold or destroyed and the population was prohibited from approaching the beach.

It was the start of Equatorial Guinea's war against the ocean.

In 1979 Macias was overthrown by a coup d'état. Together with a group of his closest colleagues he fled into the jungle with the nation's cash reserves, somewhere between 60 and 150 million dollars, which he hid in a bamboo hut.

In the subsequent skirmishes with the coup leaders, the hut was burned to the ground with the entirety of Equatorial Guinea's currency reserves inside. Macias was finally tracked down, brought before a military tribunal and executed at the Black Beach prison in Malabo.

His nephew Teodor Obiang Nguema took the throne as the country's new dictator. In the course of President Obiang's more than 30-year reign, "members of the inner circle have amassed unparalleled wealth through corruption in the form of extortion, embezzlement and theft".[2]

In the mid-1990s the country established an international ships register, probably to satisfy the Obiang clan's insatiable appetite for foreign currency. The register, which was administered from Cyprus and Miami, swiftly attracted a small fleet of blacklisted vessels.

According to Lloyd's List, as many as 40 ships were sailing around with forged papers from Equatorial Guinea. The US coast guard considered every ship with the country's flag to be suspicious and immediately boarded such ships were they to sail into US waters. In an alarming number of cases, the coast guard found serious violations of international standards. But it was the tragic fate of the four-masted schooner the *Fantome* – "The Phantom" – which would make Equatorial Guinea's shoddy flag of convenience famous all over the world.[3]

Built in 1927 by the flamboyant Duke of Westminster as the *Flying Cloud*, the ship was one of the last great traditionally-rigged sailing ships – and one of the most luxurious privately owned yachts in the world. The Greek shipping magnate Aristotle Onassis purchased the yacht as a wedding present for Princess Grace of Monaco, but Onassis never received an invitation to the wedding, so instead he left the boat to rust away in an anonymous port in Germany. Finally, the *Fantome* ended up as a charter boat for luxury tourists in the Caribbean – and with a home port in Africa's sweaty armpit: Malabo, Equatorial Guinea.

The last time anyone saw the proud rigging of the *Fantome* standing tall on the horizon was 28 October 1998. As the ship departed from port in Omoa, Honduras for a six-day cruise in the Caribbean, the tropical storm Mitch was building up more than 1,600 kilometres away, but it was moving with a violent and unpredictable force. The *Fantome* returned to port to let its passengers disembark before it plunged north towards the Gulf of Mexico in search of shelter from one of the most deadly and destructive storms ever to occur in the Western hemisphere. Ashore, it could risk being crushed while docked; the chances of managing the hurricane were greater at sea. But it was as if the hurricane was following in the wake of the schooner. The *Fantome* quickly ran into winds of 160 kilometres an hour, 12-metre waves ploughed across the bow, from the bridge the captain stared straight into the eye of the storm.

The ship and the crew of 31 were never found and the automatic emergency beacon was never activated. A few weeks later, after the hurricane had died away, some pieces of life rafts that had been torn to bits were found, along with parts of a wooden stairway and life vests with the inscription *Fantome, Malabo*.

After the wreck, the owner, Windjammer Barefoot Cruises in Miami, admitted that they had registered the ship in Equatorial Guinea for tax reasons. In Equatorial Guinea's name, the captain and the officers had received a licence and the required certifications without having passed a single exam. Everything was handled by an agent in Miami.

It was the flag state's responsibility to investigate the wreck; it was never done. Equatorial Guinea's representative in Miami made reference to newspaper articles and a report from the American coast guard. That would have to do. In the years following the *Fantome* tragedy, the toothfish poachers began registering with the bandit regime in Equatorial Guinea. The *Kunlun* was added to the register in 2004, at the time under the name the *Thule*, before the ship disappeared again two years later. But the shipping company still continued to use the flag, in all likelihood because they did not believe that Equatorial Guinea would react. When the *Sam Simon* discovered the ship in the Southern Ocean, the name plate was clearly legible: *Kunlun, Malabo*.

For the investigators of Interpol and the bureaucrats following along with the chase from land, it will be a nightmare if the *Thunder* sails into Equatorial Guinea. Then the ship will very likely slip through the fingers of the judicial system once and for all.

For Hammarstedt, the nightmare has a different quality. The worst scenario would be to chase the *Thunder* into a port where he and the ship will be put under arrest, while the officers of the *Thunder* will be free to saunter away from the quay and board the first flight to Spain.

35

MAYDAY
GULF OF GUINEA,
APRIL 2015

Darkness has descended abruptly upon the Gulf of Guinea, and at a mere 5 knots the *Thunder* glides like a shadow into the night. Earlier in the day the *Thunder* and the *Bob Barker* crossed the equator, at lunchtime an airplane appeared on the radar and a few hours later they passed a pod of Risso's dolphins.

As the watchstander team on the bridge of the *Bob Barker* is preparing for another hot and uneventful night, they suddenly see that a light is switched on near one of the bulkheads on the *Thunder*'s quarterdeck, and then several cones of lights dancing restlessly across the blacked out deck.

"19:03 – Activity observed on *Thunder*. Moving flashlights and unusual deck lights on," quartermaster Alexis "Lex" Rigby writes in the ship's log.

Then she asks Captain Hammarstedt and first mate Adam Meyerson to come to the bridge.

"What do you think, Adam?" Hammarstedt asks.

"They are definitely up to something. Anything else on the radar?" Meyerson asks.

"Nothing," Rigby replies.

Ever since they left the Antarctic, Hammarstedt and Meyerson have been concerned about the *Thunder* receiving assistance from another vessel. The name and position of all ships that come within range of the radar are recorded in the logbook. So far only a few commercial ships have passed. They are closer to land than they have ever been in the course of the chase.

The past few days Hammarstedt has been feeling uneasy. He has just sent an email to Interpol and explained that they are located less than a day's sail away from both Annobón in Equatorial Guinea and the tiny island state of São Tomé and Príncipe.

"I strongly suspect that the FV *Thunder* will make port call in the next coming days," he warned.

Will this be the night when he will really be tested? Are the crew of the *Thunder* preparing for a rendezvous with another ship? Or are they going to dump the fish they have on board before going ashore?

"Maybe they are getting ready to fish again," Meyerson says.

He navigates the *Bob Barker* closer to the *Thunder* and passes around a powerful set of night vision binoculars to see whether anything is being thrown over the side. They believe there is a conveyor belt running from the rear hatch of the *Thunder*. When the nets are hauled in, the fish is transported through the ship and into the fish factory. Have they put this conveyor belt into reverse to discharge the frozen fish back into the ocean? But the only movement to be seen on the quarterdeck is that of the cones of light and diffuse shadows.

"If you are concerned that they are going to throw something in the water, you can just shine a spotlight off to port. Don't know what good it is going to do. If they throw frozen stuff over, we're just going to pick it up and throw it back on, you know what I mean?" Meyerson says.

"The fish is just going to sink. It is frozen. Not much we can do," Hammarstedt says.

"Look what a light does to us," Meyerson says and quotes Luke the Evangelist: "Remain vigilant at all times."

"Let's get to half a mile and sit there. Keep an eye on them, see if there is any activity on deck," Meyerson says.

"19:42 – Suspicious activity continues on aft deck. Media alerted and on standby," Lex Rigby writes in the logbook.

Then Hammarstedt goes to bed.

He is sick and tired. He downs a cocktail of painkillers and two types of antibiotics in an attempt to wipe out a powerful infection. He daydreams that he is home in his flat in Söder in Stockholm, fantasizes about lying on solid ground and hearing the rain pound against the roof, but he has promised to follow the *Thunder* to the bitter end. Sea Shepherd's entire credibility is on the line. "We will not back down," is one of the organization's slogans.

He is unable to sleep; he has a gnawing, uneasy feeling that at dawn something is going to happen.

In the darkness of the great cabin, he relives the most brutal duel he has ever taken part in throughout his many years with Sea Shepherd. Amidst icebergs and turbulent seas in the Antarctic in February 2013, he navigated the *Bob Barker* in between the floating whale factory ship the *Nisshin Maru* and the tanker the *Sun Laurel*. The tanker was going to refuel the queen vessel of the Japanese whaling fleet. Hammarstedt wanted to block it. Nobody would change their course and when the *Bob Barker* glided into the wash of the ten times heavier whaling vessel, Hammarstedt lost control. In the turbulent ocean the agile Sea Shepherd vessel slammed into the side of the *Nisshin Maru*.

In the collision the *Bob Barker* listed dramatically to one side and for a few slow seconds it seemed that the ship would be vanquished by the colossal forces of the sea. Then the *Bob Barker* straightened up and remained jammed in between the whaler and the tanker while the water cannons on the *Nisshin Maru* poured water down the *Bob Barker*'s smokestack in an attempt to drown the engine. Finally, the captain of the *Sun Laurel* manoeuvred the tanker out of harm's way.

Pictures of the collision in the Southern Ocean are hanging on the walls of the *Bob Barker*'s lounge. The series has become a veritable symbol of the swift and trim ship's role in Sea Shepherd. But it was a battle that Hammarstedt would prefer not to relive; the collision and the turbulence produced by the duelling ships' movements and the propellers' heated revolutions had been so violent that he had problems walking for many days afterwards. If a ship arrives with fuel for the *Thunder* tomorrow, the crew will expect him to lead them into another uncompromising confrontation. And he is now in a part of Africa where help is very likely far away if something catastrophic were to occur.

Before he falls asleep, he thinks of Joseph Conrad's descriptions of the wild African coast that lies in wait to the east.

"Watching a coast as it slips by the ship is like thinking about an enigma. There it is before you, smiling, frowning, inviting, grand, mean, insipid, or savage, and always mute with an air of whispering, 'Come and find out'."

Tomorrow is D-day, Hammarstedt thinks. And nothing will ever be the same again.

The first rays of sunlight throw a warm, reddish-brown glow across the ocean as a new watchstander team comes up onto the bridge of the *Bob Barker*.

The officers have been following the *Thunder* through the binoculars all night. Now it's the Communications Officer Stefan Ehmann who discovers something strange – from a distance it looks like there are small figures, each wearing a bright orange coloured garment of sorts, moving about on deck. And something is hanging over the side: a jack ladder, the rope ladder that is used when someone is going to board or disembark from a ship while at sea.

"All right, I want you to get Peter," the third mate Anteo Broadfield orders.

Are they planning to put a dinghy into the water? They are now within the exclusive economic zone of São Tomé and Príncipe, but still far away from shore and they won't be able to make it there in a dinghy. Is another ship coming to pick up the crew? No other vessels are visible on the radar screen and the dinghy on the *Thunder* is still hidden beneath the blue tarp.

"There is nothing on the radar, mate. I've gone up and down on the range scale," Anteo Broadfield says as Peter Hammarstedt comes up onto the bridge and takes hold of the binoculars.

"How odd," Hammarstedt says.

On board the *Thunder* the day begins as usual but several of the crew also have the feeling that something is about to happen. But what?

Captain Cataldo is usually sulky and aloof and never calls the crew in for a meeting in the messroom to inform them of what he is thinking and planning, but the past few days he has been even more reserved and secretive than usual. Now and then he has taken a couple of the Spanish officers with him into the communication room on the bridge. Then they have shut the door. Several of the other officers have noticed that the *Thunder* had its course set for São Tomé. The fuel tanks are almost empty, they have less than 15 tons left, enough for two days propulsion at 10 knots.

When a few days earlier the cook was told to make a shopping list, they understood that they were approaching the end of the voyage and that they would soon sail into the closest country, the tiny island state of São Tomé and Príncipe.

During the first hours of the morning it is Cataldo who stands lookout. He comes to the bridge wearing a new, clean T-shirt he bought at the tax-free shop in Singapore. A new shift will start at eight o'clock. Seated in the messroom are the head of the fish factory, the Chilean José Rubincio Carrion Alvarado, and a couple of Indonesian crew members. They eat and drink coffee and tea. There are still plenty of provisions in the galley.

Then they hear the ship's alarm. Captain Cataldo comes running down to the messroom and asks Carrion to wake up the engineer Luis Alfonso Morales Mardones and the rest of the crew. The Chilean Mardones had a shift in the engine room until four o'clock in the morning. After his shift he lay in his berth watching a film. Now he gets to his feet, puts on his life vest and baffled, goes up on deck. Another of the ship's engineers, a 32-year-old Indonesian, was awakened by the alarm. He climbs down the stairs to the engine room and sees that the main engine is half submerged in water. Chief engineer Agustín Dosil Rey and first engineer Luis Miguel Pérez Fernández are down in the engine room. They ask him to come on deck immediately. What has happened?

There is no ship other than the *Bob Barker* in sight, not a thing between the Devil and the deep blue sea. It is 4,000 metres straight down, in the middle of a lustrous ocean surrounded by an empty horizon.

Captain Cataldo makes his way through the narrow corridors past the Indonesian crew's cabins, knocking hard on the doors. Some of the crew are already awake, and in the chaos that ensues, the half-dressed and sleep-dazed deck crew members collide with one another. The two deck officers, the Portuguese Manuel Agonia Dias Marques and Spanish Manuel Ricardo Barcia Sanles, leap straight out of their berths and go below deck to get the entire crew out of what can quickly become a death trap. They scream that the ship is sinking and that they must put on life vests and come up onto the quarter-deck. In the course of a few agitated minutes the entire crew is on deck and the officers start loosening the life rafts.

From the bridge of the *Bob Barker* the Sea Shepherd officers watch as the quarterdeck of the *Thunder* is filled with bodies dressed in orange. Is it raingear or life vests? Can it be a drill? Hardly. In the course of 110 days, Sea Shepherd has not seen a single emergency drill on board the *Thunder*.

"How strange," Hammarstedt remarks.

He sends an officer to wake up the ship's photographer Simon Ager. What's happening must be documented.

"There's a dude at the top of the ladder and there's a whole lot of people on the port side staring at the water," the ship physician Colette Harmsen says while holding the binoculars steadily focused on the *Thunder*.

"Yes, they are wearing life vests."

"How weird," Hammarstedt says.

Then the radio crackles.

"*Bob Barker*. It is *Thunder*," a high-pitched sharp voice says in stammering English.

It is the same voice that Hammarstedt has communicated and argued with previously. He is sure it's the captain, but he still doesn't know what he looks like or his name. Luis Alfonso Rubio Cataldo has never introduced himself by name in their radio conversations and he has stayed indoors to elude being captured by Sea Shepherd's many cameras.

"*Thunder. Bob Barker.* Go ahead," Hammarstedt answers.

Cataldo quickly gives up his attempt to speak English and requests that they communicate in Spanish.

"*No hablo español. Espera un minuto,*" Hammarstedt responds. He asks Meyerson to take the wheel and maintain secure distance between the ships while he summons the Spanish-born Alejandra Gimeno.

Cataldo comes on the radio again, Gimeno translates from Spanish.

"He says they've got a problem and that they're sinking."

"Ask him if it is mayday?"

"Mayday, mayday," can be heard from the radio's channel 16, the international distress and calling channel, before Gimeno has time to translate Hammarstedt's question.

"Say that we have received their mayday and that we are standing by to assist in any way."

Before Gimeno has a chance to translate Hammarstedt's message, a peeping can be heard on the bridge of the *Bob Barker*, two high-frequency, piercing alarm signals.

"That's their distress call," Harmsen says.

Somebody on the *Thunder* has pressed the panic button – the so-called DSC-distress signal that will be picked up by vessels and rescue services in the area.

Cataldo calls up the *Bob Barker* again. He explains what is happening.

"He wants us to launch a small boat to help them to recover the crew," Gimeno translates.

"Tell him that we are launching a small boat," Hammarstedt says.

Then he presses the alarm on the *Bob Barker*. A series of five short rings is the signal for the crew to drop everything they are doing and go to their action stations.

"Just keep doing circles. We've got to get a boat in the water. Quick as we can," Hammarstedt says to Meyerson.

While the crew of the *Thunder* begins climbing down the side of the ship and into the life rafts, Hammarstedt calls Captain Sid Chakravarty on the *Sam Simon*.

Chakravarty immediately sits down at his computer and starts sending emails. Soon Interpol and the authorities in Nigeria, Norway, Australia, New Zealand, the USA, Great Britain and South Africa have been alerted.

"You've got the bridge, Adam," Hammarstedt says to Meyerson.

"Wasn't expecting this this morning," the *Bob Barker*'s second-in-command mumbles.

Hammarstedt must make a few difficult decisions and he has to make them quickly. Shall he fill up the *Bob Barker* with the crew from the *Thunder*? There are almost twice as many of them and they have thrown chains and a smoke shell at his crew. How dangerous can they be?

And if he takes the shipwrecked seamen on board, where will he put them? In the bow? With a helicopter deck astern, there is limited space on the *Bob Barker*. Hammarstedt instructs two of his crew to take notes. Everything that happens now is to be documented. Then he gives the order for the *Bob Barker*'s dinghy *Gemini* to be sent out to the life rafts and asks Gimeno to call up the *Thunder* again and ask what has caused the ship to sink.

"How much time does he think he has?" he says to Gimeno.

What if the mayday situation is a prank? What if the captain is trying to dump the Indonesian crew so the officers can make a final desperate attempt to escape with the *Thunder*? He won't let the shipwrecked seaman on board the *Bob Barker* now. Hammarstedt wants to wait until the *Sam Simon* is in position in a few hours. He doesn't like what's happening; he doesn't trust the officers on the *Thunder*.

"The *Sam Simon* is going to be here in about two or three hours. I don't want to rush to get these guys on here. The weather is good, it's nice and calm. I don't want them to leave these guys behind on us and then they take off. So, we put a boat in the water and we keep that with them and we see if they need anything. Then we wait until there is another boat on the scene," he says.

Scarcely ten minutes have passed since the mayday signal and Hammarstedt is already convinced that the drama unfolding before him is being staged.

"They have probably scuttled the ship," he says to Meyerson.

"Yeah."

"Everything that happens on the radio must be noted. Everything. Every word."

Now it seems as if the *Thunder* is lying lower in the water, but the ship is not listing.

The *Thunder*'s life rafts fill up as one by one the crew members climb slowly down the ladder. The engineer Luis Alfonso

Morales Mardones loses his foothold and falls into the water and must be hauled up into the raft by his arms. Some of them perch on the sides while others seek shelter under the tarp. Deck Officer Manuel Ricardo Barcia Sanles suddenly stands up, climbs back up the rope ladder, runs through the corridors and into the officers' cabins and retrieves suitcases. Everything has been packed. Once back on deck he throws them over the gunwale and down into the life rafts, and then he fetches some bottles of water before descending into the raft again. The first two life rafts are cut loose from the *Thunder* and slowly drift away from the ship.

Captain Cataldo has still not left the bridge. Chief engineer Agustín Dosil Rey is also there. Dosil Rey speaks English, but he stays away from the radio, choosing to let Cataldo handle the communication.

Over the radio Cataldo tells the interpreter that the *Thunder* is on the verge of losing its electricity and that water is flooding into the engine room. He explains that there are 40 men on board and asks that Sea Shepherd launch its dinghy immediately so they can save his crew.

"The ship will sink in 15 minutes," he says over the radio.

Hammarstedt does not believe that the *Thunder* is headed for the bottom of the ocean so quickly and asks Meyerson to follow all movements on the radar.

Hammarstedt's dream was to follow the *Thunder* into a port where the local police and Interpol would be standing by with handcuffs and available jail cells. Now he must in all likelihood save the crew, while the evidence of the illegal fishing activity disappears into the almost 4,000-metre depths. But a mayday signal has been sent, and has very likely been picked up by many. As a captain he must handle the emergency situation correctly.

A trawler does not suddenly begin to take in water when the weather is good and the wind quiet. But what kind of captain sinks his own ship? How desperate are they? And what can he do to secure any remaining evidence that must still be on board the *Thunder*, such as fish, computers, logs, telephones, nautical charts and fishing gear?

He must try and outwit Cataldo, get him into a life raft as quickly as possible. Then he will have better control over the situation.

"Tell him that there is another ship coming," he says to Gimeno.

"OK, OK," Cataldo answers over the radio and explains that he saw another ship on the radar early that morning. So did the watchstander team on the *Bob Barker*. At 3:35 AM the container ship the *Thasos* sailed onto the radar, but then continued on, disappearing into the night. The brief rendez-vous with the Greek cargo ship gives Hammarstedt an opening. Perhaps it will be easier to lure the *Thunder*'s captain down into the life raft if he believes he will be rescued by somebody other than Sea Shepherd?

"I wonder if they finally ran out of fuel? This is so crazy. What a thing to wake up to," Meyerson says.

"I bet the fishing log disappears with the ship," Hammarstedt says.

From the *Bob Barker*'s dinghy the *Gemini*, Lex Rigby reports that the crew of the *Thunder* is fine in the life rafts.

"They have water, they have food, they are waving. Everyone is OK," she reports over the radio.

Rigby, who grew up in the Midlands of England and became fascinated by the ocean from watching David Attenborough's nature programmes on the BBC, is on her fourth mission to the Antarctic. At Sea Shepherd crew members can ascend quickly through the ranks if they can withstand cold, winds and turbulent seas and Rigby, who signed on as a sailor, is now a quartermaster and one of Peter Hammarstedt's most trusted colleagues.

Sitting in one of the life rafts that are silently drifting on the light breeze is first mate Juan Antonio Olveira Brion. He is wearing a black fleece jacket and a life vest and looks worn out and furious, as if he is the only one on the raft who understands that this adventure can end very badly for the *Thunder* crew. He has good reason to be concerned.

Lex Rigby thinks back to the day when a man wearing a ski mask threw a length of chain that hit the ship's photographer Simon Ager. Could the man in the raft be "the Balaclava Man"?

There are still at least five men on board the *Thunder*. The ship is lying lower in the water and has begun tilting slightly towards starboard. Hammarstedt calls up the bridge of the *Thunder* once more.

"You have to pick up the crew from the life rafts. They are frightened and nervous," Cataldo chides.

"We will tow them over to *Bob Barker*," Hammarstedt says.

"OK. This is an emergency. You must take them on board; otherwise you are breaking the law."

From the dinghy Hammarstedt receives word that there are three men standing on the deck of the *Thunder* smoking. They don't appear to be in any hurry to abandon the sinking ship.

"The crew has been in the water for 20 minutes. Take them on board," Cataldo continues over the radio.

"Tell him to calm down. Tell him to handle his sinking ship. Jesus Christ," Hammarstedt exclaims.

"I'll be the last to disembark. I am waiting for you to save the crew," Cataldo says.

The captain of the *Thunder* repeats himself over and over and Hammarstedt grows more and more angry. He has had enough of the charade. The usually so even-tempered Sea Shepherd captain is on the verge of running out of patience.

"This guy's a clown. Just theatrics."

The young photographer Alejandra Gimeno has been Hammarstedt's voice when he communicated with the bridge on the *Thunder*. Again she finds herself in the midst of a duel between the two captains, trying to navigate a storm of abusive language. It is an emergency and communication is about to break down. Gimeno is convinced that Cataldo is playing a game. He wants to keep the argument going until he is sure that the *Thunder* will sink to the bottom with the evidence.

"We take no one on board before the chief engineer and the captain have left the ship," Hammarstedt says.

"You are not following procedure. If anyone else is listening to this conversation, you will be fined," Cataldo answers.

"An hour ago you said that your ship will sink in 15 minutes. Get off the ship now," Hammarstedt roars.

There are still only 35 people in the life rafts.

Peter Hammarstedt sees a possibility to send some of his own crew over to board the *Thunder* and secure evidence, but first he wants to be sure that there are no crew on the ship. Two hours remain before the *Sam Simon* will arrive.

"Tell him to get off the ship. It's sinking," Hammarstedt repeats.

"Why are you still filming? Why don't you rescue us?" Cataldo replies.

"Tell this son of a bitch that his crew has attacked my crew. I cannot take anyone on board before everyone is in the life rafts."

Gimeno translates everything with the exception of "son of a bitch".

"You are at risk of being sued. This is very, very serious," is the response from the *Thunder*.

"Tell him to get off his fucking boat. We can deal with this later. He is not taking this seriously."

"OK. *Bob Barker*. I will send word that you are refusing to rescue us."

"Fine. He can sue us when we get to port. This is fucking ridiculous. He needs to come on board so I can talk to him personally. This is theatrics."

"Take care of the crew. We are professionals, we are not terrorists," Cataldo answers.

"I am so tired of this guy. Tell him that this is the quickest rescue in maritime history. I could get his crew on in two minutes if I had to. I'm done talking on the radio unless it is an emergency."

36

A WEIRD DREAM
THE GULF OF GUINEA,
APRIL 2015

The *Bob Barker*'s chief engineer Erwin Vermeulen starts forming a bold plan. He wants to board the sinking *Thunder*. The Sea Shepherd officers are certain that the captain wants to make sure that the *Thunder* is so far under water that the ship can't be saved before he gets into the life raft.

"He is not going to let anyone on. One hundred per cent," Hammarstedt states.

"I am completely sure it's staged. Destruction of evidence and a last ditch attempt to get off," Vermeulen says.

"We are meeting every moral obligation we have here," Hammarstedt maintains.

"I 100 per cent agree," Meyerson chimes in.

"As long as we keep checking on them, it is fine. At least now we know that he's the captain – the guy with the moustache," Vermeulen says.

From the dinghy Lex Rigby reports that the *Thunder* crew is still fine, that the Indonesians are smiling, friendly and chain-smoking.

"How are they going to deal with a non-smoking ship?" Meyerson wonders.

Over the radio they can hear the captain of the *Thunder* speaking with someone in the life raft; he asks the person in question to make sure his bag doesn't get wet.

"This situation is just like the Twilight Zone. If my boat was sinking, I wouldn't be arguing about this stuff," Hammarstedt says.

Then Sid Chakravarty calls from the *Sam Simon*. He has been in contact with the Nigerian authorities. They advised the *Bob Barker* not to let anyone come on board before there is another ship on the scene.

"Persons in distress may be armed/hostile and could use request for assistance to disrupt your efforts towards bringing her to justice," Captain Warredi Enisuoh of NIMASA, the Nigerian maritime administration and safety agency, writes in an email to the Sea Shepherd captain.

Officially, it is the authorities of Nigeria who are now coordinating the rescue operation. The Navy, Air Force and the maritime rescue coordination centre in Lagos have been alerted and are standing by. Enisuoh has also asked the authorities of Equatorial Guinea, São Tomé, Cameroon and the Democratic Republic of the Congo to make preparations to assist Sea Shepherd. The atmosphere on the bridge of the *Bob Barker* becomes calmer. The officers look out at the crew of the *Thunder* in the two life rafts.

"Maybe we should get them some sodas? Red Bull?"

"That will make them angry. Nothing with caffeine," is the opinion of the ship's physician Colette Harmsen.

"Let's give them Valium," Meyerson suggests.

The two life rafts floating between the *Thunder* and the *Bob Barker* bear the name *Ming No. 5, Ulaanbaatar*, one of the *Thunder*'s many identities. In the intensifying heat, the crew of the *Thunder* eat oranges and drink soda. The empty bottles are thrown into the ocean. The Sea Shepherd crew in the *Gemini* try to fish them out. Both the fishing pirates and activists have the ocean as their place of work, but the similarities end there.

Soon the hunters and the hunted will be on the same ship.

"Tell him that the shipping director in Nigeria has said that we will stand by. Another boat gets here in two hours," Hammarstedt says.

"How far away is the next ship?" Cataldo wonders.

"25 nautical miles," Hammarstedt replies.

He neglects to tell him that it is Sea Shepherd's the *Sam Simon* who is heading towards them.

"Is it a ship that wants to pass us?" Cataldo asks.

"I don't know. We will ask the Nigerians. Tell him that Nigeria is coordinating now and that we are taking our orders from them," Hammarstedt says.

Cataldo tells Gimeno that the battery in the radio he is using to communicate will soon be dead.

"Tell him to get off his damn boat. This guy is a joke," Hammarstedt says.

While Hammarstedt tries to lure Cataldo into the life raft, the chief engineer Erwin Vermeulen is ready to board the *Thunder*.

"It is not the *Titanic* nor the *Kursk*. Nobody is going to go down for it," he says.

"James Cameron is a supporter," Hammarstedt responds with a smile.

The Canadian director behind the two largest box office successes in history, *The Titanic* and *Avatar*, in March 2012 was the first to undertake a solo descent of the 11-kilometre depths all the way to the bottom of the Mariana Trench in the Pacific Ocean. But nobody on the bridge of the *Bob Barker* has any particular faith in the idea that Cameron will dive 3,800 metres for a fishing vessel in the Gulf of Guinea.

Cataldo comes on the radio again and asks how far away the other ship is now.

"12 nautical miles," Hammarstedt answers.

He explains that the ship will arrive in an hour.

"Illegal, illegal," Cataldo answers in Spanish. Again he demands that Hammarstedt bring the crew of the *Thunder* on board the *Bob Barker* and points out that the law requires that the first vessel to arrive at an emergency situation must rescue the shipwrecked seamen.

"He's saying he's going to sue you," Gimeno says.

"I'm so tired of this asshole," Hammarstedt replies softly so the radio won't pick it up.

"He says we can leave if we want," Gimeno translates.

"We are not leaving. We are coordinating on orders from Nigeria. Tell him to disembark so he can save his god damn life," Hammarstedt says and continues: "Just ignore him. And tell him that it is illegal to sink his own ship. I am so tired of this asshole," he says again, this time loud and clear.

He feels that he is starting to gain the advantage over Cataldo.

"He's not going to be happy when he finds out that the second boat is the *Sam Simon*," he says to Meyerson and Vermeulen.

The bridge of the *Bob Barker* is filled with laughter.

"This guy's a clown," Hammarstedt states.

"If he goes down with his own ship, it would be like that scene in *Cape Fear*," Meyerson chuckles.

In Martin Scorsese's action thriller, Robert De Niro plays a mad rapist who is chained to a burning houseboat and drowns.

Cataldo stands on the bridge of the *Thunder* holding a pair of binoculars and staring in the direction of his nemesis on the *Bob Barker*. Cataldo is not planning to accompany the *Thunder* to the bottom of the ocean and now it's high time that he get himself into the life raft. In São Tomé a hotel bed and flight tickets to Lisbon await him. Everything has been arranged.

At the same time, he knows that Hammarstedt and Sea Shepherd are in contact with Interpol and authorities on all continents. He has received regular updates from his wife in Viña del Mar in Chile, and he knows what's at stake. If they can just reach Europe, get away from this nightmare. Will the other ship that is approaching offer a solution? He takes the radio with him and climbs down the stairs from the bridge of the *Thunder* for the very last time.

While several of the crew are taking selfies in the life rafts, the *Sam Simon* comes within range of the radio receiver on the *Bob Barker*. Hammarstedt and Chakravarty discuss the next step. They are still afraid that the officers who remain on the *Thunder* will sail away as soon as Sea Shepherd begins picking up people from the ocean. Five practised seamen can easily navigate the *Thunder* alone. Then the *Bob Barker* will have to resume the chase of the pirate ship while Chakravarty and the crew of the *Sam Simon* will be left alone with 35 men. That won't do.

There is only one solution. Everyone has to get off the *Thunder* before anyone can be rescued. That is the condition. And then it happens: Cataldo and the last of the *Thunder* officers climb down into the last life raft and cut it loose from the trawler. Cataldo has the handheld radio with him. He has seen that another ship is approaching and confirms now that everyone has left the ship.

"Is it the *Sam Simon*?" he asks.

"Yes," Hammarstedt replies.

"Where is the other ship?" Cataldo wonders.

"The *Sam Simon* is the other ship," Hammarstedt says.

Again the laughter booms on the bridge of the *Bob Barker*.

"You behaved like a coward," says a dispirited Cataldo.

"Whatever. Just ignore him. I'm really done with this guy."

The duel between the two captains appears to be over. One of them is on the way to the African nightmare of his life, the other to international fame and admiration.

Hammarstedt asks the officers in the *Gemini* to do a head count of the crew in the life rafts; he wants to be sure that everyone has disembarked before he sends anyone on board the sinking ship. It is not easy to gain oversight. The sides of the life rafts are high; many of the crew are seated under tarps to protect themselves from the ruthless sun. They count 39. Shouldn't there be 40? The *Thunder* officers are dissatisfied. They complain about Sea Shepherd filming them.

As the *Sam Simon* sails in towards the site of the shipwreck, Captain Sid Chakravarty prepares himself for how he will handle the shipwrecked seamen. He will help them on board and one by one position them on the quarterdeck. All the doors leading into the ship will be secured and everyone will be frisked for knives and other weapons. He will simultaneously maintain contact with the authorities in Nigeria and São Tomé.

Both the Sea Shepherd captains believe it would be best if a Nigerian naval vessel picked up the castaways and took them to Lagos, where they can stand trial. And what about São Tomé and Príncipe? Can they send a coast guard vessel? Chakravarty doubts that the authorities of the poor island state have a vessel large enough to transport the entire crew. The most likely outcome is that the *Sam Simon* will have to transport the pirates into the port in São Tomé escorted by the *Bob Barker*. Then somebody must be prepared to receive them there.

The *Thunder* is now even lower in the water and is listing a few degrees toward starboard.

Chief engineer Erwin Vermeulen on the *Bob Barker* and third mate Anteo Broadfield gather up flashlights, GoPro cameras, communication equipment and backpacks. Hammarstedt asks them to remain on the bridge of the *Thunder*. He is afraid that the radio won't work other places on board the trawler. Hammarstedt is feeling stressed. He knows that the feat Vermeulen, Broadfield and the ship's photographer are going to perform now can be mortally dangerous. If they are on the *Thunder* when the ship goes down, there is nothing that can save them.

"This is like a weird dream," he says to Meyerson, who pinches his arm.

"We're awake. Right?"

The three activists dressed in black climb up the same rope ladder that the *Thunder* crew used to evacuate the ship. Below them, Cataldo sits in the life raft watching everything with an incredulous look on his face.

The youngest of the three, Anteo Broadfield, is the first to step onto the *Thunder*'s deck. Vermeulen follows behind him and the photographer Ager, who holds a GoPro camera on a tripod in his hand and another attached to a strap around his head. He is nervous and tense. How much time do they have before the ship becomes unstable and sinks?[1]

They find a passageway along the broadside and make their way past the wheelhouse and up to the quarterdeck. The listing of the ship is now so appreciable that they have to lean towards the port side as they run towards the entrance to the officers' cabins and the bridge. On the first door on the

left are the words *jefe de máquinas*. It is chief engineer Agustín
Dosil Rey's cabin, one of the most trusted employees of the
Thunder's ship owner. It is empty and clean. So are the other
officers' cabins. The *Thunder* is well maintained, a great ship,
Ager thinks before he climbs up to the bridge. There it is
also neat. Broadfield and Vermeulen run into the navigation
room, tear open drawers and cupboards, and find a white
smartphone and a digital camera which Ager stuffs into a
backpack. There is a logbook lying on the desk in the navigation room. Broadfield finds several blank logbooks in a small
storeroom in the navigation room, but there is clearly a lot
that is missing.

Where is the fishing log?

Where are all the laptops?

"What did you find?" Hammarstedt asks over the radio.

"Mobile phones and charts. Cartons and cartons of
Marlboro cigarettes," Broadfield answers.

"Leave the cigarettes. Take the phones."

In a drawer in the navigation room there are two diction-
aries – Spanish-Russian and Russian-Spanish. On a previous
voyage, when Cataldo stayed home in Chile, the *Thunder* had a
Russian captain. There are a couple of computer monitors and
a printer in the room and an old-fashioned calculator. All the
instruments and electronic equipment on the ship appear to
be in good condition, but it is obvious that the *Thunder* has
been in service for a long time. In a drawer in the navigation
room Vermeulen finds a stack of nautical charts. Perhaps
they can tell them something about the *Thunder*'s movements
before they were chased out of the Antarctic?

While the trio searches the bridge of the *Thunder*, Adam Meyerson and the press officer Michelle Mossfield study the captain of the *Thunder* through a pair of binoculars. He is sitting on the side of the life raft and gesticulating. Cataldo is clearly not happy that Sea Shepherd is now on board the *Thunder*.

"It's pretty good if you can be cocky when your ship is sinking. He runs his mouth like nonstop," Meyerson says.

"Blue baseball cap. He's got like a goatee. Does he look cocky to you?" Mossfield asks.

"He would be cocky in LA," Meyerson says.

"Fuck. Excuse my language," Mossfield says.

They also see that a couple of the Indonesians in the life rafts are vomiting. Mossfield has some good Japanese seasickness tablets that she found on the *Sam Simon*. Nobody wanted to take them because they didn't understand what was written on the label. Mossfield got hold of a translator and solved the mystery. A guinea pig vouched for them.

"They're really, really good," she says.

Now the crew of the *Thunder* can have them.

The radio crackles again.

"We have a bunch of charts and a computer," Broadfield says from the bridge of the *Thunder*.

They have found the computer in the communications room.

"You have five minutes. Then get off the boat. Bring the PC with you," Meyerson replies.

Hammarstedt and Meyerson don't want the three on the *Thunder* to go below deck.

"It's a ship no one knows the inside of. I don't feel comfortable doing it," Hammarstedt says.

But Vermeulen and Ager are already on their way. Ager climbs down onto the quarterdeck and trots one lap around it. He sees that somebody has left behind a blue jacket. The *Sam Simon*'s dinghy the *Echo* has also reached the *Thunder*. Together with the *Gemini* it circles the sinking ship. The crew is ready to receive the materials from the *Thunder* and to respond with the speed of lightning should Vermeulen, Broadfield and Ager need help. Ager throws his backpack with the telephone and camera inside down to Lex Rigby in the *Gemini*. Then he goes back to the hallway leading into the officers' cabins and the bridge. He is handed a stack of charts and documents, runs out onto deck again and tries to find a good place from which to throw it all down to Rigby. Then he circles around a little before finding the broadside's lowest point, the same place where two months ago they saw the crew of the *Thunder* hauling up fish. He throws the charts and a couple of folders down from the upper deck. Some of them are taken by the wind and end up in the ocean. Rigby fishes the wet documents out of the water.

Then Ager and Vermeulen climb down the few steps leading to the middle deck. They register that all the bulkheads and doors on deck are wide open – the exact opposite of what they should be if the captain wanted to prevent the water from spreading throughout the ship.

They find a door and stairway leading further down into the depths of the ship. First they come to the fish factory where the catch is cleaned, gutted and prepared for freezing. It is pitch dark, but in the beam of light from the flashlight, they can see that the factory is clean and neat. Ager is starting to grow worried.

"I can't see fuck all," he says to Vermeulen.

They are below deck and have no control over what is happening to the ship. What if it suddenly capsizes? Will they have time to get out?

They keep running towards the back of the ship. Vermeulen still has a tiny hope of saving the ship by stopping the leak, but to do so he must find the engine room. He has a pretty clear idea about what has happened. There are powerful ducts running into the engine room that channel water in from the ocean to cool down the engine. On these ducts there are a couple of heavy valves that can be opened to allow seawater to flow slowly into the engine room. Being an experienced ship's mechanic, he knows that opening these valves is the safest way to intentionally sink a ship.

The sound of water splashing about in the bottom of the ship rises towards them and they find the hatch leading down into the engine room. It too is wide open.

"Look here," Vermeulen says.

"Shit, man," Ager answers, following right behind him.

"It is going to be impossible to get down there now."

The water is about to fill up the entire engine room. In a short while it will rise through the hatch and fill the rest of the ship. Vermeulen takes a few steps down the steep stairway. He wants to try filming down in the darkness.

"Watch out! Looks like there's a bit of a current in there."

"There is a workshop here on the left which is flooded. There is no way we are going to get inside. The water is almost up to the ceiling of the engine room," Vermeulen says.

"Yeah, yeah. Let's get back outside," says Ager breathlessly.

Staying put would be foolhardy. They quickly climb up the stairs again and into the large, open area amidships where nets, materials and floats are stored. One more task yet remains. Where is the freezer facility where the fish is stored? They are reluctant to leave the sinking ship before securing a fish.

On the port side of the deck they find a hatch that is boarded up. When Broadfield realizes that it is nailed shut, he starts tearing off the boards. Beneath a bucket full of cigarette butts and empty Marlboro packets Vermeulen and Ager find another hatch. It is too heavy and they are unable to get it open.

"There must be another entryway," Vermeulen says and runs into the dark hallway of the ship together with Ager while Broadfield continues searching up on deck.

In the messroom there is a frozen chicken thawing on the counter, but they can't find an entrance to the cold storage.

"Fuck, man. Do we have to wait for this piece of shit to sink," Ager says.

The *Thunder* is listing more and more all the time. How much time do they have?

They find another entrance to the fish factory. The floor is slick and slippery, Vermeulen stumbles, skids and falls into an aluminium rinsing tank.

"Like fucking ice skating," Ager says before reaching out his hand to haul his friend back onto his feet.

On the bridge of the *Bob Barker* they see that somebody has pulled up the rope ladder that was hanging over the *Thunder*'s gunwale. Is there still somebody on board?

For the first time in the 110-day chase, Meyerson is visibly stressed and upset. He calls Vermeulen up several times, but the latter doesn't answer.[2]

"Not getting anything back from them now," he says to Hammarstedt.

Then Vermeulen replies.

"Just want to make sure that it was you guys who pulled up the pilot ladder on the *Thunder*."

"No, we didn't," Vermeulen tells Meyerson.

"Tell them to get off," Hammarstedt orders.

Simon Ager shivers. Has someone stayed behind on board to make sure the ship can't be saved? Is there somebody waiting in the darkness inside?

"It might be Anteo, to get into the fish hold," Vermeulen says over the radio to Meyerson.

"Roger that. I just don't want anyone sneaking up behind you. Just like an episode of Scooby Doo."

Vermeulen makes contact with Broadfield. He confirms that it was a false alarm.

"It is confirmed. Anteo pulled up the pilot ladder," he says to Meyerson.

While Vermeulen, Ager and Broadfield are sweating on board the *Thunder*, Meyerson and Mossfield have caught sight of a flock of birds.

"Where did all those birds come from? They look like cranes," Meyerson says.

"They were sitting on the *Thunder*. It's so strange," Mossfield says.

"Why did they come here all of a sudden?"

They are unable to agree about what type of bird it is, but Meyerson believes it can be a sign that the *Thunder* is about to go down.

"If we see those birds again, it's time to get off the boat."

"Let's tell them to get off in five minutes," Hammarstedt says.

"I told them that ten minutes ago," Meyerson says.

"Give them a reminder."

"It is going to roll that way, too – like right onto them," Meyerson says.

"The end of the *Thunder*," Hammarstedt says.

Meyerson starts singing an old classic by The Doors.

"This is the end, my only friend …"

"But it is not really my friend, though. I kinda hate that boat."

"Really?" Colette Harmsen asks.

"Have you gotten the Stockholm syndrome?" Meyerson laughs.

On board the *Thunder* Broadfield has found a small hatch leading down into the cold storage room. With Vermeulen's help, he now pulls the rope ladder through the ship. They attach the ladder and Broadfield climbs down into the darkness. Woven polypropylene bags full of fish are floating around in cold, grey water. There is water dripping from icicles hanging from the ceiling. Since the power went out on the *Thunder*, the fish has begun to thaw. Broadfield grabs hold of one of the bags and attaches it to a rope. They pull it towards them and tear it open. The head and tail of the fish have been removed, but it looks very much like a toothfish. They throw it over board into one of the dinghies.

As Vermeulen and Ager jump to safety in the dinghy, Broadfield runs one last time into the sinking ship. They have forgotten to take the folders they found on the bridge. Then, after 35 minutes on board, all three are about to disembark from the sinking ship.

Thousands of sailors and fishermen have been on board the solid trawler that was launched in Ulsteinvik, Norway almost 50 years ago. On the bridge of the *Bob Barker* they now count the draft marks on the *Thunder*. The ship is lying very low in the water. The end is near.

"That was the eeriest fucking thing, man, going in there," Ager says.

On the *Bob Barker* the cook has cleared out some space for the fish in one of the freezers. This is highly out of the ordinary on a ship where only vegan food is served. The ship's physician and veterinarian have prepared formaldehyde to preserve the fish so a DNA test of the carcass can be done.

When Vermeulen, Broadfield and Ager climb on board the *Bob Barker*, Hammarstedt welcomes them on the deck. He wants a report immediately.

"There were emergency suits lying on the bed. Suitcases packed, but left behind there. No logbooks. One computer, charts, mobile phones. They deliberately opened the hatches to let it flood. They had plenty of food on board. Chicken everywhere, even defrosting in the galley," Vermeulen says.

"You need to type up a witness statement immediately," Hammarstedt says.

He knows that this can be important in a potential criminal case against the *Thunder*. Sea Shepherd has hours of video footage, and they have recorded the communication with the *Thunder*'s captain, but the most important thing of all is the testimonies of the three who have been on board.

"Everything that can flood was unlocked. Only the personal fridges were locked," Vermeulen says, and he adds: "I'm dying for a beer!"

A good deal of what they have just observed on the *Thunder* indicates that most of the crew on the trawler were caught off guard when the alarm went off.

"Maybe a few of the officers knew, but the crew didn't. They had suitcases, but they left them," Vermeulen says.

They also made another interesting discovery. Throughout the entire chase the Sea Shepherd photographer has tried to take photographs of the officers on the *Thunder*. As soon as somebody appeared on deck, Ager pointed his telephoto lens at them and started snapping away. The pirates have clearly done the same thing. In a drawer on the bridge they found pictures of the crew of the *Bob Barker*.

Hammarstedt and Vermeulen climb the steep stairway up to the bridge of the *Bob Barker*. There Hammarstedt takes a quick look at the take from the *Thunder*, which includes some cheap mobile phones.

"These look like the phones drug dealers have," he says.

"Yeah. Expendables," Vermeulen answers.

Hammarstedt is relieved. They have secured telephones and computer equipment that can give Interpol information about who the *Thunder* captain has communicated with on land. Perhaps the answer to the identity of the owner is to be found in these phones? Sea Shepherd has also documented how the officers on the *Thunder* have left doors and bulkheads open, thereby clearing the way for the water pouring onto the ship. And last but not least, they have secured a fish specimen. He feels certain that it is a Patagonian toothfish.

But the day is far from over. Where shall they take the crew? To Nigeria? São Tomé?

Sid Chakravarty prepares to receive the pirates on board the *Sam Simon*. He is concerned about how the crew of the *Sam Simon* will manage to deal with the pirates, who outnumber them two to one. He asks Hammarstedt if he can borrow four brawny men from the *Bob Barker*. What Chakravarty fears most is that the *Thunder* crew will try to come up onto the bridge and take control of the *Sam Simon*. For a moment he considers zip-tying the hands of the ship-wrecked seamen.

"Sure you need that? They seem pretty quiet," Hammarstedt says.

"I will keep that as an option when I see how the mood is," Chakravarty says.

None of the Sea Shepherd shipmasters have ever transported prisoners at sea. They agree to proceed slowly. Chakravarty will bring the captain on board first. He will talk to him to get a feeling of the mood before he lets the rest of the crew climb on board – one by one. But what will they do when everyone is on board? Set their course for São Tomé immediately? Or should they wait until the *Thunder* sinks?

While Hammarstedt and Chakravarty are discussing their options, Colette Harmsen comes up onto the bridge. She has taken care of the fish.

"I had to change my shirt because I hugged a fish. I still smell," she says.

Hammarstedt asks her to tape up the freezer and label it "do not open".

What kind of birds were they that appeared in the sky around the *Bob Barker*? Meyerson doesn't know. They look like cranes. What are they doing so far out at sea?

"They are not seabirds," he says to Simon Ager, who has come up onto the bridge. Ager doesn't have an answer.

"Anyway, today is the day for the two beers I have been saving," Meyerson says.

"This show is going to be bigger than *Whale Wars*," Ager answers.

"It was like the fanciest fishing boat when it was built," Meyerson says.

Anteo Broadfield has also come up onto the bridge. He is

impressed with the ship that is now slowly sinking right before their eyes.

"The hull was massive. The accommodation was sweet," he says.

Hammarstedt is sitting in the communications room and talking with journalists. After Sea Shepherd sent out a press release, the telephone has been ringing off the hook.

On the bridge of the *Bob Barker* they are still struggling to absorb the day's events.

"It is our ship now. Let's save it and sell it to Greenpeace," Meyerson chuckles while looking at the sad sight. "I had a dream that we would see a big black puff of smoke and then the *Thunder* sinking. We didn't see the big black puff of smoke, but it is sinking, so I guess half of my dream came true. What a waste for them and for the ocean. It is a huge waste of everything to watch it end like this," he says.

The *Thunder*'s stern is pitching heavily against the gentle waves, agitating the water up on the deck. The old pirate does not have a chance, the water is beating against the stern and the quarterdeck is almost at the same level as the water surface.

"There you go. Drink it down, baby," Meyerson says.

Hammarstedt stares steadily out at the ocean.

"I can't believe it."

"Look what you did, Peter. Good on you," Harmsen says.

"But the ship is still in pretty good shape. It's worth millions. And they are still willing to do that. I can't understand what they gain," Vermeulen muses.

"How much trouble can they get into?" Meyerson wonders.

"I don't know. Maybe it's too much fish to throw overboard. I don't know," Hammarstedt says.

"Remember that they are really out of fuel. They have nothing left. Maybe they didn't know what to do anymore?" Vermeulen says.

"Maybe," Hammarstedt says.

And what happens now, after the *Thunder* is gone? Will Interpol come to São Tomé?

"I just put out an email and said that we need immediate advice on where to take these guys, and we are waiting for a reply to that," Hammarstedt says.

He has also asked Nigeria to send a naval vessel to escort them.

"We'll see. Hard to do a rescue and media and a TV show, but we are getting there. I am going to see if anyone replied. You OK, Adam? I know you haven't gotten any sleep or anything."

"Yup. I'm fine. This is what I saved myself for. This is why I have been so lazy for four months," Meyerson chuckles.

The crew of the *Thunder* have been in the rafts for more than five hours. Two life rafts are tied together with a rope. It is midday and the hot sun is beating down. Sid Chakravarty is on his way over to the *Bob Barker* for a final conversation with Hammarstedt before the pirates are taken on board the *Sam Simon*.

"They are going to be angry," Colette Harmsen says.

"I know the Spanish are dangerous. Let's hose them down with the fire hose," Meyerson suggests.

On the bridge the telephone continues to ring. Now it's the Australian ABC News who wants to talk to Hammarstedt, but he is in a meeting with Chakravarty. The journalist has to wait and becomes angry.

"We'll have to schedule our sinking better next time," Meyerson laughs as he navigates the *Bob Barker* closer to the *Thunder* so Ager and the other photographers can take the best possible pictures when the ship sinks.

On the bridge of the *Bob Barker* two of the crew are studying Cataldo, the *Thunder*'s captain, who is sitting on the side of one of the life rafts. They can see that he is still talking and gesticulating.

"He looks like such a cock," Harmsen says.

"I wonder what his story is?" another woman on the bridge of the *Bob Barker* marvels.

"He looks like the guy from *American History X*, but with more hair," Harmsen says, thinking of the American actor Edward Norton, in one of his most famous parts as a violent neo-Nazi in the film from 1998.

Hammarstedt and Sid Chakravarty have decided what they are going to do and Hammarstedt gives Meyerson a quick briefing: "*Sam Simon* is going to take on the *Thunder* crew. Gonna start with the captain. Sid is going to debrief him, then take on the rest. Then we are going to escort them to São Tomé," he says.

"I have pictured this ending in a lot of different ways. This wasn't one of them," Meyerson replies while staring at the sinking ship.

"I've driven people to drink before, but I've never driven them to sink."

Broadfield ponders over all the fishing gear he saw on the *Thunder*.

"They had enough gear to fish for a long time. A lot of nice wet weather gear," he says to Meyerson, who is looking at the many Indonesians sitting in the life rafts.

"These guys probably had the best paid fishing job in all of Indonesia, and we ruined it for them. Crime does pay," he says.

"I have never seen a ship sink before in real life. If anyone wants to say goodbye to the *Thunder*, then this is their last chance."

When Hammarstedt returns to the bridge, he sees that water has begun to flood the deck of the *Thunder*. He picks up the ship's interphone and makes an announcement for the crew of the *Bob Barker*.

"Attention all crew. Attention all crew. Looks like the *Thunder* is going down."

Then the crew comes up onto the bridge to bid a final farewell to the ship they have been following for 110 days. At 12:52 PM, the *Thunder* lies down in the ocean. It is as if the hull just rears up. First, the water floods over the section furthest back on the quarterdeck, then it pounds in against the panes on the starboard side of the wheelhouse. The keel rises 80, and then 90 degrees. In a short while only two of the hawse holes are visible, like two eyes taking a final glimpse of the sky before retiring after 46 years of service. The air that is pressed out of the inside of the ship creates a column of water several metres high, like a geyser. As the front part of the bow is swallowed, the ocean turns a turquoise colour. Then the sea silently closes up around the *Thunder* and seals the ship's 3.8-kilometre journey down to its grave.

Several of the Indonesians start chanting loudly, almost like football supporters encouraging their team to make one final effort: "*Thunder, Thunder, Thunder.*" The Spaniards are silent.

"Let's stay clear of that little spot," Hammarstedt says to Meyerson.

"Where did the birds go?" Meyerson asks.

"They came over to us," someone on the bridge says.

"That was the end of the campaign," Vermeulen states.

"We've been staring at that stupid boat for four months. And it is gone. I don't even know where I'm going anymore. 'Cause all I did was follow them idiots. Now I have to navigate and choose somewhere to go. Put the radar on 12 nautical miles instead of a mile and a half," Meyerson says.

"I don't know what to do with my life. I feel like the Grateful Dead when Jerry died."

"What were they thinking?" Harmsen marvels.

"They weren't thinking, they were sinking," Meyerson says.

37

A LAST RESORT
GULF OF GUINEA,
APRIL 2015

It is no coincidence that it is the boatswain Giacomo Giorgi who is waiting to receive Captain Cataldo as he climbs up the pilot ladder and onto the low quarterdeck of the *Sam Simon*. The heavily tattooed and brawny Italian is the most frightening welcome the ship has to offer.

Before signing on with the *Sam Simon* Giorgi ended his career as a vocalist in a hard-core band by screaming "I'm not afraid today, I won't be afraid tomorrow" at a dark, rock club in Rome. With Giorgi as head of the welcoming committee, Captain Sid Chakravarty wants to give the pirates the impression that he is completely in control.

When the entire crew of the *Thunder* is on board, they will be two against one. All day long he has been pondering over what he will do. Should he zip tie their hands? Lock them inside cabins? Shut them out on deck?

For the time being he wants to keep the crew on the quarterdeck and escort the three top officers – the captain, the fishing captain and the chief engineer – to separate cabins.

After Cataldo has been frisked, Chakravarty tells him that he wants to have a conversation with him.

The short and stocky captain of the *Thunder* with buzz-cut hair and a dark, stubby beard is dressed as if he is on his way to the nearest beach pub: a black T-shirt bearing a Heineken advert, over his right shoulder a small backpack and on his head a purple visor cap with a dragon motif and the word "Singapore" embroidered on the stiff brim.

"What about passports?" Chakravarty asks.

"*Pasaporte*? No. It was very, very fast," Cataldo stutters in shaky English.

"Oh? It took six hours to sink," Chakravarty counters.

"Very, very fast," Cataldo repeats.

"Can I have your name?" Chakravarty asks.

"Alfonso."

"Can you write it for me? Help me with the spelling? And can I have your date of birth and nationality, please?"

"What is date of birth?" Cataldo inquires.

Chakravarty's Spanish interpreter comes to the rescue, and the details are scribbled down on a piece of notepaper. Then Cataldo reluctantly agrees to be escorted inside the ship to a cabin, but before he leaves, he turns to face Chakravarty and waves his arms.

"No camera. OK?"

"I cannot control the cameras," Chakravarty responds.

That is a white lie, but the *Sam Simon* captain wants to document everything that takes place. Under his T-shirt he has hidden a small microphone and all of Cataldo's outbursts are being recorded.

When he enters the cabin, the captain of the *Thunder* receives an unpleasant surprise. The lock on the door has been taken apart and reinstalled so it is faced the opposite way; Sea Shepherd wants to lock him inside. Cataldo emphatically insists on being escorted back onto the deck.

"Capitan, you cannot lock me inside a cabin," he says to Chakravarty.

"Then you have to stay outdoors. I need all the passports," Chakravarty says and asks to see the contents of Cataldo's backpack.

"No, no. You are not the police," he protests.

"This is Dutch law. You are on a Dutch ship," Chakravarty answers.

"We are not terrorists. There are personal items in the bag," Cataldo says in Spanish.

But Chakravarty does not give in. He wants above all to avoid having Cataldo establish authority on board. If the 40 pirates should decide to take over the ship, there is little the 23 Sea Shepherd activists can do. For the moment Cataldo seems most frustrated about his having been completely outsmarted, Chakravarty thinks.

"OK, OK. You can check my bag. Captain to captain," Cataldo says.

"No cameras!"

The two captains and the interpreter go through the door leading to the workshop on the *Sam Simon*. While Cataldo opens the backpack, Chakravarty asks what happened to the *Thunder*.

"There was a ship coming and then: BOOM!"

The *Sam Simon* soon resembles a prison hulk. One by one the Indonesian crew climb onto the deck, some barefoot, others wrapped up in warm work jackets. They are all polite and taciturn. Some seem confused. Others are clearly relieved.

The far more dejected Spanish and Latin American officers have bags and suitcases with them in which their clothes have been neatly folded with care. In response to questions they mumble their names before moving on to line up side by side with their backs to the camera lenses.

In Cataldo's backpack, Chakravarty has made an interesting find.

"Is this your seaman's book? Can I have a scan of the first page?"

"No. Personal," Cataldo replies.

The seaman's book is a personal document in which a seaman's history at sea is recorded. The ships he has sailed with, the length of his service time at sea, and where he has been. Chakravarty wants to know as much as possible about Cataldo and the rest of the *Thunder* crew and tells him that he needs the passports and ID papers of the crew to notify the authorities in São Tomé. But Chakravarty also wants to give as much information as possible to Interpol and the police, who will hopefully be waiting for them when they arrive at the port.

"Where are all the passports? I don't believe that you don't have them," he says.

Cataldo shakes his head.

"I am the captain. I am the authority on board," Chakravarty says.

"You know the rules. The international laws," Cataldo answers.

"These are the *Sam Simon* rules."

On the quarterdeck the Sea Shepherd crew wearing white rubber gloves inspect the bags and suitcases of the ship-wrecked seamen who climb on board. Nobody has a passport or seaman's book with them, but Chakravarty doubts that they are gone.

He continues to put pressure on Cataldo, who complains that his crew were left stranded on the ocean for far too long before they were rescued and that they became seasick and cold.

"Can I check your pockets?" Chakravarty asks.

"OK. Can I have communication with my family?" Cataldo asks.

"We will drop you off in São Tomé. You can communicate from there," Chakravarty answers.

"Very important to talk to my family, but *por favor*, no camera," Cataldo requests.

Chakravarty does not want to let Cataldo borrow the satellite phone; he suspects that the captain of the *Thunder* wants to call somebody else entirely than his family in Chile.

Again Cataldo starts to ask if there are other ships nearby.

"We are the only option. No one else is coming," Chakravarty says.

"Where's the merchant ship that *Bob Barker* talked about?" Cataldo asks.

"There is no other ship. We have tried for a British warship and the Nigerian Navy. No one else will come."

"OK. OK," Cataldo answers, and then recalls that he left his sunglasses in his cabin on the *Sam Simon*.

Now he wants them back.

Chakravarty goes up to the bridge to speak with his officers.

"Phew! The captain is intense. He is a bit touchy about being locked in his cabin," he says before returning to the quarterdeck to resume the conversation with Cataldo.

Now he is standing with the logbook from the *Thunder* in his hand. It was found in the bag of one of the other officers, and Cataldo demanded that it be given to him. Chakravarty wants to see it, but Cataldo refuses.

"What is this? Security, security. This book is personal for the ship. For me and the company. Log book, position, navigation," he says and asks Chakravarty to calm down.

"Don't tell me how to run the security on my ship," Chakravarty answers in irritation.

He never receives the *Thunder*'s log book but when the crew of the *Sam Simon* go through the contents of a black waste bag that first mate Juan Antonio Olveira Brion has brought up onto the quarterdeck, they find all the passports for the crew. Captain Cataldo continues to refuse to hand over the passports and Chakravarty would prefer not to use force against the crew of the *Thunder*, who outnumber them, even though there has not been much indication that Cataldo has enough authority over his crew to order a mutiny. A Nigerian military plane is also circling above the site of the shipwreck.

Chakravarty has asked the pilot to fly low over the *Sam Simon* a couple of times. He explains to the crew of the *Thunder* that the military plane is on site to help with clearance of the crew.

Captain Cataldo continues to insist on borrowing the satellite telephone. And it is not his family he is going to call now, but a ship agent in São Tomé.

"I make the calls. It's my ship," Chakravarty replies.

"You need to understand for me. I need to call to my agency. Two minutes. Three minutes. Finished," Cataldo asks in his broken English.

"The ship agency is not going to come to rescue you. It is you and me."

"My idea is very, very good," Cataldo responds.

With his passport in his pocket and an obliging assistant on shore, Cataldo still sees an opportunity to escape. He has to speak with the local ship agent to ensure that a speedy exit from the African island has been planned, an island which on the map resembles nothing more than a pinhead far out in the Gulf of Guinea.

"No agency," Chakravarty says.

"Your ship has sunk, my ship is still floating."

38

THE ISLAND OF RUMOURS
SÃO TOMÉ AND PRÍNCIPE,
APRIL 2015

São Tomé and Príncipe is the island of rumours.

The rumours fly from the small shacks that serve cheap beer along Rua 3 Fevereiro, they are catapulted through the enthusiastic clamour of messengers and offers at the market-place, they multiply and spread outside the always muddy station for the New York-yellow taxis and continue on into the comfortably air-conditioned Café Central with its sweet baked goods and dark, bitter coffee. Once in a while the rumours penetrate the porous walls of the courthouse and legislative assembly and perhaps the presidential palace. The rumours are tales of corruption and fraud, of ordinary family dramas, incredible fishing expeditions, terrible fishing expeditions, business opportunities and run of the mill meanness and idle gossip.

The rumour about Wilson Morais is that he is a robber and a murderer who killed one of the money changers at the bus station and that he later drove around the streets of São Tomé with the corpse seated in the passenger seat. He did this, also according to the rumours, up until the excursion came to an end with a long-term stay in the city's only jail.

What can be confirmed about Wilson Morais with certainty is that together with his father he runs the bustling and apparently successful shipping agency Ecuador, and that he is a street smart, at times very jovial, but also secretive man with good contacts and knowledge of most of what is going on in São Tomé.

In mid-March, Morais received a phone call from Spain. A fishing vessel was on its way to São Tomé and they needed assistance. Ecuador had formerly taken on assignments from Spanish fisheries companies without asking too many questions and he accepted the commission. A few days later an email arrived containing details about the ship's owner, the company Royal Marine & Spares, explaining that the trawler the *Thunder* would be arriving at the island state for maintenance and a crew rotation. Morais was sent the necessary ship's documents and crew lists to clear the ship's arrival and acquire visas, hotel rooms and airline tickets for the crew.[1]

It was a wholly ordinary commission for a ship agent. It was more out of the ordinary that the ship owner also wanted to flag the ship in São Tomé.

Only a dozen ships have their home port on the island state's black-listed ship's register. Morais contacted the coast guard to arrange the papers and formalities so the *Thunder* could be assigned a new home port.

While Morais waited for the client to sail into São Tomé harbour, he received a phone call from the harbour master, who told him that as unbelievable as it might seem, the ship was about to sink. Wilson Morais immediately jumped into action and called up another ship in the area to organize a rescue operation but soon learned that a vessel was already in place and the situation under control.

The rest of the day he prepared for the crew's arrival and had time for merely a few restless hours of sleep before he had to drive down to the harbour and jump on board the coast guard vessel that would bring the shipwrecked seamen to land.

In the darkness, a short distance away from the perfect, half-moon shaped Ana Chaves Bay, which forms the approach to São Tomé, he could make out the silhouette of a ship with a camouflage pattern on the hull and a cartoonish wolf-jaw on the bow. The 55-metre-long *Sam Simon* made São Tomé's modest coast guard vessel the *Águia* – the Eagle – look pitiful.

While the enlisted seamen stood by with one hand on the rail of the *Águia* and the other on their automatic weapons, Wilson Morais hopped on board the *Sam Simon*. He went straight to the *Thunder*'s captain and fishing captain and in a peaceful corner of the ship he told them that minivans would transport the shipwrecked crew to luxury hotels near the airport.

Fishing captain Lampon sat down and ducking his head, packed his few belongings. Chakravarty had asked the photographers of the *Sam Simon* to watch over Lampon with particular care. The latter was the only one of the Spanish officers who wore a wristwatch on his right arm, as had "the Balaclava Man", the man who had thrown the chain length and steel pipe at the Sea Shepherd crew.

But Lampon had had enough of all the attention. He stood up, looked directly into a camera, reached out his arms and exclaimed loudly "*puta mierda*" – bloody cunt.

Then he climbed into the coast guard vessel without saying a word to the crew who had rescued him.

The ship owner's representative in Spain had given Wilson Morais instructions to get the officers of the *Thunder* out of the country as quickly as possible. The tickets for Lisbon were already booked. The next evening at 7 PM, they would mingle with the tourists at São Tomé and Príncipe's international airport and be lifted out of their lives' worst nightmare.

If everything went according to plan.

39

48 HOURS
SÃO TOMÉ AND PRÍNCIPE, APRIL 2015

He is awakened with a start by the telephone. The public prosecutor Kelve Nobre de Carvalho glances quickly at the clock and establishes that it is five in the morning. On the other end of the line is São Tomé's chief of police; he seems clearly elated. The police station is full of foreigners from a shipwreck, he explains.

Kelve Nobre de Carvalho finds his glasses and puts on a shirt, trousers and shoes and before getting into his car he has time to down a quick cup of coffee and give clipped responses to his wife's questions.

"There's been a shipwreck," he replies.

The air is still cool when he gets into his car and drives the few kilometres between his home and the police station. Beneath the almond trees on the esplanade he sees women balancing woven baskets and plastic tubs containing fruit and vegetables on their heads; from time to time he glimpses the shadows of the first morning joggers. Now and then the headlamps are reflected in the pupils of vagrant stray dogs.

Life starts early in the morning in São Tomé, before the all-consuming heat descends upon the island.

The sight that greets him at the police station in the capital São Tomé surprises him. Several of the shipwrecked seamen are well-dressed; the majority of them even look happy. The Asians smile and joke. The rest of them, whom Nobre de Carvalho presumes come from Europe, are more aloof.

The young public prosecutor has never heard of the *Thunder* wanted by Interpol or the chase that has been underway at sea for almost four months. Life as a public prosecutor in Africa's second smallest country with a mere 200,000 residents is comfortable and laid-back. One out of three residents lives in São Tomé, the only densely populated area on the two islands that can be called a city. Here Nobre De Carvalho investigates three or four murders per year, a few robberies and a corrupt politician or two. And then there are the constant banana thefts.

The first thing he does is to collect the passports of the shipwrecked seamen, then he asks the local Interpol contact to check whether arrest warrants have been issued for any of the seamen. Then he fingerprints them.

To keep the crew on the island, Nobre de Carvalho must open a criminal case and for the time being he has no opinion about whether the seamen he has before him are the victims of a shipwreck or if they have committed some kind of crime. He is at a loss. In the course of 48 hours he must decide whether he will let the crew go or open a formal investigation. The latter option is the most difficult. The crime scene is lying at the bottom of the ocean.

At the police station he also meets Wilson Morais, the secretive ship agent who is the one in São Tomé who knows the most about the *Thunder*. Morais has bought sandwiches, mineral water, cigarettes, juice, cakes and biscuits for the crew. In the afternoon, after the preliminary, fumbling interviews, Morais will transport the shipwrecked seamen to the hotels by the airport. The next day he will drive the crew to the island's only airport and put them on a plane to Lisbon and freedom. But the armed policemen who are monitoring the seamen's movements at the hotels and the ambitious public prosecutor's involvement give Morais a disturbing feeling that his plan will go up in smoke. For the time being that is a thought he keeps to himself.

Perhaps it is a coincidence that determines the fate of the *Thunder*'s crew in São Tomé. The business lawyer Pieter van Welzen from the Netherlands is sitting in the shade by the swimming pool of the five star hotel Pestana near São Tomé's esplanade when he reads the first article about the wreck of the *Thunder*.

After having spent a holiday in São Tomé and Príncipe on an impulse many years ago, he fell in love with the peaceful group of islands. The multilingual van Welzen is now São Tomé's consul in the Netherlands, co-owner of a culture centre on the island and in the process of building a house in the capital. He has also become a kind of mentor for the younger public prosecutor, Nobre de Carvalho, whom he finds to be sharp, committed and fearless and among the few in São Tomé who dare to challenge the small power elite in the country.

On the Internet, van Welzen sees that the wreck of the *Thunder* has made the international news. He doubts that his friend the public prosecutor understands the kind of complicated case that sailed in during the night. The public prosecutor has done criminal investigations of thefts, but never illegal fishing, he has investigated corruption, but never human trafficking and environmental crime. He fears that the case could prove to be an ordeal for his friend.

If the authorities in São Tomé are going to investigate the shipwreck, they must quickly establish contact with Interpol. And they must get hold of witnesses of the incident – Sea Shepherd, van Welzen thinks. From the hotel he writes an email to Sea Shepherd's European headquarters in his own home town of Amsterdam and offers to assist with the case. The next day he receives an answer from Captain Sid Chakravarty on the *Sam Simon*.

"The best thing to do at this stage would be to send a message to Interpol in Lyon," Chakravarty writes, and includes the phone number of the Interpol agent Mario, who he knows is ready to move out.

"It would be incredibly important for Interpol to investigate the Captain and Fishing Master before they leave. The ownership of the *Thunder* must be established before these men disappear and Interpol is waiting for the invitation to assist," he writes in the email.

After Pieter van Welzen has briefed him and the Director General of Public Prosecution about the case, public prosecutor Kelve Nobre de Carvalho decides to start an investigation. It would have been simpler to drop it. It is not their ship, not their crew, not their company and the *Thunder* has not been fishing in São Tomé's waters. But he has witnesses and after the Director General of Public Prosecution called the telephone number they received from Sid Chakravarty, Interpol's Incident Response Team is on its way.

The Wednesday flight to Lisbon takes off without the crew of the *Thunder* on board. At the hotels the shipwrecked seamen are starting to get nervous. They sleep in soft beds, splash around in the swimming pools and the ship owners have sent money for new clothes and toiletries, but they still have armed police on their heels. In the evenings dangers both real and imagined are mixed up in confused discussions: prison and yellow fever, Interpol and malaria.

Several of the *Thunder*'s officers know that the ship was wanted by Interpol, but how much does the young public prosecutor know about them? The local defence attorney hired by the ship agent Morais tries to reassure them, first with a yellow fever vaccine, then cautious optimism.

"Everyone will be able to travel home soon," he says.

For three of the officers of the *Thunder* life will soon turn pitch-dark.

40

THREE CONDEMNED MEN

SÃO TOMÉ AND PRÍNCIPE,
APRIL 2015

Five days after the wreck of the *Thunder*, three Interpol agents land in São Tomé. The team is led by the energetic Portuguese agent Mario, who has followed the voyage of the *Thunder* from the moment the ship was found until it sank. With him from Lyon he has a specialist in human trafficking and from Lisbon a policewoman who speaks fluent Indonesian.

The agents are not authorized to wave hand guns around, interrogate suspects or force anyone into handcuffs. They don't arrest people, don't operate prisons, don't own the intelligence information they collect and cannot make statements on behalf of the member countries. When an Interpol agent appears at a crime scene, he is there to assist the local police.

Interpol's Project Scale will for the first time assist a nation in bringing up criminal charges against fishing pirates.

After having informed himself of the details of the local investigation, the Interpol agent sees that just about everything has been done incorrectly. The interrogations of the

Thunder crew are superficial; the police have asked the deck crew, chief engineer and captain all the same simple questions. In several of the interrogations the suspect's country of origin was not even established. But what really puzzles him is the arrangement of the furniture in the interview room. Where the suspect is supposed to sit, there is a tall chair. Where the policeman is supposed to sit, there is a lower chair. It's almost as if the crew of the Thunder are being treated like celebrity guests, not like suspects in a criminal case, they think.

In the subsequent interrogations, the crew and officers will be gathered in a big room and nobody is to know who will be interrogated or when. When an interrogation is finished, the suspect is to be led out of the building without having the possibility to speak with those who are still waiting.

The public prosecutor Nobre de Carvalho witnesses how the Interpol team first goes to work on the furnishings. Pictures and other removable objects on the walls that can be used as a weapon are taken down. The Indonesians are to be interviewed as witnesses and the room and the atmosphere is to be pleasant and relaxing. With the officers, it will be different. They are suspects and the atmosphere in the room must be serious and oppressive. They will sit on hard, low chairs. And between the suspect and head of interrogation there will be a solid table that is wide enough to prevent the suspect from throwing a punch.

They start by interviewing the Indonesian crew. Both Sea Shepherd and an expert in human trafficking from the University of Auckland have alleged that the crew may be victims of involuntary servitude. Although the Interpol team doesn't believe the allegations, they must be checked out. A ship owner who wants a crew to sail to the most remote and dangerous maritime regions on the planet wants loyal seamen he can trust, capable and experienced men who know how to work effectively in the inhospitable climate of Antarctica, Mario thinks.

In the course of the interviews it becomes clear that the Indonesians are not victims of human trafficking. They have received wages, they have posted messages on Facebook, and they have communicated with their families in Indonesia. The Interpol investigators find no evidence of the Indonesian crew having been subjected to any criminal violations.

When the fishing captain Juan Manuel Patiño Lampon enters the interrogation room, he is wearing reading glasses, shorts, flip-flops and a T-shirt.

This is the moment the investigators have been looking forward to.

Lampon is tall, corpulent and has beard stubble. His facial expression is impenetrable and his gaze is so full of rage that the investigators believe he will soon break down and cry. Lampon sits down on the edge of his chair, as if he is preparing to make a quick exit or for a tussle. When he is offered a bottle of water, he declines with a hand movement.

Sixty-one-year-old Juan Manuel Patiño Lampon has been shaped by more than 40 years at sea; he is a proud and uncompromising fisherman and the *Thunder*'s alpha male. It is the man who wears his watch on his right wrist, the way "the Balaclava man" did, and who in the course of four months has not said anything but *"puta mierda"* – bloody cunt – to Sea Shepherd. He was the man who made the important decisions and decided where they would sail and fish.

First, the investigators will compliment Lampon on the gillnets he has constructed. When Mario met the Sea Shepherd ship the *Sam Simon* in Mauritius a mere two months before, he studied the nets Lampon deployed in the Banzare Bank. He was impressed with the construction and knows that the *Thunder*'s fishing captain is a master of the craft. The best fishing captains leave their signature on the 15–20 kilometre-long nets, which are spliced together to catch as many fish as possible and simultaneously to make them easy for the crew to handle. For a fisheries investigator, the net construction can tell him just as much about the perpetrator as DNA on a bloodstained carpet can tell a homicide investigator.

After having warmed Lampon up with the compliment, they will get him to admit that he has been fishing illegally. That is the strategy.

Before each interrogation of the officers, Mario has prepared 40 questions, depending upon the kind of role the suspect had on the *Thunder*. Now he takes head of interrogation Nobre de Carvalho out into the hallway and tells the young and inexperienced public prosecutor that they must throw out the manuscript and devise a new plan. After having read Lampon's body language, the Interpol agent understands that he won't tell them anything of value if they confront him aggressively. He knows the *omertà* culture from which the fishing captain comes. They must try to set a trap.

Back in the interrogation room, Nobre de Carvalho first asks open and harmless questions in an attempt to get Lampon to relax.

"How many times have you sailed with the *Thunder*?" he asks.

"This was the first," Lampon answers.

This was the answer they had been hoping for. The Interpol agent snaps to attention and starts leafing through the folder of intelligence information he has brought from Lyon. Inside it there is a crew list showing that Lampon has been on at least three trips with the *Thunder*. His first answer is a bald-faced lie. Kelve Nobre de Carvalho repeats the question, this time slowly enough so it cannot be misunderstood.

When Lampon gives the same answer, the Interpol agent sees an opportunity to make him crack. He leans toward Nobre de Carvalho and says loudly:

"We must start a criminal case against Captain Cataldo. He claims that Lampon has been on more than one voyage. The captain has clearly lied and wronged Lampon's name."

The investigators receive the response they were hoping for. The fishing captain asks for a chance to change his answer. He has been on several voyages, he admits.

Then he starts talking about the missions, the nets and the fishing. This is information that can be useful if the Spanish authorities should decide to investigate Lampon, but which won't have any consequences for the fishing captain in São Tomé. He hasn't been fishing in São Tomé's waters and the country has no laws enabling the court to penalize a foreign citizen for fishing illegally in international waters. Therefore, they allow Lampon to travel home to Ribeira.

Even though he is the ship owner's and the fishing master's puppet, it is Captain Luis Alfonso Rubio Cataldo who is legally responsible for the ship.

"Investigate the case as a suspicious accident, not as illegal fishing," is the advice Nobre de Carvalho receives from the Interpol agent.

The young public prosecutor must find the person responsible for sinking the ship and the pollution of São Tomé's waters. Then he must find the person against whom criminal charges can be brought for the ship's sailing under forged papers. Who will be allowed to leave and who must stay is already becoming clear to Nobre de Carvalho.

From the luxury hotel Pestana first engineer Luis Miguel Pérez Fernández posts photographs of himself in the swimming pool on Facebook. "*Qué bonito*" – how lovely – his wife at home in Ribeira comments. In his home town, friends and family "like" the picture of the man they haven't seen in almost five months. But suddenly the first engineer stops publishing updates from his life in the tropics. While 37 of the *Thunder*'s crew are granted permission to leave São Tomé, the passports of Pérez Fernández, chief engineer Agustín Dosil Rey and Captain Luis Alfonso Rubio Cataldo are confiscated.

They are informed that they cannot leave the island.

Captain Cataldo makes a final attempt to extract himself from the problems. Alone and unannounced, he turns up at the office of the public prosecutor Nobre de Carvalho and tells him that he has a family at home in Chile, that he is an ordinary man who is trying to feed his wife and children. He didn't know anything about the documents being forgeries, he claims. When this doesn't work, he tries to place the blame for the shipwreck on the engineers, but the public prosecutor doesn't believe the Chilean captain's stories.

In São Tomé it is said that the conditions in the prison are so favourable that if you are gaunt going in, you will be fattened up by the time you leave. This is meagre comfort for three forsaken men.

During the investigation of the *Thunder* shipwreck, disturbing things begin to occur in the life of public prosecutor Kelve Nobre de Carvalho. On his way to work at eight o'clock in the morning, the domestic servant calls and tells him that some strangers are inside his house. In the bedroom she found the public prosecutor's suits torn out of the wardrobe and strewn across the floor. Beside the pile of clothes was a one-litre tin of petrol. Somebody wanted to burn the house down, but the domestic servant surprised the intruder, who ran off. In the weeks that follow two policemen sleep in the public prosecutor's house.

One week later he is awakened at night by the sound of splintering glass. When he goes out onto the dimly lit square in front of the house, he sees that the windscreen on his car has been smashed.

There is a dog lying on the ground with a broken leg. That could of course have been a coincidence.

41

THE LUCK OF THE DRAW
CAPE VERDE, MAY 2015

At the end of May Peter Hammarstedt is in Cape Verde, where Sea Shepherd has one of its permanent bases. In the Porto Grande Bay outside the city of Mindelo he notices a ship. Hammarstedt loves ship stories and every time he sees a vessel he wants to know more about, he jots down the name – *Itziar II*. Then he Googles it.

The stories he reads about the *Itziar II* are astonishing. The ship rocking peacefully in the turquoise water outside Mindelo has been blacklisted for 12 years for illegal fishing in the Southern Ocean. Hammarstedt realizes that the *Itziar II* could have been one of "The Bandit 6".

A dinghy transports him out to the ship. The windows are broken, the hull is shedding rust, there are piles of woodwork on the deck and the interior has been ripped out. Local fishermen who paddle past in a canoe tell him that the ship has now been taken over by Mindelo's vagrants. In the evening they often see a fire lit on deck.

Hammarstedt sends an email to Interpol and tells them about the find, and then he takes a taxi to the airport. As he is driving down the coastal motorway along the Porto Grande Bay, he looks out toward the decrepit pirate to bid a final farewell, but now there is another ship in the water beside it. It is painted white and has brownish-orange streaks of rust running down the hull from the scuppers. There is something about the profile of the ship; he is sure he has seen it before, many times, while he was preparing for the search for "The Bandit 6".

Before he boards the plane to Lisbon, he calls one of the Sea Shepherd activists in Mindelo and asks him to take a dinghy out into the bay to take a photograph of the ship.

"Make sure that nobody sees you!" he warns.

When Hammarstedt lands, he goes straight to the hotel and checks his email. He studies the photographs from Cape Verde, then he checks Interpol's website. There is another name on the ship that was photographed just outside Mindelo, but he is certain that it is the *Songhua*, one of "The Bandit 6".

He calls the fisheries officer Gary Orr, New Zealand's man in Operation Spillway. When a groggy voice answers the phone, he remembers that it is the middle of the night in New Zealand.

"I am so sorry for waking you up," Hammarstedt stammers.

"Don't be sorry. I'm getting up," Orr replies when Hammarstedt has told him the story from Cape Verde.

Half an hour later Orr calls back.

"I am 100 per cent sure it's them."

Hammarstedt goes into the bathroom of the hotel room and gets a plastic cup, and then he goes to the minibar and plucks out a small bottle of whiskey. As he celebrates by himself in the silence of the hotel room, he is filled with amazement over the luck of the draw. He spent half a year of his life tracking down and chasing the *Thunder*; now he found one of "The Bandit 6" by chance.

The next morning he flies home to Stockholm. As he is retrieving his baggage, he receives another email from the photographer in Cape Verde. There is now a third ship beside the *Itziar II* and the *Songhua*. This ship also has a strange name, but when he sees the pictures, he is sure that it is the *Yongding*. Again he calls Gary Orr in New Zealand, who confirms his find.

There is a yellow flag flying from the foremast of the *Yongding*, a signal from the captain that there are no contagious diseases on board and that the crew is waiting for the customs officers to inspect the ship so they can go ashore. For Hammarstedt it means two things: the crew is still on the ship and there is definitely no toothfish to be found in the cold storage room. He is right. When the police of Cape Verde board the two ships, they don't find any fish.

The crew that goes ashore from the *Yongding* and the *Songhua* are a motley group of Spaniards, Indonesians and Latin Americans. Most of them travel on to the airport, but some of them get no further than the many bars found in Mindelo. There they celebrate with beer, Johnnie Walker and the local liquor *grogue*. When they come to a few days later, the morning-after sets in. They are broke and there will be no salary from the ship owner in Spain. The interior, provisions and electronic equipment on the *Songhua* and the *Yongding* end up on the black market in Mindelo. Some of them manage to drag themselves to the airport, others continue the party.

Peter Hammarstedt knows nothing about the drinking binge in Mindelo, but he can scarcely believe his own good fortune. When he finished Operation Icefish, two out of six pirate vessels were put out of commission – the *Thunder* was gone for good and the *Kunlun* under arrest in Thailand. Now only two remained – the *Viking* and the *Perlon*.

Sea Shepherd has already commenced the preparations for Operation Icefish 2, but when they receive the news that the *Perlon* has also been apprehended, they drop it.

When Sea Shepherd found the *Thunder* on the Banzare Bank, the *Perlon* was nearby. Hammarstedt's record-breaking chase could just as well have been a search for the *Perlon*, but while the *Thunder*, *Kunlun*, *Songhua* and *Yongding* were being tracked down and chased throughout the Antarctic summer, the *Perlon* managed to stay out of sight. At the end of April its luck ran out. At the Australian Cocos Islands, the ship was boarded by armed agents dressed in black from Australia who seized ship documents, the contents of computers and papers. Then the agents alerted the authorities in Malaysia.[1]

Two weeks later, a mere three nautical miles south of Tanjung Bulat on the south-eastern tip of Malaysia, the Spanish fishing captain tried to transship the fish onto a barge. But a Malaysian patrol vessel sailed up alongside them while the operation was underway, and the jig was up.

For the authorities of Australia and Malaysia this was a huge victory. For the first time in the long-standing battle against the pirates in the Antarctic they could confiscate the fish. The captain of the *Perlon* had not applied for a transshipment permit. It was a violation of Malaysian law.

The captain and the crew had to pay 1.6 million Malaysian ringgit – 400,000 dollars – in fines to avoid prison time. 270 tons of Patagonian and Antarctic toothfish were sold at auction for 5 million ringgit – 1.25 million dollars. The 64-year-old *Perlon* was sold as scrap metal.

When the crew of the *Perlon* receive their sentences, the *Songhua* and the *Yongding* are still in Mindelo. The ships have been dry-docked, repainted and appear to be ready for a new mission, but Peter Hammarstedt calms down by telling himself that the police still have them under surveillance.

"I think they're a long way off from leaving and doubt that an Operation Icefish 2 will be necessary," he writes to the authors.

A week later he has changed his mind.

42

THE ESCAPE
PHUKET/DAKAR,
SEPTEMBER 2015

It looks like a reckless disappearing act, but in reality it is preposterously simple. One day the *Kunlun* is suddenly gone. Five men board the ship, start the engine, raise the anchor and cut and run, away from port fines, arrest orders and Thai battleships. Six hundred and fifty-six tons of steel wanted by Interpol and captured in Thailand, missing without a trace.

When fishing captain José Regueiro Sevilla navigates the *Kunlun* away from the tropical holiday island of Phuket on the morning of 8 September, he has with him 181 tons of Patagonian toothfish that were seized by the authorities a half year ago. In the fuel tanks the *Kunlun* has recently received, with the approval of the port authorities, 80,000 litres of bunker fuel.

It's almost as if the authorities in Phuket want the ship to disappear.

When the news of the escape reaches Peter Hammarstedt, he doesn't know whether to laugh or cry.

"Sigh …," he writes in an email to the authors.

Then he fires off a torrent of abuse on Sea Shepherd's website – not against Thailand, but against two nations he thinks should have done a great deal more to stop the ship and seize the catch.

"When we criticized Australia and New Zealand for not arresting the *Kunlun* at sea, authorities in those two countries assured the international community that the most effective tool in the fight against these poachers was port state controls. If the vessel had been arrested by Australia or New Zealand, the catch would never have been returned. Instead, Australia and New Zealand's unwillingness to arrest the *Kunlun* and seize its catch at sea has allowed this poaching operation to continue, and to profit from its crimes," the Sea Shepherd captain writes.[1]

Then Hammarstedt and Captain Sid Chakravarty decide to take on the search for the *Kunlun*.

Since he had to leave the *Kunlun* in the Southern Ocean a few months before, Chakravarty has pondered a great deal over the ship. Now the *Kunlun* is the perfect prey for Operation Icefish 2, a daring outlaw on the run, more famous and notorious than the *Thunder*. The next few days Chakravarty studies recent satellite photos of the *Kunlun*'s possible escape routes, but he doesn't see anything resembling the white painted fugitive.

Sea Shepherd's flagship the *Steve Irwin* is prepared for another expedition to the shadowlands to search for the last two members of "The Bandit 6" – the *Kunlun* and the *Viking*.

Most of those involved in Interpol's Operation Spillway are extremely disappointed with the authorities in Thailand. One man comprehends, someone who has worked closely with the Thai fisheries authorities, Glen Salmon with the Australian AFMA. He shrugs off the critique from Hammarstedt and Sea Shepherd.

"For some there is no other acceptable outcome than these boats getting sunk and the master going to jail for the rest of his life. Most countries don't have laws like that. They haven't fished in your waters, your laws are not strong and you are not going to get a seizure of the vessel or a large financial penalty, just some sort of a fine, maybe. That is not good enough for the rest of the world," he says.

"When this vessel went out of their port, it was probably the best day of their lives. It was like an albatross hanging around their neck."

In Thailand the authorities point accusing fingers at one another. Neither the port authorities, the customs officers nor the Navy want to take the blame. Finally the charade comes to an end with the transfer of three customs agents in Phuket.

While the pursuers argue among themselves, the *Kunlun* sails towards Dakar with a hand-picked crew who are experts at not attracting attention. All electronic equipment that can disclose the position of the vessel is turned off, and a new name is written on a steel plate and attached to the railing by simple wires. When the ship arrives in Senegal, its name is the *Asian Warrior*.

At the harbour in Dakar the 181 tons of toothfish are loaded into containers and shipped to Vietnam on one of the container ships of the world's largest shipping company, the Danish Maersk. The bill of lading states *Thon en vrac congele* – frozen tuna fish in bulk.

Had Interpol known that the *Kunlun*'s sister vessel the *Yongding* had stolen into Dakar and unloaded 268 tons of toothfish worth EUR 3.5 million a few months before the

Kunlun came to the same harbour, they would also have known where to search for the ship.

Yet again "Tucho" and his sons "Toño" and "Naño" Vidal are one step ahead of their pursuers.

Then fishing captain José Regueiro Sevilla makes a mistake that will be enormously costly for the Vidal family.

After having spent half a year getting the ship and fish out of Phuket, then a couple of months sailing across the Indian Ocean and up the western side of the African continent, on the evening of 1 December, José Regueiro Sevilla boards an Iberia flight in Dakar. It is the only direct flight from the West African country to Madrid and the quickest route home for Sevilla and the four others who have been on the *Kunlun*'s final voyage.

Four hours later they land in Madrid. When Sevilla passes through the Schengen control, the alarm goes off.

Everyone who shows their passport at the Schengen control in Madrid is checked every day against the Spanish police's database of wanted persons of interest and criminals. And now the Spanish police investigators are secretly monitoring José Regueiro Sevilla's movements, but Sevilla doesn't learn about this. It is his employer the police are interested in.

After all the hardships and months at sea, had Sevilla only spent a few extra hours on his trip home to Spain by stopping over in France, Portugal or any other Schengen nation and shown his passport there, the Spanish police would probably never have noticed that he arrived from Dakar.

Now they know where to search. And yet again, random events conspire against the Vidal family.

When Sevilla lands in Madrid, a Spanish police investigator is meeting with two fisheries officers from Senegal in Interpol's headquarters in Lyon. As soon as the investigator receives word that Sevilla has just arrived from Dakar, he tells the two Senegalese officers that they very likely have a vessel wanted by Interpol in their harbour. When they come home, the Senegalese officers find a ship that fits the description – the *Asian Warrior*.

Now things happen quickly. The containers of toothfish from the *Kunlun* are traced to the North Vietnamese seaport Haiphong. There they are stopped and inspected by local authorities. Then samples of the fish are taken to confirm that it is Patagonian toothfish and not tuna fish, as stated on the bill of lading.

At the seaport in Haiphong the inspection officers behave as if it were an ordinary control procedure so the owner of the cargo won't suspect that Interpol and the Spanish police are involved.

For one year the cargo of frozen toothfish has been on a circumnavigation of the world from the Southern Ocean to Thailand, then around the entire African continent, past the Horn of Africa, across the Indian Ocean and into the South China Sea before ending up in Vietnam.

All this for a few million euro.

43

THE UNLUCKIEST SHIP IN THE WORLD

SÃO TOMÉ AND PRÍNCIPE, SEPTEMBER 2015

As Peter Hammarstedt walks down towards the Palace of Justice in São Tomé, a light pink colonial building by the Ana Chavez Bay, he feels slightly uncomfortable. He is dressed in a black suit and tie, the only suit he owns. He found it in a dustbin in Söder in Stockholm and paid a tailor a few kroner to repair the lining. Five months after the shipwreck of the *Thunder* he will stand face to face with Luis Alfonso Rubio Cataldo for the first time. On the beach below the Palace of Justice he observes the remains of abandoned ships sticking up out of the sand like rusty bones.

Hammarstedt and Sea Shepherd's photographer Simon Ager are the first to arrive at the courtroom. The tall windows and heavy wooden benches give the room the appearance of a church. Hammarstedt ponders over whether or not he should shake Cataldo's hand but he believes the man may interpret this as a sarcastic gesture. He decides to refrain.

As Cataldo enters the courtroom, Simon Ager raises his camera. The *Thunder* captain rushes towards him but Ager wards off the attack by placing one hand against Cataldo's chest. Then the *Thunder* captain continues towards Hammarstedt. With his chest pushed forward and clenched fists, he leans over him. Hammarstedt raises his hands above his head. In the background he hears Cataldo's defence attorney scream and he leans back in his chair. The attack will appear even more violent if he demonstrates the he's not going to defend himself, he thinks.

But the blow never comes; mumbling, Cataldo returns to the dock, where he sits staring into the shimmering hot and humid air.

During his testimony the *Thunder* shipmaster states that he feared for his life for 110 consecutive days.

"You were two days from port and you feared for your life. Why didn't you go into land?" the judge asks.

"I had my orders."

"But you are the one responsible for safety on board. For you that must be the most important thing?"

"I had my orders," Cataldo repeats.

But he refuses to reveal whom his orders come from.

The judge shakes his head in resignation before asking the next question.

"Who do you work for?"

"I don't know," Cataldo replies.

After the first day of the trial, when Hammarstedt returns to the secluded bungalow by the beach, he notices that the hotel grounds are not properly fenced in. In his room he checks the window and wonders if he would hear it should somebody try to break it open.

After the incident earlier in the day, four policemen carrying MP5 machine pistols and wearing bulletproof vests stood guard in their respective corners of the courtroom. But on the way out, when Cataldo laid eyes on the Sea Shepherd activists in the cool patio on the courthouse's ground floor, he launched another attack. Now Hammarstedt is starting to worry about his own safety. Cataldo and his men are staying at a hotel not far away.

The thought of an inebriated and vindictive Cataldo causes Hammarstedt to call the public prosecutor Kelve Nobre de Carvalho and request police protection. They agree that an agent from the federal police force will keep an eye on Cataldo, see how much he consumes at the bar and call if he should leave the hotel.

Hammarstedt is just about to fall asleep when somebody knocks on the door. He can't see who it is, but he is sure that it is Cataldo. Gripped by fear, he picks up the water pitcher on the nightstand and jumps out of bed. For 110 days they were separated by an abysmal sea and a few tons of steel. Now there was only a thin wall.

"Who is it?" he called out.

"Open the door," is the reply from the other side while the knocking continues.

"Who is it?" he repeats.

"*Tranquilo*," is the reply from the other side of the door.

It turns out to be the police agent, a giant of a man who went by the nickname "Africa".

"Tomorrow I will follow you to court. When the pirates see us together they will never touch you again," he reassures him.

When Hammarstedt crawls into bed again, it's as if the sheets are vibrating in time with the hammering of his pulse.

On the second day of the trial, Peter Hammarstedt is the first witness called to testify. The three defendants seem far less tense. They enter the courtroom joking and laughing. Chief engineer Agustín Dosil Rey sits leaning forward with his elbows resting on his knees and keeps his eyes glued to Hammarstedt. The first engineer Luis Miguel Pérez Fernández stares mainly at his own shoes, and does not look up all day. Captain Cataldo allows his gaze to rest on the view outside the window. For seven hours they will continue, without a recess, without lunch and without water.

Hammarstedt has decided to paint a picture of the fish poachers as a criminal organization and mentions the fishing captain Lampon's business partner, who was apprehended in possession of two tons of cocaine.

"These three were not involved. Somebody on the ship was," Hammarstedt stresses.

Chief engineer Agustín Dosil Rey looks at Hammarstedt as if he is a leper. Every time Hammarstedt mentions Interpol, the chief engineer rolls his eyes.

"You don't represent Interpol. What gave you the right to follow this ship? Did Interpol ask you to follow them?" the defence attorney asks.

"No, we came across a criminal act and followed the ship," Hammarstedt answers.

To the question of the consequences of the *Thunder*'s wreck, Hammarstedt replies that the oil will start leaking out of the wreck.

"You sell fishing permits to the EU. This destroys the opportunity to do so. São Tomé is a natural habitat for sea turtles and you are investing in ecotourism. These people are destroying that for you. How can you put a price on the country's ecotourism?" Hammarstedt asks.

At that moment, Hammarstedt is sure that the chief engineer is going to stand up and knock him down. A stenographer is seated on a wooden bench against the wall and diligently writing down every word with a ballpoint pen.

The *Thunder* officers' defence attorney Pascoal Daio got his education at the prestigious university La Sorbonne in Paris, has formerly been a Supreme Court Judge and is a highly esteemed man in São Tomé. His strategy is to discredit Sea Shepherd, to portray the organization as terrorists and a kind of ISIS of the environmental movement. He accomplishes this by showing a series of YouTube videos of Sea Shepherd and the *Bob Barker* in confrontations. Many of the videos have been published by Sea Shepherd supporters. When he shows the near-collision between the *Bob Barker* and the *Thunder* in February, Cataldo gets to his feet, clicks the heels of his shoes together, and holding his hands behind his back, he takes the floor.

"I have never been so afraid. I was sure that my crew and I would die," he says.

Then Hammarstedt speaks up.

"What Cataldo is saying is absurd. The film shows that the *Bob Barker* is sailing at full throttle astern to avoid being hit. We saved them! It's not certain they would be here had it not been for us. Every day for 110 days we reported to the police. We saved them. We gave all the evidence to Interpol. We came to São Tomé at our own expense to testify. Captain Warredi Enisuoh of the Nigerian coast guard stated that never before have two ships sacrificed so much to stop a ship. That is why we are here," Hammarstedt says.

"Why didn't you put in at port?" the judge asks Cataldo again.

"I had my orders," he answers.

"Who did you report to?"

"I don't know."

After their initial optimism the three defendants seem battered and resigned. There is no Spanish or Chilean consul present during the trial. Also Cataldo's attire surprised Hammarstedt. He has come dressed in dungarees and a blue shirt unbuttoned at the neck. Beforehand he had imagined the ship owner would hire a local tailor to sew the captain a suit. The first engineer Luis Miguel Pérez Fernández scarcely utters a word. Most of the time he stares at the floor, now and then he glances up to send Hammarstedt a look of contempt. The impression is that the three have been left to manage on their own. Nonetheless, they are clearly protecting the ship owner.

Throughout the entire trial they categorically deny having sunk the *Thunder*, but cannot give any sensible explanation for why the ship is now resting on the bottom of the ocean off the coast of São Tomé.

"Why did the *Thunder* sink?" the judge asks in closing.

"It was a perfect day to sink a ship," Hammarstedt replies. "And they thought they could get away with it. Either the *Thunder* was sunk intentionally, or it was the unluckiest ship in the world," he continues.

During his entire testimony the three defendants listened to Hammarstedt's explanation without moving. Now all three of them nod in approval. As if they want to say: Yes. The *Thunder* was the unluckiest ship in the world.

44

THE JUDGMENT
YELLOWSTONE, OCTOBER 2015

When he wakes up, there is hoarfrost on the tent canvas. After packing up the tent, Peter Hammarstedt gets in the car and drives south through Yellowstone. From the window he sees the sulphurous vapour rising from the hot springs. It's as if the earth is alive. When he catches sight of a bison, he stops the car and gets out. He is finally on the holiday he dreamt about during the search for the *Thunder* half a year ago.

While he is silently observing the grazing animal, his mobile phone chirps. It's a message from Sid Chakravarty.

"Everyone was sentenced. They got three years in prison. EUR 15 million in fines," the message says.

"What?" Hammarstedt answers.

"Cataldo and the officers. They were sentenced to three years in prison."

Hammarstedt sits down on a rock. The chase of the *Thunder* has reached its final conclusion. Now he stares out across the shining mirror of water on the lake before him and feels a trembling joy over the fact that Captain Cataldo must spend the coming years behind bars.

45

PRISONERS' ISLAND
SÃO AND PRÍNCIPE,
JANUARY 2016

They are like two pinheads in the enormous Gulf of Guinea, spit out of the sea and covered by a labyrinthine rainforest. Since the equator and prime meridian meet here, São Tomé and Príncipe are somewhat justified in calling themselves a kind of global midpoint. In reality there are few places located so far from the attention of the world as Africa's second smallest nation.

Four months have passed since the officers of the *Thunder* were sentenced for having operated with forged documents, sinking the ship and contaminating the waters of São Tomé. Captain Cataldo and his men have not paid the fine of EUR 15 million, and neither are they to be found in the country's single prison, a facility described as being "tough but not life endangering". And it seems as if nobody knows with any certainty where the prisoners have gone.

Public prosecutor Kelve Nobre de Carvalho explains that Cataldo and his men have lodged an appeal and are living in a house "somewhere or other" in the city. In a corner of the office some of the evidence from the *Thunder* case lies tossed into a heap.

"One day something strange happened. I was sitting at the café by the esplanade reading a book. Without my knowledge, the three from the *Thunder* had picked up my tab. The next time I ran into them, I told them that that was attempted bribery and that I would send them straight to prison if it happened again. It is really not usual for a defendant to pay the restaurant bill of a public prosecutor," he says.

"Is it possible they have escaped?"

"This island is a prison. Nobody gets out of here. Sometimes I see them, at a café or outside the bank," Nobre de Carvalho says.

From the perspective of an ordinary visitor there is not much to do in the capital city of São Tomé. By the old fort on the coast there are enormous granite statues of the Portuguese explorers João de Santarém and Pêro Escobar, who went ashore on the island in 1470 and found it uninhabited. The explorers maintained that the island was a suitable place from which to trade with continental Africa, but the first colonists perished from malaria and tropical diseases. The next wave of Europeans who went ashore were deported criminals, prostitutes and 2,000 Jewish children who were taken from their parents in Lisbon and forced to convert to Catholicism. The fortune hunters also came, those who were seeking to profit from trading in slaves and spices. On the island they discovered fertile volcanic soil, ideal for cultivating cocoa. In the early 1900s, São Tomé was the world's largest manufacturer of cocoa and was called "the chocolate islands". The cocoa plantations, of which there were more than 800 on the islands, were owned by the feudal lords from Portugal. The workers were brought from Angola and Cape Verde and worked under contracts stipulating conditions that amounted to slave labour. After the liberation from Portugal in 1975, the Portuguese plantation owners fled, taking with them their knowledge of operations, and soon the nationalized plantations were invaded by the jungle and relentless deterioration. Now 90 per cent of São Tomé and Príncipe's revenues come from developmental aid, the largest amount in the world per capita, and the national budget is at the level of the annual results of Snapchat. With EUR 15 million in debt to the state, Captain Cataldo and his men have to be some of the most valuable assets found on the island.

In the hours preceding the wreck of the *Thunder*, a large sum of money was transferred from a bank in Singapore to the local bank in São Tomé. The money was intended to cover hotel costs, food and airline tickets for the crew and officers. The local ships register had also received a request to have the *Thunder* flagged in São Tomé. The enclosed documents were forgeries. The man who handled the money and paperwork was the *Thunder*'s local ship agent, Wilson Morais. The family's agency is the oldest and most respected on the island, but the young Morais' reputation was dubious. He is now the *Thunder* owner's most trusted man.

We meet him on a corner by the marketplace. He tells us that he has to continue down to the harbour.

A ship has come in that needs supplies.

"I like shipping. It's exciting, you know," he says, pressing down on the accelerator of the battered Japanese pickup. A walkie-talkie dangles from the mirror, and under the driver's seat he has a black plastic bag full of cash.

"I have to pay with cash for just about everything on this island," he says, reaching his hand down into the bag beneath the seat and passing a wad of bills to one of his assistants, who is waiting outside the car.

"I can't give my people a break. Most of them are lazy, so I have to supervise them. I'm telling you. There's no time for this shit, man. They don't want to work hard. Sometimes I talk to them in a very tough way," he says.

"The owner of the *Thunder* isn't stupid, you know. They looked for a port with a low profile. The plan was for the ship to remain here for three or four months of repairs, then they would find a local crew to start a new season," Morais says.

"I work directly with the owner. The owner sends money to the families every month and he pays for all the officers here in São Tomé," he explains.

"The money sometimes comes from a bank in Singapore, but we deal with José Manuel Salgueiro. He is the one giving the orders. Everything goes through him," he says.

José Manuel Salgueiro's name and telephone number were found on the bridge of the *Thunder* just before the ship sank. The Spaniard has been an operator for a number of ships that were fishing illegally in the Southern Ocean and has a close affiliation with the Galician ship owner Florindo González and *la mafia gallega*.

"I can't go into any more detail. The owner is the owner," Morais says.

Wilson Morais explains that he still sends his invoices to Royal Marine & Spares, the company in Nigeria which one year before was denounced as a fraud by the authorities in the country.

"I just do my job. Let's finish up with this and have a beer. OK?"

A gang of young boys who are busy polishing an old Toyota point towards the villa at the end of the street and shout: "The pirates, the pirates."

By the beginning of October, Wilson Morais had had enough of skyrocketing costs. He had made outlays of more than EUR 10,000 a month to cover hotel rooms for the three officers of the *Thunder*. He had also had difficulties having the costs reimbursed by the *Thunder*'s owner. On a by-way near the esplanade he found a villa for rent. The house had been the property of the military. Now it had been taken over by a speculator, was guarded by a security guard and equipped with domestic help and a swimming pool. In addition to renting the house for Cataldo and his men, he provided them with a small motorcycle so they could get around on the island.

In the beginning the mood between the three convicted criminals was tense; Cataldo had tried to deflect the blame for the wreck onto the engineers. Sometimes Morais would drop by with a case of beer to alleviate the tensions between them.

Now Cataldo comes walking up to the gate. He opens it slightly and tells us that he is not allowed to speak while the appeal of his case is ongoing.

"I have pictures of Sea Shepherd that show what they really do," he says, as if he held the trump card he never had the chance to play before somebody knocked over the table.

Neither the Spanish nor the Chilean authorities have asked to have the prisoners extradited. Now it seems as if the three officers have been left to their own devices and the luxury prison. But Cataldo is still unflinching in his loyalty to the owner.

"One day I'll show you. Then I'll tell the true story," he says and returns to his luxury prison.

"It's a paradox," Alex the interpreter says, who always has a sharp quip to make about life in São Tomé. "While the prisoners are living a life of luxury, paid for by an unknown source, through a hidden bank account, the population is struggling to survive."

Soon São Tomé begins behaving evasively. The telephones are silent, meetings are postponed, the director of the coast guard appears to have sunk into the ocean and the public prosecutor Kelve Nobre de Carvalho is suddenly so busy that one would think a wave of banana thefts had washed over the island. Nobody seems to know where the documents, judgments and court records of the *Thunder* case are found. Nobody is allowed to talk, nobody answers the phone and nobody can tell when Cataldo and his men will receive their final sentence.

On the beach by the courthouse there is a group of young people sitting with their hands around their ankles and staring out at the sea as if the incoming tide is going to bring with it a few surprises.

"They are sitting here and waiting for the saviour. And the saviour is an NGO," the interpreter Alex says in his customary caustic manner.

The judge who found the three officers of the *Thunder* guilty and who oddly enough is also responsible for the appeal is standing outside the courthouse. At the sight of us he runs towards a car, jumps in and disappears. He stops a short distance up the street, close enough to be able to see us but far enough away to be able to take off if we should run towards the car.

When we call him, he says that he is not allowed to speak to us.

"The judges know their rights, but they are not as well informed about their duties," the interpreter Alex says.

In the city centre, the ocean air has eaten away at the old colonial buildings, rendering them porous and ramshackle; on some of them the effect has been the same as a grenade. At Café Central the owner sits playing sudoku at her regular table, something she has been doing without cease since her husband recently passed away. At his office next door, the defence attorney Pascoal Daio is working on the appeal for the officers of the *Thunder*.

"Who owned the *Thunder*?"

"I don't know. This house belongs to me, but the *Thunder*, no, I have no idea ..."

In the evening we go to the bar Pico Mocambo, a well-maintained colonial building in a lush garden where they serve pungent, homemade rum. Suddenly a massive, frowning voodoo mask of iron falls down from the wall. A piercing shriek follows. It hits the table top and the hand of a female tourist from Portugal. Wailing, she leaves the bar with three broken fingers.

It is "The Martyr's Day". Ship agent Wilson Morais loads up the car with beer and mobile phones and invites us to come north on the island to take part in the commemoration.

"Cataldo and the two others declined the offer to come along," he said. "They are simultaneously stressed and bored. All they do is talk about their families and surf the Internet. I asked if I could get them something to alleviate the stress, ha ha … But they always say no."

Along the road the eternally green wall of the jungle recedes and is replaced by a more open landscape, like a savannah. In the village of Fernão Dias what appears is a chaos of processions, local musicians and overdressed politicians crowded together around improvised stalls offering grilled fish, corn on the cob and squid. "The Martyr's Day" is a commemoration of the Batepa massacre of 1953, the tragedy that would change São Tomé.

It started when the colonial government formed an ambitious plan for the urbanization and modernization of São Tomé as a means of attracting more white settlers to "the province". Soon, a rumour was spreading through the plantations that the governor wanted to use forced labour to implement his visions.

During the first, incipient protests a policeman was hacked to death with a machete, followed by a wave of violent retaliations nourished by a growing paranoia within the colonial regime. The sale of machetes and knives was suddenly prohibited and those who fled into the jungle were followed and locked into overcrowded cells where they were forced to fetch water in defecation buckets and were fed rotten beans. Those who did not die from torture and illness were overcome by thirst, suffocation and malnutrition. In the drying rooms of the cocoa plantations prisoners were burned alive. In Fernão Dias a work camp was established where the prisoners received the task of "emptying the ocean". They were chained together in pairs, equipped with buckets, and forced down to the water's edge to retrieve water that they had to pour out in the sand. Those who collapsed were thrown into the ocean. More than 1,000 people are said to have been killed during the massacre, which led to a new nationalist movement and later to independence for São Tomé and Príncipe.

On the way home from the commemoration, we end up stuck in a tailback. Wilson Morais holds in the clutch and guns the engine, as if that is going to help us advance more quickly. Suddenly he steals the march on us, telling us the rumour with which we have not yet confronted him: That he is said to have killed a money changer and driven around the city with a corpse hidden in the car.

"Has anyone told you that I've been in prison?" he asks. "It was a damn foolish thing I did. I learned my lesson and I don't like talking about it."

Then he starts talking.

"A friend of mine knew some Russians who were on the island. They carried out transport commissions for the UN and were going to spend a few days off bird-hunting in the jungle. But they had no weapons, so I rented a semi-automatic shotgun from some acquaintances in the military. The day I brought back the gun, a friend and I stopped out in the bush to test-shoot it. He started. After having fired off a few rounds he gave me the weapon. I thought it was empty and pulled the trigger. But there was still ammunition in it and I hit him in the chest."

Then he lifts his hands off the wheel and shows us how he had held the gun.

"It was an accident, but I panicked, ran away and tried to hide. But it only took a few hours before I was arrested. It was a bloody stupid thing …"

The friend died instantaneously, leaving behind two young children. Wilson Morais spent three years in prison. He is still paying a monthly sum to the children of the deceased, he solemnly declares.

"Every now and then Cataldo and the Spaniards ask about the conditions in the prison. I haven't tried to hide that I've been there."

Once back in the city, Wilson Morais invites us to a meal of grilled fish and a couple of beers at one of the outdoor restaurants found in rows beneath the breadfruit trees in the city park.

"The Spaniards are starting to get fat," Morais says. "Captain Cataldo goes to the gym at least, even to the disco-theque. The others just sit inside, surfing and eating. I'm afraid they will lose their minds soon."

For the two engineers from the *Thunder*, Agustín Dosil Rey and Luis Miguel Pérez Fernández, it is yet another bad day. One of the 450 miserable days the two have spent together since the *Thunder* set out on its final voyage. On the way to the Miguel Bernardo bakery they are stopped by the police. They haven't paid the annual vehicle tax on the small motorcycle the agent Morais acquired for them. The debt of EUR 15 million increases by a few more euros.

When Wilson Morais introduces us to the Spanish prisoners, they make it clear beyond any doubt that they don't want to talk. They go to the bakery every morning on the small motorcycle that looks like it is about to buckle beneath their weight.

They are now staring silently, each in a different direction, out towards the market place, towards the row of yellow New York taxis, towards the pack of vagrant dogs scampering around in the garbage that has accumulated along the curb of the sidewalk. They sit here every day, like two forgotten old men waiting for the final judgment.

4 6

THE MAN FROM MONGOLIA

SINGAPORE, FEBRUARY 2016

The *Thunder*'s journey was concealed by layer upon layer of lies and conspiracy. The ship was assisted and protected by anonymous agents, insurance companies, banks, corrupt servants and flag states that wanted their cut of the poaching revenues. Four of "The Bandit 6" sailed under the red and blue flag of Mongolia, the most unlikely shipping nation of them all.

"The *Thunder* became a huge problem," says Tamir Lkhagvademberel, the director of the Mongolia Ship Registry.

We meet at a luxury restaurant in Singapore. The director is a husky and smiling middle-aged man incessantly fingering his gold-plated phone. He has five employees with him who listen to the conversation in silence. They were the ones who were going to punish the *Thunder*'s owner and officers if they broke the law or investigate the ship if it should get into an accident. Mongolia's Navy consists of a tugboat on a lake in the north-western part of the country. It is manned by a crew of seven, only one of whom can swim.

"We have a bad reputation. That is something we are working hard to get rid of, but it is difficult to be removed from the black list. It will take us at least three years," the director says between mouthfuls of lamb shank.

For ship owners there are a number of good reasons to sail under flags of convenience like the Mongolian. It is cheap, the ship owners are spared the annoyance of public regulations, can hire inexpensive and non-union labour and avoid taxes and cumbersome environmental and safety regulations. And they don't ask owners hiding behind shell companies in tax havens any intrusive questions.

For somebody who runs a business which for years has been accused of hiding criminals, Tamir Lkhagvademberel seems surprisingly straightforward and naive – like his own path to the top of the Mongolian shipping industry.

In the winter of 2008 he flew from Ulan Bator to Berlin and from there on to Oslo. He didn't know much about the Norwegian capital, but managed to find his way to the university, where he presented his wish to become a student. Preferably within the tourism and travel industry, he said.

The only documents he had with him were a diploma from a hotel management vocational school in Singapore and a tourist visa. After having received a polite rejection and advice to apply through ordinary channels, he travelled on to Sweden and the University of Uppsala. There too his attempts at acquiring acceptance as a student were unsuccessful.

Back in Mongolia he gave up on his dreams of higher education and found a job in the Ministry of Transport, where eventually he was appointed ship's registrar at the Mongolia

Ship Registry – the ship registry of a country located 1,300 kilometres from the closest port. The registry was the idea of Mongolia's Prime Minister Nambaryn Enkhbayar and was to give its clients "excellence in registry and marine services". What he did was to rent out Mongolia's sovereignty to a private company, allegedly to procure revenues for the country's treasury. He appointed his daughter as head of the office. Since few ship owners wanted to travel to the edge of the Gobi Desert to register their ships, the Mongolian ship registry was based in Singapore.

When Tamir Lkhagvademberel arrived at the ship registry's austere offices in Singapore's Chinatown, one of his first tasks was to register the fishing vessel the *Kuko*. In the registration papers, the old *Vesturvon* has undergone an impossible transformation: the ship was no longer built in Ulsteinvik in Norway in 1969, but rather in northern Spain 20 years later. On paper the hull is two metres shorter and five tons heavier. While the ship is registered in Mongolia, it is also listed in the Nigerian ships register under the more well-known name of the *Thunder*. The ship owner in Galicia had secured two sets of papers. For him it was a perfect system, while for the authorities who were trying to follow the ship's pillaging missions in Antarctica, it was a nightmare.

Tamir Lkhagvademberel has no reasonable explanation for how so much could go wrong at the same time.

From the ministry in Ulan Bator, he has been told to use the meeting to create a better impression of the ship registry. A few years ago the registry's director was caught cheating at a casino in Florida. But that wasn't the worst of it.

The country was accused of having registered anything that would float at a low cost. Mongolia-registered ships were constantly being seized or were mixed up in life-threatening or fatal accidents.

Before Mongolia started selling its flag, the ships register of Cambodia was the preferred banner of international criminals. The register was owned by the private company Sovereign Ventures, which had close ties with North Korea. After several episodes involving ships smuggling narcotics and weapons, Cambodia was forced to shut down its register. Sovereign Ventures bought its way into the Mongolia registry instead, which was quickly suspected of hiding North Korean and Iranian ships in violation of the international sanctions regime. Before long the Mongolian shipping escapade came to be viewed as a serious security threat.

"Mongolia appears to have no problem renting out its flag to weapons proliferators, criminals and other shady figures who endanger the security of the United States and its allies," Director Peter Pham wrote in an analysis for the Nelson Institute for International and Public Affairs.[1]

"We had no experience with shipping; this was a first step towards the maritime industry. Some of the ships we registered became a headache for us. The USA and NATO pressured us to get rid of the North Korean ships and we also threw out agents who worked with blacklisted ships. We had to do something about our reputation," Tamir Lkhagvademberel says.

The pirate vessels' owners paid USD 3,000 to sail under the Mongolian flag. Nonetheless, the registry's sales volume did not exceed 1 million dollars in 2015, according to Lkhag-vademberel. That is barely enough for payroll, rent and living expenses in one of the most expensive cities in the world. If they are not earning money on it, why does Mongolia have a ship registry?

"Mongolia wants to become a shipping nation. We hope that more Mongolians will purchase their own ships in the course of the next few years," is Lkhagvademberel's attempted explanation.

Under pressure from Australia, Lkhagvademberel removed the *Thunder* and the other fishing vessels from its registry.

The ship registry's financial director, the company's only woman, is explicitly sceptical about the meeting.

"Why are we actually sitting here and talking to you?" she asks.

Five silent men look up from their plates and wait for an answer.

We drive to the offices of the ship registry in Chinatown. At the office the director has an equestrian statue of Djengis Khan.

"We once had the largest fleet in the world," he says.

Even by the loosest of definitions, it must be admitted that it has been a long time since Mongolia was a shipping superpower. In the thirteenth century the Mongolian fleet was wiped out by a typhoon in an attempt to invade Japan. More than 4,000 ships and 100,000 soldiers are said to have disappeared.

In Mongolia the *Thunder* operated with three different identities. The ship was registered under the name the *Wuhan No. 4* in July 2012. According to Lkhagvademberel, the registration of the *Wuhan* was made possible by a disloyal servant at the registry, who gave the *Thunder*'s owner what he needed in the way of papers, stamps and signatures without registering the ship in the official registry. What is odd about the ship's certificates that Lkhagvademberel gives us as documentation for the *Thunder*'s two Mongolian identities – the *Kuko* and the *Wuhan No. 4* – is that the most important defining feature on a ship – the so-called IMO number, which follows a ship from its christening to the scrap heap – is not included on either of them. What is even more curious is the *Thunder*'s third identity in Mongolia. On the *Thunder*'s final voyage the life rafts were marked with the name *Ming No. 5, Ulaanbaator*. There is no *Ming No. 5* in the Mongolian registry, according to Lkhagvademberel.

The streets of Singapore are hot, clean and full of life. There are hundreds of ships in the harbour waiting to unload their containers. The shipping traffic is overwhelming and chaotic, but so non-bureaucratic that Singapore is constantly cited as one of the simplest places in the world to do business. The pirate fleet's silent service providers are also hiding in the midst of this commercial whirlwind. Here they procure provisions, spare parts and fuel. Here they also find their ship agents.

In their explanations after the wreck of the *Thunder*, the officers stated that it was the Singapore company Thong Aik

Marine Enterprises that represented the owner of the ship. Some also implied that the company owned the *Thunder*.

"No, no, no. We are not the owner of this vessel. If we were, we would not have been sitting here right now," a harassed representative for the company shouts into the telephone.

Then he hangs up.

47

THE LAST VIKING
INDONESIA, MARCH 2016

It is the crew of a merchant vessel who discovers the *Viking* first. The easily recognizable, blue-painted pirate lowers anchor north of Bintan Island in Indonesia. The discovery quickly becomes an intelligence report that is sent to the Indonesian Navy. A short time later a military helicopter is airborne and soon confirmation arrives that it is the world-famous fishing vessel that is now in Indonesian waters.

The first pirate on which a wanted notice was issued is the last to be apprehended.

The worn out and disillusioned crew of the *Viking* have sailed straight into Indonesia's war against illegal fishing. While other nations hand out fines and prison sentences, Indonesia brings out the big guns. By the time the *Viking* is forced in to port at a naval base in Bintan by a battleship, the Indonesian authorities have sunk 170 foreign fishing vessels in less than two years.

"It's simpler for us now," explains Rear Admiral Achmad Taufiqoerrachman, who led the operation against the *Viking*.[1]

"Before we sometimes found ten ships fishing that were functioning on a single fisheries permit, but because there was so much double-dealing on the part of the companies that owned the vessels, we never succeeded in proving which nine were fishing illegally. Now we just say: This is illegal," he says when we meet him in Jakarta a few days after the *Viking* has been apprehended.

And the new shoot-first-ask-questions-later policy works, according to the rear admiral.

"The number of illegal vessels in our waters has been drastically reduced."

Indonesia is the country in the world hardest hit by illegal fishing. The authorities estimate that there are 5,000 illegal fishing vessels lurking in the island nation's waters at any given moment. The country loses at least 5 billion dollars annually on the looting, according to the authorities.

That is why combating the fishing pirates is one of the main tasks of Rear Admiral Taufiqoerrachman and the Indonesian Navy. It is also the reason why Indonesia has a special elite group investigating illegal fishing, a group that reports directly to the president.

For Indonesia the fight against pirate fishing is deadly serious and the *Viking* is actually irrelevant.

"I informed the Minister of Fisheries that we had found the *Viking*. 'Oh yeah! Blow it up today,' she said. I explained that the ship was wanted by Interpol and that we should wait until they come to Indonesia so we can carry out a joint investigation," Taufiqoerrachman says.

The Indonesian investigators and the Interpol team from Norway who go on board the *Viking* a few days later find that the officers have cleaned up well. There is not a document to be found from later than 2013 and outdated and destroyed electronics equipment fills the shelves on the bridge. It is not surprising. Five months earlier, armed Australian agents boarded the ship in the Indian Ocean. The officers on the *Viking* have had plenty of time to dump evidence into the ocean.

There is little information on the bridge that can incriminate the owner, but the investigators make finds that tell them about life on board the *Viking*. They discover several well-stocked medicine cabinets containing antibiotics still within their expiration date, tools to perform simple surgery, a little perused edition of *Don Quixote* and dozens of flags – the most well-worn is North Korea's red, white and blue.

They also find documentation that sheds light on the *Viking*'s odd relation with war-torn Libya –and with the abandoned pirate ship that Peter Hammarstedt found in Cape Verde.

When in 2013 Norway requested that Interpol issue a notice on the *Viking*, the ship was named the *Snake* and was allegedly flagged in the North African country. There the owner had procured a ship's certificate that was incompetently translated into Arabic and stamped with the coat of arms of Libya's former King Idris, who ruled until 1969. It was obviously a forgery.

When the Interpol team ransacks the *Viking* in Indonesia, they find a stamp on board containing a spelling mistake: the word "Discrict", not "District". A stamp with the identical spelling mistake was also found on board the abandoned pirate ship in Cape Verde. And that isn't the only connection between the two ships. Both have a relation to a dead ruler from Libya.

On board the pirate vessel in Cape Verde the investigators found an IMO number which had previously belonged to a tuna fishing vessel owned by one of the sons of Libya's deceased dictator Muammar al-Gaddafi, a vessel that was sunk during the NATO bombing of the country.

"There was somebody who knew that the Gaddafi vessel had disappeared in the chaos in Libya. And they took advantage of that," says an officer from the Interpol team.

Given the currently prevailing chaos in Libya, this is a puzzle that it is unlikely they will manage to solve, but in the opinion of the inspection officer, the story illustrates just how far the pirates are willing to go to dupe and confuse the authorities.

Forged documents and bizarre relations with Libya contrast strikingly with the books the investigators find in the captain's wretched cabin. He likes poetry. And in quiet moments he has sharpened his wits working on complicated sudoku.

Two mopeds transport us through the naval base on the island and to an open grassy plain screened off by sail canvas. It is an intensely clear day; the *Viking* is moored by the quay a few hundred metres away and surrounded by soldiers. From a distance the ship seems to loom large, almost impressively. A 70-metre ship, the *Viking* is the largest of "The Bandit 6".

Then the crew is led out of a barracks and across an open field, in a silent line. They plod along slowly, wearing the same grungy T-shirts they had on when they were arrested a few days before. Captain Juan Domingo Nelson Venegas González is first; the Chilean's body is agile and his expression is alert. When he sits down, he greets us with a forced smile. Around us stand half a division of naval officers listening to every word that is spoken.

"I didn't hear about Interpol until we arrived here. We have been in two or three ports without anything happening. Then you figure everything's OK, right?" he begins.

According to the captain, the last voyage on the *Viking* was a diabolical trip. The ship remained docked at a shipyard in Bangkok for a long time with a broken gearbox and when they went south in September, she was boarded and inspected by the Australian Border Force northwest of Christmas Island.

After they had been fishing for a few weeks, the ship's generator broke down. Instead of going to their usual delivery sites in Angola, the Congo and Sri Lanka, they had to dump 20 tons of rotting fish into the ocean. Captain Venegas claims that it was cod and not toothfish. With the generator out of order the bilge pumps didn't function either, which made the Burmese crew uneasy and nervous. At one point there were incidents of insurgency and attempted mutiny on board. Because no incomes were generated from the fishing, the ship owner stopped paying. Now six months had gone by since the Burmese crew and the officer had received their wages.

"The owner has not even given us money for food. I have to pay for that out of my own pocket," Venegas complains.

The owner of the *Viking* he describes as a "guy from Singapore named Eric Tan", but says that the ship is registered with a Nigerian company.

"The only thing I know about the owner is that he has disappeared. Nobody can find him and I don't know why he has abandoned us. I am in a lot of hot water because of him. We have only just learned that our papers are forgeries. Everything is fake, the flag, the documents. I trusted my boss. Isn't that what you're supposed to do?"

"So you're innocent in all of this?"

"I'm not innocent. I am the captain.

"If you'd Googled the *Viking*, you would have quickly discovered that the ship was wanted."

"We don't have Internet on the ship. The owner says it's far too expensive. Besides I have more important things to do than surf the Internet."

At first he doesn't answer the question about whether he has been in Antarctica. After a few seconds of silence, he looks up.

"I know there's ice in the Antarctic, but I've never seen it. There are many good fishing grounds between the 42nd and 43rd parallels. Both shellfish and cod," he says.

When we show him a picture of the *Viking* near the ice edge in the Antarctic, he nods, uncomprehending.

"How long have you been a seaman?"

"Don't ask me. I can't stand to think about it. I've been a farmer, worked in cold storage facilities, with fish farming and shellfish farming."

"When did you go on board the *Viking* for the first time?"

"Everybody asks me that but I am under incredible pressure from all sides. I can't even remember my children's birthdays any longer."

"But you know the ship well?"

"Give me any fishing vessel at all and in the course of 12 hours I will know all the ship's details from top to bottom. The engine, the generators, ballast, the bridge. Everything. But if you give me a battleship, I won't be able to understand anything," he says.

"I don't want the owner to die, but I do want him to suffer like me. I thought a suitable punishment would be to put him in a chair and pour honey over him. Beneath the chair I'll put a bucket of ants. Then the ants will crawl up and eat their way through his ass," he says, leans forward and looks down at the grass.

"Funny, right?"

The base commandant stands up and signals that the meeting is over.

"I was at the wrong place at the wrong time. Whether I'll have to spend months or years in jail, I don't know," Captain Venegas says and is led out of the shade, across the scorching heat of the grassy plain and over to the *Viking*. The next day he will sail the ship for the last time. Then the old pirate vessel will meet its destiny, the bomb enthusiast the Minister of Fisheries Susi Pudjiastuti.

On 14 March 2016, the Minister of Fisheries flies journalists and ambassadors to the beautiful Pangandaran Beach in Java with her own airline company Susi Air. The *Viking* rests on a sandbank waiting for its executioner.

"This is Indonesia's contribution to the global community in the endeavour to eliminate illegal fishing," the fisheries minister says.

Then there is an explosion.

48

OPERATION YUYUS
GALICIA, MARCH 2016

Every day Antonio "Tucho" Vidal Suárez gets into his grey
Land Rover and drives the short distance from the elegant villa
on the hill overlooking Ribeira and down to the harbour. After
having visited the fish market he continues to his favourite bar,
the Doble SS, an unpretentious establishment with five tables
and a long bar. Together with a couple of long-since-retired
old salts, he kills a few hours playing cards. Then he ends the
day with a coffee while he makes a few business calls at one of
the tables outside. "Tucho" has retired, but every time the
family convenes to make an important decision, it is still
the patriarch who has the last word, the "Mafia fishermen's
godfather", as some people call him.

"Tucho" doesn't see what is hiding in the shadows. By the
bar a plainclothes policeman is covertly taking photographs of
him. The telephone has been tapped, and many of his routine
movements are followed by eyes he cannot see. Hidden video
cameras have been installed by the entrance to the shipping
office. When on the rare occasion he manoeuvres the expensive Bentley out of the underground garage, an anonymous

vehicle follows behind him. When he fills the car up with petrol, there is a stranger nearby.

After "The Bandit 6" was chased and boarded in the Southern Ocean, the Spanish minister of agriculture, food and the environment summoned the director of the environmental crime division of the national police force of the Guardia Civil for a meeting.[1] They were having problems with a criminal family in the north, she explained.

When the Guardia Civil investigator Miguel and three of his colleagues are put on the case, they know virtually nothing at all about illegal fishing and the Galician fishing mafia's operations in the Antarctic. But after having consulted with environmentalists, fisheries experts and Interpol, a clear image begins to emerge of who is involved in the looting of the Antarctic. After a few months, the Guardia Civil agents travel to Galicia to take a closer look at the suspects: The Vidal family, Florindo González and Manuel Martínez Martínez. They check the offices and residences of everyone involved and then make a decision.

The first target of Operation Yuyus is the Vidal family in Ribeira.[2] They have the most ships and hands down the worst reputation of all. The havoc wreaked by the Vidal family was so blatant and the international pressure on Spain to investigate them so great that it was an embarrassment for the Spanish authorities.

For the undercover police from Madrid, the Vidal family seems more like ordinary white collar criminals than a mafia organization. But who knows, one of the undercover agents thinks, perhaps it will blow up tomorrow?

From endless hours spent on stakeouts they have established that the brothers Manuel Antonio "Toño" and Angel "Naño" Vidal Pego seldom go out for lunch, but instead have homemade sandwiches at the office and that both have an affection for the car make Porsche. "Toño" has a large Cayenne, while "Naño" is most satisfied in the sports model 911. But that is hardly a crime.

For months they have tapped the telephones of several of the shipping company's employees, but the results have been disappointing. None of the conversations have been about the pirate vessels.

However, the investigators have found informants with detailed knowledge of the Vidal family's business and register of sins in the Antarctic, and who know where conclusive evidence against the family is to be found. But Miguel wants to hold off on securing this. First, they will launch a full-scale raid on the offices and residences in Galicia.

The investigation remains under wraps until the Guardia Civil starts checking the bank accounts of the Vidal family's companies in several Spanish banks. A bank employee warns the Vidal family's financial director that the police are sniffing at their finances. When Guardia Civil picks up on the warning from a phone tap, they decide to move in immediately.

Early in the morning of 7 March 2016, 50 Spanish police officers and two Interpol agents get into their cars. They have with them two tracker dogs that can sniff out hidden cash. It is the largest offensive against the Galician fishing mafia ever. And it has been planned down to the most minor detail.

One team sets out for an office in the city of A Coruña, while two other teams drive towards Ribeira. When they have reached the Barbanza peninsula, some of the cars turn off the motorway, heading for the Vidal family's fish oil factory near the city of Boiro. The rest of the cars continue driving another 20 kilometres along the gentle curves of the motorway leading to Ribeira. At exactly nine o'clock all the teams make their move.

By the time Miguel is inside the office in Ribeira with a search warrant in his hand, he is sure that he is expected. During the first few minutes the atmosphere is nervous; one of the staff is punching a number energetically into the telephone. The two computer specialists from Interpol receive the passwords for the computers and start mirroring the contents.

In drawers and cupboards Miguel and his colleagues find several dozen mobile phones and SIM cards. When he looks down into a box containing 30 SIM cards from Spain, Portugal and Thailand, Miguel understands why the telephone tap has not produced results. The shipping company's people have been constantly switching telephones and communicating by Skype and Telegram, programs on which it is possible to delete messages a short time after they have been sent.[3]

Although the Guardia Civil will never find these messages, Miguel is satisfied with the find. The Guardia Civil wants to attempt to prove that the ship owner family Vidal and some dozen co-workers are an organized crime syndicate and it is only people with something to hide who replace the SIM card every time they communicate with one another, he thinks.

The Guardia Civil also makes another interesting find – a dozen passports belonging to little brother Angel "Naño" Vidal Pego. The passports are filled with stamps from Singapore, Malaysia, Thailand, Indonesia and Vietnam. It would seem that "Naño" has been responsible for the shipping company's operations in Asia.[4]

After they have ransacked the offices in Ribeira, A Coruña and the fish oil factory in Boiro, the investigators travel to the homes of the two most important individuals in the shipping company – the father "Tucho" and the eldest son, "Toño".

When they ransack the father's villa in Ribeira, they let the dogs loose. In the large cellar facility under the villa they sniff at "Tucho's" Bentley, the grey Land Rover he uses on a daily basis and his wife's Mini Cooper, but they find nothing of significance.

After the action against the Vidal family the Guardia Civil procures another search warrant. And this time Miguel knows they will find concrete evidence.

When the *Kunlun*, *Yongding* and *Songhua* were on a mission in the Southern Ocean, every week they sent detailed reports to Vidal's insurance broker in Vigo, the company ARTAI Corredores de Seguros. The reports confiscated by the Guardia Civil state how many kilos of toothfish the ships had fished in the course of seven days and how much the fish was worth. Every week the value of the cargo the rusty wrecks had in their cold storage rooms increased. It did not take long before the catch – the white gold – was worth far more than the ships. And these were valuable commodities the Vidal family wanted to insure.

They had flagged the ships in rogue states and hidden the holding companies in tax havens but the detailed insurance reports documenting the illegal fishing were sent to an office in Galicia.

Greed was the shipping company's Achilles' heel.

When Miguel adds up the totals from the many reports, he figures out that the *Kunlun*, *Yongding* and *Songhua* in the years from 2010 to 2015 have fished 5,800 tons of toothfish, for a documented value of EUR 81 million. Based on information from the Guardia Civil's informants, it cost the shipping company around EUR 2 million a year to send the three ships to the Antarctic. The shipping company also had costs for port calls, warehousing and transport of the fish in Asia, but the profits were nonetheless astronomical.

Miguel cannot help thinking of everyone who has contributed to keeping the enterprise going for so long. Flag states, ship agents, port authorities, banks and insurance companies. Everyone must have known what they were taking part in, he thinks. The *Kunlun*, *Yongding* and *Songhua* had been blacklisted for years, but nonetheless, large European companies such as British Marine and German Allianz had sold insurance to Vidal's pirate fleet.[5] When the Guardia Civil turned up at the office of the insurance broker in Vigo, it was hardly necessary to mention the possibility of accomplice liability. ARTAI immediately cooperated with the police.[6]

Miguel is very satisfied with the evidence the Guardia Civil can present to the special national court of justice in Madrid. They have the insurance reports showing the amount of fish, the documents the Spanish fisheries authorities confiscated the previous year, an enormous amount of materials confiscated by the Australian authorities when they boarded the *Kunlun* and videos from New Zealand showing the *Kunlun* fishing in international waters. They know that the ship's documents the captains have presented to the authorities in several countries are forgeries and they have crew lists with the names of Spanish citizens who have been on board the ships. After they received access to bank accounts in Spain, they also learned a lot about the Vidal family's business model, not to mention, what has happened to all the money.

The shipping company has used the following method to launder the money back into Spain. When the fish was removed from the ocean, it was owned by the same company that owned the ship – companies registered in the tax havens of Panama and Belize. Then Vidal sold the fish to a company they personally controlled in Switzerland. The Swiss company then resold the fish to the buyers. Based on the confiscated materials, the Guardia Civil has identified ten companies in Hong Kong and Taiwan that bought toothfish from the Vidal family's Swiss company. After the settlement was deposited into an account in Hong Kong, the money was forwarded to the Vidal family's Spanish companies. There millions have been spent on financing investments in real estate, renewable energy and the fish oil factory in Boiro – the same factory with a large sign on the entrance gate proclaiming that the EU and the Spanish authorities have contributed EUR 6.6 million in subsidies. The white gold was used to build a business empire for the future.

By studying bank accounts and private consumption, the Guardia Civil investigators discover that large sums have also gone to the financing of private luxuries – big houses, expensive flats and extravagant cars. The rental of "Naño's" Porsche 911 alone costs EUR 5,000 a month – far more than the salary of an experienced investigator for the Guardia Civil.

On the afternoon of 7 March, the neighbours in Ribeira watch in shock as members of the powerful Vidal clan are arrested and shipped off to remand prison in the capital of the province A Coruña and in Madrid. The patriarch "Tucho", his two sons, daughter, son-in-law and the shipping company's financial director are charged with environmental crime, money laundering, document forgery and being part of a crime syndicate. A few days later the six of them are released after having paid bail amounting to a total of EUR 600,000.

"Tucho" returns to the card table at his favourite bar the Doble SS.

49

THE TIANTAI *MYSTERY*
THE SOUTHERN OCEAN/
MALAYSIA/SPAIN, 2012–2016

For Peter Hammarstedt the *Tiantai* was the symbol of the brutality of the pirate ship owners who were looting the Antarctic. A floating coffin at the bottom of the world with a hull ill-equipped to withstand the powerful forces of the Southern Ocean. When he was travelling around fundraising for the search for "The Bandit 6", he always concluded with the story of the refrigerated cargo ship that disappeared and presumably took the entire crew with it down into the depths.[1]

Later both the police and insurance investigators have tried to solve the mystery of the *Tiantai*. They still don't have all the answers, but there is one thing they know for sure: the distress alert that was triggered in the Southern Ocean when the ship disappeared was a hoax.[2]

The strange story of the *Tiantai*'s short life as a pirate vessel starts on a tempestuous day in January, north of the Shackleton ice shelf in the Antarctic in 2012. The ship that a fisheries officer from Australia spots through the rain and the wind has three large cranes on deck and a high wheelhouse astern. It resembles neither the pirate trawlers nor the large research vessels they now and then encounter down by the ice edge in "the Screaming Sixties". The ship has no business being here, thinks the experienced inspector who calls up the unidentified ship.

The man who introduces himself as the captain explains that he is from Thailand and that there is a crew of 20 on board, including two Spaniards. They sailed from Singapore a week ago and the next stop is Zanzibar, he explains in broken English.

That's an odd story, the fisheries officers think. It makes no sense to sail down to the Antarctic when you are travelling from Singapore to Zanzibar.

"What do you have as cargo?" the officer asks.

"No cargo on board now."

"If you have left Singapore and are going to Zanzibar, why have you come down this far South, Sir?"

"Ahh, please repeat again. Over," the captain replies.

"If you left Singapore one week ago and now in 45 days you will be in Zanzibar, what do you expect to pick up as cargo, Sir?"

"Yes. Correct!" the Thai captain exclaims.

"What will be your main form of cargo when you tranship in Zanzibar?"

"I don't know."

When the officer asks for the contact information of the company that allegedly owns the ship in Tanzania, there is silence on the radio.

The experienced Australian fisheries officer has had enough of the charade.

"Sir, I believe that you are transshipping or are attempting to transship fish caught illegally within the CCAMLR zone. What you have said to me and what we have seen will be recorded and given to the Tanzanian Government and other CCAMLR members. Do you wish to make any further comment?" the officer asks.

He receives no answer.

Two months later, a surveillance plane sees the *Tiantai* being towed past the Australian Christmas Island by an old acquaintance, the *Kunlun*. They are headed for Indonesia, not for Zanzibar, as the captain had claimed.

The sight of the *Tiantai* and the *Kunlun* together confirms the suspicion. The *Tiantai* is a newcomer in the pirate fleet in the Southern Ocean. It is probably the mother ship of a fleet of fishing vessels that have been observed in the vicinity of one another for many years – the *Kunlun*, *Yongding* and *Songhua*.

The *Tiantai* is blacklisted.

There are two different versions of the story of the *Tiantai*'s final voyage in March 2014. One version – the maritime declaration – was submitted to authorities and insurance companies, while the other was written down by hand on small pieces of paper by a man who witnessed the shipwreck.

The maritime declaration, which is officially written by the Indonesian captain of the *Tiantai*, starts like this: "16 March. The voyage south was without incident. It should be noted that we observed a few isolated icebergs."

Three days later they are close to the ice edge northwest of the Australian research station Casey. There the *Tiantai* meets its sister vessels the *Kunlun*, *Yongding* and *Songhua*. In the course of a few days, 589 tons of frozen fish are offloaded onto the *Tiantai*. In the middle of the night the crew hears something bang against the hull on the port side. They see that a half-submerged ice floe, about 90 metres long and 40 metres wide, has hit the side of the ship. The crew checks the hull thoroughly but can find no damage.

When they start navigating closer to the *Kunlun* in the early morning hours to receive the last of the fish, the *Tiantai* starts behaving strangely. There is something wrong with the balance of the ship, and they discover water in one of the cargo holds.

They discontinue the transshipment and ask for help with draining the ship. Then the captain sets his course northwest to find a place with calmer weather conditions where they can attempt to save the vessel. In the course of the next day, the amount of water in the cargo hold increases. They try to find the leak, but it is impossible. The cargo hold is now full of ice cold water and heavy bags of frozen fish are floating around chaotically. The captain asks his colleague on the *Kunlun* if he can borrow an extra bilge pump.

On 26 March, the weather grows worse. The ship is unstable and difficult to manoeuvre, and the crew starts to get nervous. The captain decides to evacuate the majority over to the *Kunlun*. Those who remain, the captain, ship mates and engineers see that now water is also pouring into the engine room. They also find water in the second of the ship's three cargo holds. Then the ship starts listing dramatically, several times they lose the power and on 29 March they give up. The engine room will soon be completely under water and the weather conditions are bad. The rest of the crew is evacuated over to the *Kunlun*.

The first story of the final days of the *Tiantai* ends here.

What happens next is undisputed.

First, the *Tiantai* keels over, then the stern is pulled under and takes the rest of the ship with it. The bow is the last thing the crew sees before the ship disappears into the ocean depths.

On board an emergency beacon is activated and the signal is picked up by the Australian chief rescue operations centre, which is responsible for rescue actions in this area. Further north, in the Indian Ocean, a large-scale search operation is simultaneously underway for a plane from Malaysia Airlines which disappeared without a trace with 239 people on board a few weeks earlier. One of the Australian planes taking part in the search is redirected to the Southern Ocean, where the emergency beacon continues to transmit the position.

When the plane arrives, all the pilot sees are some scattered remnants of wreckage in the turbulent waters. In Australia the conclusion of the medical experts is disheartening: Nobody could have survived for more than a few minutes in the freezing cold water. And it is impossible to make contact with the ship owners.

Another plane is sent to the region, which is located more than 3,000 kilometres from the Australian mainland. A substantial distance north of the shipwreck site, the pilots spot a fishing vessel. It is the *Kunlun*. Nobody responds to the pilots' call, but the sight of a pirate ship they know is collaborating with the *Tiantai* gives them hope that the crew on the wreck were saved.

When the *Kunlun* reaches Malaysia a mere month later, the ship is welcomed by the local authorities, representatives for the insurance company and an inspector from Australia. When the inspector sees the crew list that the captain of the *Kunlun* hands over, he recognizes several names he knows were crew on the *Tiantai* when the ship was inspected the year before. It would seem that the crew was rescued.

But what has actually happened?

The investigators hired by the *Tiantai*'s insurance company, the German Allianz, are from Spain. They have previously investigated the wrecks of Spanish-owned pirate vessels. There have been a suspiciously large number of such shipwrecks, but as long as none of the ships' officers make any admissions, it is very difficult to confirm suspicions of insurance fraud. There is no evidence. The scene of the incident is gone.

The officers they are interviewing now work for the disreputable Galician mafia. The investigators know that these are tough men who are paid to lie to port authorities and customs officials, men who live and work side by side in a floating community at the bottom of the world. Four ships and 100 men, all part of an industrial crime operation, month after month, year after year.

There are no deviations between the accounts of any of the officers on the *Tiantai* and the *Kunlun* that are recorded in the maritime declaration, which soberly concludes that the wreck was the result of a force majeure – an extraordinary event for which neither the captain nor the crew could be blamed.

Had the captain of the *Kunlun*, the Peruvian Alberto Zavaleta Salas, told the story he has written down in tiny handwriting on several scraps of paper, it's possible that the Vidal family in Ribeira would not have received a payment of EUR 5.5 million – 1.6 million for the ship and 3.9 million for the fish – in compensation after the wreck of the *Tiantai*.

Two years will pass before Zavaleta Salas discloses his version of what happened when the *Tiantai* sank. He will then be broke and unemployed, living in his home city of Chimbote in Peru. Every time he Googles his name, he is reminded that the Vidal family made him the scapegoat on the *Kunlun*.

"They have taken advantage of me, tricked me and hurt me," the Peruvian now says about his former employer.

He sends a written testimony to the authors of this book and to the Spanish Guardia Civil.

This is Alberto Zavaleta Salas' story of the wreck of the *Tiantai* in the Antarctic.

The *Tiantai* is an unending engine breakdown, a bad purchase and it is impossible to sell the ship, one of the ship owners' trusted men from Ribeira explains to Zavaleta Salas as the *Kunlun* sails towards the Southern Ocean.

On the first day they load 20 tons of fish onto the *Tiantai* and receive fuel in return. For the next few days they fish as usual. No fish is ever transshipped from the *Songhua* and the *Yongding* to the *Tiantai*, as stated in the maritime declaration, but on 22 March, around 50 tons of fish are hoisted from the *Kunlun* onto the refrigerated cargo ship.

Again there are problems with the engine of the *Tiantai*, and for several days the *Kunlun* tows the larger refrigerated cargo ship slowly north while the officers monitor their progress on the sonar. Two experienced engineers from Spain are now down in the engine room of the *Tiantai*. On 27 March, at 6:44 PM, in a location where the ocean is so deep that the sonar doesn't reach the bottom, the chain is cut. The two Spanish engineers are picked up by a dinghy.

Then the waiting begins.

Zavaleta Salas, who throughout the entire episode is on the *Kunlun*, understands what is going to happen.

They are going to get rid of the ship.

He has a strong suspicion of what has been going on down in the engine room of the *Tiantai* during the past few days. There are huge pipes running through the room that bring in seawater to cool off the engine, pipes with valves that can be opened so that water flows into the ship in a controlled manner.

The weather has been good, but now the wind is starting to pick up. The Spanish officers are standing along the railing, and taking pictures every time a wave hits the refrigerated cargo ship, pictures that will be given to the insurance company to convince them that the conditions were rough. At the same time they make bets about how long it will take for the *Tiantai* to disappear.

They remain in the area until the ship is gone. When it disappears, Zavaleta Salas estimates that there are 70–80 tons of fish on board, not 589 tons, as was reported to the insurance company, fish for which EUR 3.9 million is paid.

When he asks one of the Spaniards why they wanted the fish in the cargo hold when the ship sank, the answer he receives is that they are worried that the insurance company will try to send somebody down to the wreck with a midget submarine. If they do so, it is important that they see fish on the ship.

Zavaleta Salas finds this to be a demented claim. The *Tiantai* is now lying at a depth of 5,000–6,000 metres, and in another position from the one they will report to the insurance company. Nobody will ever find the ship.

Two days later they throw the emergency beacon overboard and then set their course for Malaysia. When they approach land barely a month later, Alberto Zavaleta Salas has the chance to see the maritime declaration for the first time. He knows very well what happened, but he and the officers are ordered to learn the story that is written down there by heart. Everyone has to tell the same story, the Spaniard whom the ship owner sent to lead the operation repeats.

When they get to Malaysia, Zavaleta Salas is nervous, but he sticks to the script.

Two years later, the Peruvian shipmaster tells what he holds to be the true story of the wreck of the *Tiantai*, in hopes that the Guardia Civil can help him file suit against the Vidal family so he can collect the money he is owed. He also hopes that he can make a few bucks on the story. He is disappointed.

For investigator Miguel and the Guardia Civil, the wreck of the *Tiantai* is already a part of the case against the Vidal family and 12 of their trusted directors, fishing captains and engineers, but Miguel is investigating the ship and the wreck as a part of a large money laundering operation. The *Tiantai* was bought with money the ship owners had earned on illegal fishing. The money was subsequently laundered, first through the purchase of the *Tiantai*, subsequently through the insurance settlement, and then once more when the ship owners bought two new ships for the insurance money and one final time when yet another ship sank under suspicious circumstances.

On 23 September 2015, the fishing vessel the *Txori Urdin* went down on a clear, pleasant day off the coast of the little island state of São Tomé and Príncipe in the Gulf of Guinea, not far from the final resting place of the *Thunder*.

There were no Sea Shepherd cameras that documented what happened when the *Txori Urdin* disappeared, but the explanation given by the captain and the officers is a veritable repetition of the explanation following the wreck of the *Thunder* a few months before.

"They heard a big boom. They didn't see anything that could have caused it, but they think it was a container," was the statement of one of the investigators who made inquiries into the wreck of the *Txori Urdin*.

While the captain and the two engineers on the *Thunder* were sentenced to pay EUR 15 million in damages to São Tomé and Príncipe, the crew of the *Txori Urdin* were picked up by a French ship and transported to the Ivory Coast. There they had to make statements to the local police, and then they were allowed to travel home.

The insurance payment of EUR 2.325 million is now in a bank account in Spain. The Spanish authorities have frozen the assets through an attachment order. If they win the case against the Vidal family, they will seize the money.

Miguel and the Guardia Civil don't need Alberto Zavaleta Salas' story to prove the money laundering. And when Zavaleta Salas tries to sell the story and his documentation to the *Tiantai*'s German insurance company Allianz, he runs into yet another closed door.

Allianz does not want to attract any more attention to the case. The insurance company sold insurance to a ship that was blacklisted, a ship in a fleet of the most notorious pirate shipping companies in Galicia, the shipping company that is now under investigation in the largest police operation ever against illegal fishing in Spain. It is a case that Allianz does not want to be associated with.

The ill-fated Alberto Zavaleta Salas waited too long to tell his story.

50

A DIRTY BUSINESS
HOBART, JUNE 2016

The *Thunder* lies shrouded in the darkness of 3,000-metre depths, colonized by micro-organisms, algae and rust-eating bacteria that are slowly consuming the hull. Interpol and Sea Shepherd call the ship's demise and final sentencing in São Tomé a breakthrough in the battle against fisheries crime.[1]

"The chase of the *Thunder* showed that there are millions of square miles of ocean that are unregulated and that you have unscrupulous people who are chasing the money," US Secretary of State John Kerry stated at a conference in Chile.[2]

Fourteen months after the sinking of the ship the owner of the *Thunder* has still not been punished.

Hobart. It was here the search for the *Thunder* began.

The rain is hammering down on Tasmania's capital on this June evening. That is perhaps why the city seems desolate and forsaken. Its neat rows of Georgian stone houses give it a touch of an English village's calm complacency. The old storage houses on the harbour are a reminder of the time when the city equipped whaling expeditions to the Antarctic. There are no guests at the Hadleys Hotel bar, but Roald Amundsen's portrait stares down from the wall.

In March 1912 Amundsen came here and was given a "miserable little room under the stairway". He felt that he was treated like a vagabond. The next day he walked over to the post office and sent a telegraph reporting the news of his conquest of the South Pole to King Haakon of Norway. Near one of the piers extending like fingertips out into the Derwent River, the Norwegian polar explorer Carsten Borchgrevink set out on his Southern Cross expedition, the first to spend the winter in the Antarctic.

Soon the former penal colony was the most important depot for Antarctica. The Secretariat of CCAMLR, the Commission for the Conservation of Antarctic Marine Living Resources, is located in an old schoolhouse in Hobart.

"This is a dirty business and we must continue to hunt down these bastards until each and every one of them is in prison and all their ships are lying at the bottom of the sea."

Professor Denzil Miller is called an Antarctic legend. He has led 15 scientific expeditions to the continent, and for eight years he was the Executive Secretary of CCAMLR.

"This is not about catching some fish. It is world-wide, organized crime. If we are going to stop them, we must be far more serious about following the money trail, where the money goes and what it is spent on. I have suggested that we establish 'red cells' with our own intelligence officers who operate completely under the radar and outside the system and who have the freedom to access tax registries and bank accounts. When it comes to crime as sophisticated as this, personal liberty does not exist. We must clean up one area at a time, chase them from place to place, stop them, harass them and investigate them. The ship owners all operate according to a simple principle: the possibility of being caught and punished is so small that it's worth the risk. And usually you can buy your way out of the problems," Miller says.

"There's no difference between stealing somebody's food and killing them. The consequence is the same, it's just a different kind of action. With one you kill a little more slowly than the other. There is therefore no reason to respect Vidal and the other ship owners as risk-takers. They are bandits. Illegal fishing is a way of breaking down moral and social structures. At the same time, it discloses people's unfathomable greed."

After a toothfish poaching vessel sank off the coast of South Georgia with 17 casualties, the autopsy report showed that most of the crew were either HIV-positive or had hepatitis.

"They were the poorest of the poor. A few years later the casualties from the wreck of the *Amur* were dumped on land near a landfill in Mauritius. That shows what kind of people are behind these operations," Miller says.

When the pirate skip the *Amur* sailed out of port in Montevideo in September 2000, it already had a death sentence. The ship was in terrible shape, the crew barely had any experience as fishermen. Off the coast of the Kerguelen Islands the ship sailed into a violent storm, two waves broke over the ship, and seconds later it was being tossed around in the breakers, listing perilously. The fishing gear blocked the evacuation routes, there were no fire extinguishers on board and the crew fought to make their way to life rafts which never opened. At first the ships in the area did not respond to the distress signals. When the disaster was a fact and a vessel came to their rescue, 14 of the *Amur*'s crew had drowned or frozen to death. The survivors and the deceased were taken on board an illegal, Russian-registered vessel. The corpses were put in the cold storage room together with the toothfish. In Mauritius both the dead bodies and those of the crew who were ambulatory, were dumped on land without papers or explanation. The ship owner later told the next of kin that they were not entitled to any compensation, in that there were neither insurance policies nor proper employment contracts.

In the years from 1996 to 2003, as many as ten ships are believed to have disappeared on their way to the Southern Ocean. They were floating coffins which seldom incurred large losses for the ship owners if they were taken down by the breakers in the Antarctic. Or by the authorities. Any crew members who were arrested were abandoned and forgotten by the ship owners.

After the Uruguay-flagged pirate ship the *Maya V* was boarded and escorted to Australia with 200 tons of toothfish in the cold storage room, the crew were let off following the payment of an insignificant fine. But the shipmaster and the fishing captain stood trial. The 71-year-old shipmaster stated that he had had two heart surgeries, had a helpless and mentally ill son at home in Uruguay and only 20,000 dollars in his retirement fund. During the time he spent in prison, the Spanish fishing captain started showing signs of clinical depression and paranoia.

Instead of paying the bail for the shipmaster and the fishing captain, the ship owners lent out the money at 7 per cent interest. Also the Chilean crew felt that they'd been left holding the bag. They had to pay fines and airline tickets out of their own pocket and at home in Chile they brought charges against the company that recruited them, the fisheries company Pesca Cisne in Punta Arenas. The company was controlled by the González family of the tiny city of O Carbal-liño in the Spanish province of Galicia.[3]

"The Spanish operators could basically be described as downright cruel."

The environmentalist Alistar Graham pronounced this judgement almost 20 years ago. Long before Interpol became involved in the search for the fishing pirates, Graham ran his own intelligence operation to find the owners behind the illegal toothfish vessels. From Hobart he operated the organization Isofish, the foremost objective of which was to expose companies and individuals who made their fortunes on "the white gold". It all started when Graham, with his irrepressible chuckle and indubitable talent for raising hell, picked up on a rumour claiming that there was a fleet of illegal toothfish poaching vessels in Mauritius. In exchange for a substantial amount of money, an open bar and a rural hiding place he sent an acquaintance to Mauritius to spy on and infiltrate the pirate fleet. After having exposed the pirate toothfish fleet in Mauritius he continued to follow the trail all the way to Galicia.

"The ships are just steel. Every morning there was somebody who jumped out of bed and decided what the ships should do. They were the ones we were going to find," Graham says from his "office" in Hobart, the pub and restaurant of the New Sydney Hotel.

Graham had developed a sly technique for extracting the truth about the illegal fishermen. He knew that he was confronting large men who carried out difficult jobs in dangerous waters and who were away from home for long periods of time. Nonetheless he wanted to send them a message: I know where you are, where you live and what you are doing.

When Graham travelled to Galicia in the end of the 1990s, he took contact with the local newspapers and provided them with information about the fish poachers and his stories about them were circulated in the local community. Then he applied pressure on the stay-at-home wives, probed and asked questions about what their husbands were actually doing. At first a hellish commotion ensued, but little by little the wives and mothers started to talk. And some of the ship owners.

"One of the ship owners told me how he had learned the business from his father and that his eight-year-old son would take over the business. He was working from a modest office in Vigo. From there he could organize fishing operations all over the world. They were not concerned about whether they were fishing legally or illegally. They just went out and did it."

"It was a hard game and no place for losers," Graham states today.[4]

In the course of a few days everyone in Vigo, Galicia's largest city and Europe's largest fishing port, knew there was a stranger sniffing around in the city.

"One morning while I was eating breakfast at the hotel in Vigo, all of a sudden two bloody enormous guys appeared beside my table. They wanted to know what I was up to. I looked up at them and thought: I'll never survive this. It was Florindo González and his brother," Graham says.

It was the same Florindo González who was sued by the unhappy crew of the *Maya V*. And the same person the Spanish private detective "Luis" had identified as the owner of the *Thunder*.

The correspondence with the secret informants who spied on the pirate fleet for many years is in the files of COLTO – the coalition of legal toothfish operators. In an email from 2004 two men are listed as the two largest poachers in the Southern Ocean: Antonio Vidal Suárez and Florindo González.

"The main thing has been to get the interest and focus of Australian, US and Spanish authorities on catching 'Mr Big' of IUU-fishing, rather than focusing on the smaller people involved … What I want to ensure is that Vidal, and González do not get away with all their actions, which have made them millionaires over recent years."

Twelve years after the letter was written, "Mr Big" is still at large.

51

THE SHOWDOWN
VIGO, OCTOBER 2016

He arrives at the agreed upon hour, leaves his all-weather jacket on the chair, stands by the window and looks out at the clouds drifting towards the city. For two days he has been talking about his life as a fisherman in the Southern Ocean. And about life on board the *Thunder*. We have agreed that the location of the meeting is to be kept secret.

"What are we going to talk about today?" he asks.

"The owner of the *Thunder*."

At first he stalls and says that will cost us more. Then he starts to tell us about the man for whom he has worked for many years, and whom he calls simply "Floro". The businessman Florindo González Corral from Galicia.

"The first ship he made a lot of money on was the *Odin*; on one of the trips to the Antarctic we brought in 480 tons of toothfish. With the profits from that fishing expedition he bought the *Thunder*. He has had at least five vessels. Sea Shepherd says that the *Thunder* has earned EUR 60 million, but it's much more than that," he begins.

"Florindo came to Singapore when we set out on the last trip. The luggage of one of the officers had been lost on the flight and Florindo paid for new clothes before we sailed south. He hired the Indonesian crew through a crewing agency in Jakarta, he just called and said: Send me 30 seamen. He treated them well and always brought them cigars when he met us at the quay. And he was also very concerned about the quality of the fish. 'You know how I want it,' he used to say to the head of the fish factory."

"Every day at four or five o'clock in the afternoon, central European time, Florino or his right-hand man José Manuel Salgueiro, called the *Thunder*. When we were in the ice he said we had to make our way to international waters. He told us that the officers of the *Thunder* should be especially observant and post two watchstanders when they rounded the Cape of Good Hope. One day Captain Cataldo was instructed to turn the *Thunder* around and attack the *Bob Barker*. Then one of the officers exploded and screamed: 'Floro can damn well come down here to crash with that damn Sea Shepherd ship himself, if that's what he wants.' Over the phone he often discussed which opportunities we had to get away and we talked about Angola, Papua New Guinea and Europe. But we didn't have enough fuel to make it all the way to Europe. At one point these conversations came to an end or were just between him and Cataldo," the seaman says.

"When they finally let us depart from São Tomé, we flew to Lisbon to be interviewed by the insurance company. Florindo, his brother and assistant showed up outside the hotel. They gave us instructions on what we should and shouldn't say. That we must not mention toothfish and that the vessel was owned by a Singapore company. The majority did as they were told," he says.

During the chaotic days following the wreck of the *Thunder*, an insurance claim arrived for more than EUR 7 million. For many years the *Thunder* was insured by the company British Marine. After the search for the *Thunder* made the international news, the *Thunder* and several of the other "Bandit 6" ships disappeared from the portfolio of the long-established company. In spite of the Interpol notice status and a history as a poacher of fish, the Spanish company Mutua Marítima de Seguros (Murimar) accepted the commission of insuring the *Thunder*. Now Murimar had received an indemnity claim for a ship that had probably been sunk intentionally and containing illegal cargo. The claim was sent from the company Estelares in the tax haven of Panama.

Estelares appears for the first time in the *Thunder* saga when the ship was registered in the small African nation of Togo in 2006 and as owner when the vessel was registered in Mongolia in November 2010. But who is behind Estelares? In the company documents from Panama three people were listed as chairman of the board, board member and secretary, respectively, in the company. Two of them work for a law firm in Panama.

"Although we help out establishing companies in Panama, we are in no way involved in operations or the business management of these companies. We are just involved in the registration and the companies' compliance with the laws regulating company registration in Panama," the company's board member, the lawyer Iria Barrancos Domingo says, who is also the president of Panama's maritime bar association.

She refuses to answer questions about who owns Estelares. The *Thunder*'s journey into the abyss was protected by a bulwark of lawyers, brokers and institutions that chose to close their eyes to the fact that they earned money on the looting of the Antarctic.

A few blocks from Plaça Catalunya in the city centre of Barcelona, Vicente Burgal operates the detective agency Global Risk Overseas. In addition to having solid expertise in the disclosure of both unfaithful servants and unfaithful husbands, the company has also investigated several suspicious shipwrecks in the Southern Ocean. Before the insurance company pays out millions to the secret owners of the *Thunder*, they want to try to get to the bottom of what actually happened to the ship. The job is assigned to Vicente Burgal.

The man who shows up at the meetings with the private detective and the insurance company's agent is Florindo González Corral. There he calls himself a representative for the owner of the *Thunder*.

In an email the Spanish private detective asks us to keep a low profile in relation to Florindo González. "What you call 'bad guys' are individuals who are widely recognized and considered important in Galicia. You must keep in mind that everyone who lives there has a family member who is involved in smuggling. Fishing without a permit is a part of their DNA and something everyone accepts. Just like bullfighting. These people receive money from the local authorities and the EU.

Maybe it sounds strange, but that's how it is," the private investigator writes.

"Every country has its own customs and codes that must be respected. If not, we won't get the results we want. Five minutes after you called Florindo, he contacted us and asked if we were the ones who had given you his phone number. He wasn't nervous, he was just irritated. Because he wants to stay clear of the sinking incident and illegal fishing. For the time being we have no documents that can prove that Florindo has financial interests in the *Thunder* or Estelares. But we know that he is the one who controls the company," the private detective continues.

A few months after the wreck, Interpol receives a letter which also identifies Florindo González Corral as the owner of the *Thunder*. They know the sender, but the source of the information is not revealed out of fear of reprisals. The letter specifies that the informant is somebody who is close to Florindo Gonzalez Corral.

"When we showed the source a photo of González Corral, he identified him as the owner of the *Thunder*. He was also the owner of the *Odin/Comet*, which sank off the coast of Mauritius in 2009. González Corral was present on several occasions when the *Thunder* put in to port in Southeast Asia, he arrived together with 'Suso' and José Manuel Salgueiro," the letter states.

The glass door to the old office building in Vigo's harbour has been smashed. The office on the first floor looks like a relic from another time; behind the curtains in the semi-dark premises are only half-empty filing cabinets and an old typewriter. These are the offices of Florindo González and his company Bacamar. In June the Spanish fisheries authorities made their move on this address. Everything was in place for Operation Sparrow 2 and this time it was the owners of the *Thunder*, *Perlon* and *Viking* who were the target of the operation. Florindo González was politely aloof during the raid. It seemed as if he had been waiting for the moment and had been advised by his lawyers to say as little as possible. The confiscated materials convinced the Spanish fisheries authorities that Florindo González was the man who controlled the *Thunder*'s expeditions.

"We know that he often travels to Malaysia to organize the logistics and to negotiate prices," says Assistant Managing Director Héctor Villa González of the inspection department of the Spanish Ministry of Agriculture and Fisheries, Food and the Environment. "We found documents that connected him to the ship. There is no doubt that it was Florindo González Corral who owned the *Thunder*."

52

THE MADONNA AND THE OCTOPUS
O CARBALLIÑO, OCTOBER 2016

The stone church Santa María de Arcos is located on the outskirts of the town of O Carballiño in the southwest corner of Galicia. Along with a few Renaissance paintings and a simple altarpiece, the church houses the statue of the Madonna of Arcos.

Every year on 15 August the Madonna is carried out of the church, placed on a beautifully decorated float and transported through the town in a ceremonious procession. The procession is led by the respected businessman and family patriarch Florindo González Otero. Behind him follows his eldest son, Florindo González Corral, then a brass band and the rest of the residents of the town. This is how it is every year.

This is the most important date on the González family's calendar. Not even a business trip to the enterprise in Chile, to the hotel complex in the Canary Islands or to a fishing vessel unloading in Asia, is a valid reason for staying away from the church on this day. Any family member who fails to attend, will never be forgiven.

A few days before the procession, there is an auction to determine who will be allowed to carry the Madonna in and out of the church. Everyone knows that the González family will win the bidding round; nobody dares to outbid them, unless the family itself grants its permission. The González family has paid almost EUR 10,000 for the right to handle the figure of the saint, but for the patriarch Florindo González Otero faith doesn't have a price. The Madonna will give the family's ships protection.

In the 1970s one of their fishing vessels sailed into a storm, the ship started taking in water and the lives of the crew of 30 were in danger. When Florindo González Otero lost contact with the ship, he went to church, said his prayers to the Madonna, promised to be true to her for as long as he lived, carry her in and out of the church, and to support the congregation financially. For that reason there is a picture of the saint in all the family's offices and ships. On the *Thunder* the Madonna figure was hanging on the bridge.

August 15 is also the day of O Carballiño's octopus festival. Although this unremarkable town is located 80 kilometres from the coast, it adorns itself with the title of "Galicia's Octopus Capital". When the Cistercian monks established themselves outside the city in the eleventh century, the coastal villages were obliged to pay tithes to the monastery. The most impoverished paid in octopus which was dried, preserved or processed in O Carballiño. Encouraged by the local octopus industry, in the 1960s the González family bought a boat to fish octopus off the coast of Morocco. They quickly expanded into cod fishing in Canadian waters and off the coast of South Africa. After having lost their quotas in South Africa, the González ships moved further south and west. Soon the family had its own fleet and freezing plant in Chile.

The family company's express philosophy was to explore new markets, and at most they owned five vessels and had 500 employees, traded and exported octopus, toothfish, cod and shellfish. Soon the family was among the richest and most respected in sleepy O Carballiño. From their profits they made donations to a football school, theatre productions, music groups and the church.

More than one year after the wreck of the *Thunder*, on 15 August 2016, the family was honoured with the city's award of distinction for its work "as a financial impetus for the region and the close collaboration with the local govern-mental authorities". During the award ceremony, the head of the family Florindo González and his eldest son of the same name stood each on either side of the city's mayor.

"We are proud and we have earned the award. It is recog-nition for having struggled for so many years," the son said in his thank-you speech.

Nobody in the auditorium noticed that the relationship between father and son was cool and aloof. The constant accu-sations that the González name was connected with *la mafia gallega* had plagued the 86-year-old patriarch for many years.

It is a mild Friday evening in October. In just a few days the foliage will begin to fall on Avenida do Parque – the best address in O Carballiño. The street is a lush bright spot in a city so dominated by dogmatic and effective 1950s architecture that tourists are advised not to visit here. On Avenida do Parque all the villas are the same, light sandstone colour with red tiled roofs and are fenced in by wrought-iron picket fences. In most of the gardens there is room for a swimming pool and a two-car garage. By the window on the ground floor of one of the villas, the enterprising son Florindo González Corral sits leaning forward and talking on the telephone.

Since we contacted him by email for the first time in March 2015, Florindo González Corral has denied having any knowledge of the *Thunder*.

"The company I represent, Frigoríficos Florindo, is a first class food commerce company, both internationally and nationally. All our activities are legal and regulated by the authorities in the countries in which we operate. I would therefore advise against your publicizing my name in connection with illegal fishing, the vessel and the company you mention. If you do so, you will be held liable for all the damage you inflict on me and my company's reputation," he writes in an email.

In a subsequent email he asks that we not mention his name at all. Then he stops responding.

Now he comes strolling calmly down the driveway. In the villa neighbourhood it's so quiet that his steps can be clearly heard. He is wearing the same type of button-down blue shirt that he wears in official contexts. In his right hand the ember of a cigarillo glows.

"We've come to talk about the *Thunder* …"

It's as if he has been waiting for this moment. He is accommodating and offers us small cigars from a box. The cigarillo, the heavy gold chain, the open shirt front and the red-cheeked face give him the look of a middle-aged man about town.

"I have nothing to do with the *Thunder*. I have no connection with the ship. I know it was an old Norwegian ship that came to Spain with papers from Panama, and then it sailed to Mauritius. There were some Asians who bought it. They were from Singapore, I believe."[1]

"You were in a meeting with the insurance company as a representative for the *Thunder*'s controlling company?"

"I had a conversation with them, but that doesn't mean that I owned the ship. I have nothing to hide," he says.

He has no explanation for why so many sources identify him as the owner of the *Thunder*, but tells us that he bought fish from the *Thunder* when the ship was called the *Rubin* and the *Typhoon*. He emphasizes that there was never any talk of poaching fish.

"I was in Mauritius when they were selling fish, but I haven't bought fish from the ship in the past 12–13 years," he says.

He reluctantly tells us about "Capitán Nemo" and José Manuel Salgueiro, the two who have been identified as his closest collaborators in the operation of the *Thunder*.

"José Manuel Salgueiro is retired and has been ill for three years. He's depressed and is not in a financial position to own a ship. We worked together in Mexico, but that was a long time ago. 'Capitán Nemo' is an agent I had contact with. There are many people who know me, many seamen. If somebody asks me for help, I help out. But there are many other problems, Chinese who fish illegally with crews who are barely paid and never allowed to leave the ship. In Galicia we have problems with narcotics smuggling, perhaps the authorities and the police should have made that a priority instead," he says and flicks the cigarillo across the sidewalk.

"But you know the story of the *Thunder*?"

"Yes. That hasn't been a good story for me. The other day I was at a party in Vigo and everyone asked about the *Thunder*. It caused problems for me with the family. They saw my name on the Internet, especially my father. We have the same name," he says.

The story that Florindo González Corral tells us on this golden afternoon is full of gaps. He also denies that he owned several of the old pirate vessels that witnesses and investigators have connected to him.

"In the end this will perhaps be a story I can tell my grandchildren," he sighs.

"What will you tell your grandchildren?"

"I don't know," he answers curtly.

"The Indonesians on the *Thunder* say that you treat them well …"

"Ha ha ha ha."

"We'd hoped you could tell us about all the conversations you had with Captain Cataldo?"

"I know that he's a captain and that the boat was chased. Now I don't think there are any boats from Galicia in the Antarctic any longer. Neither is there any market for illegal fish," he says.

The twilight steals into O Carballiño, "don Florindo" looks at his watch, tosses the third burned down cigarillo onto the sidewalk and rests his hand on the wrought-iron picket fence.

"Let's hope that this story will soon come to an end," he says as his good-bye.

53

THE FINAL ACT

When the *Thunder*'s second engineer Luis Alfonso Morales Mardones came wandering into his home town of Valparaiso in Chile, he believed that the worst was over. The story of the wrecked pirate ship had sparked the interest of both the local media and the engineer's vindictive ex-wife. Now he would have to pay off an old debt.

Mardones lived in a modest house on the ridge of a steep ravine in Cerro Cordillera, one of the hills surrounding the seaport on the Pacific shore. When we knocked on the door one spring day in 2016, the neighbours told us they hadn't seen him in months. The only trace of Mardones was an article in a local paper. "The Story of a Pirate" was a character assassination carried out by his former wife. According to his ex-wife, Mardones had served 18 years in the Navy, but was kicked out when it became known that he'd initiated a relationship with a transsexual. After that dishonourable discharge, he signed up on a fishing vessel, subsequently became a pirate and boasted of the huge sums of money he earned on the *Thunder*. She was obliged to provide for herself and her children by working as a street clown, she explains.

Now her ex-husband was going to pay. After the article, Mardones disappeared from Valparaiso.

In September 2016 the *Thunder*'s Captain Luis Alfonso Rubio Cataldo came home to his fashionable apartment in the seaside resort of Viña del Mar outside Valparaiso. Cataldo and the two Spanish officers never had to serve their sentences in the São Tomé prison. Although they lost the appeal, they were allowed to leave the island without paying the fine of EUR 15 million. Their local ship agent Wilson Morais tells of how he was left to foot a substantial bill for rent and services he had carried out for the pirates. The shipping company suddenly stopped responding to his emails. The young public prosecutor Kelve Nobre de Carvalho had ambitions of following the money trail left by the *Thunder*, but the web of tax havens and dodgy flag states involved in the *Thunder* saga proved too complicated to penetrate. Instead, he sent a letter to authorities in Madrid requesting assistance in collecting the EUR 15 million fine from the ship owner. Asked by the authors who he identified as the ship owner, he named Florindo González.

The investigation against Florindo Gonzalez Corral is still ongoing.

"He is in the oven. Cooking slowly," one of the investigators says.

Most of the crew of "The Bandit 6" ships were young and underpaid men from Java who were presumably puzzled by the fact that their officers so frequently wore ski masks. In March 2016, we are on the way to the province of Tegal to hear their stories from the *Thunder*'s last journey. While we are waiting in Indonesia's capital, Jakarta, we are ambushed: A fight has broken out over the stories of those who lived in the very bottom of the *Thunder*. A research assistant at a university in New Zealand, Elyana Thenu, warns the crew of the *Thunder* against meeting us. And she does so by spreading a dose of lies that frightens the crew into silence.

"We have found out that one of them is a journalist, but the other has ties with the Norwegian government. You should know that Mr Glenn has discovered this through his friends outside of New Zealand. The Norwegian government is working closely with Interpol, who wants to crack down on illegal fishing," she writes in a Facebook message to the crew.

To prevent the meeting, she threatens them.

"You will all be punished in accordance with international maritime law. I would therefore ask everyone who is in contact with these men from Norway not to speak with them," she writes on Facebook.

"Please cancel the appointment," Thenu virtually orders.

"Mr Glenn", the man who was referred to in the email, is Dr Glenn Simmons, a scientist and specialist in human trafficking at the University of Auckland. He was the one who claimed that the Indonesian crew was very likely held on board the *Thunder* against their will, a story Sea Shepherd spread all over the world to draw attention to the chase. The Interpol agents found no evidence supporting this claim when they interviewed the crew in São Tomé. A few months after the 30 Indonesians returned to Indonesia, Simmons and Thenu interviewed several of them. The interviews are part of a research project and the crew clearly made some admissions.

"You stated that you knew it was an illegal ship and that nonetheless you chose to work there to earn money. That's not legal," Thenu writes in the message where she warns them against us.

Now everything will get better, she promises.

"We [Mr Glenn and I] want to help you find a better life."

It is a perfect lie for frightening the Indonesian crew into silence. Several of them have now been hired by fishing vessels off the coast of West Africa.

Back home in Chimbote, Peru the *Kunlun's* Captain Alberto Zavaleta Salas received several emails from the Vidal system in which he is urged to delete all correspondence with the shipping company. And he is asked to keep his mouth shut if anyone should call. After our meeting in Lima, Zavaleta Salas decided to collaborate with the Spanish police. Until he finds work on a ship, he subsists on odd jobs as a painter. A number of the other captains of "The Bandit 6" vessels explain that they are struggling to find work in the aftermath of all the media attention surrounding the pirate vessels.

In September 2016 in Indonesia, Captain Juan Domingo Nelson Venegas González and the chief engineer of the *Viking* are charged a fine of 2 billion Indonesian rupiahs. They are unable to pay it and must serve a four month jail sentence.

After the wreck of the *Thunder* Captain Warredi Enisuoh of the Nigerian coastal administration, NIMASA, went on holiday in Norway. At the turn of the year 2015–2016, he and a number of chief executives were implicated and later charged in a corruption case at NIMASA. Tens of millions of dollars are to have vanished from the coastal administration's office. Warredi Enisuoh has pleaded not guilty in this case on which at the moment of this writing there has not yet been a final ruling.

In Ribeira Antonio "Tucho" Vidal Suárez is seated as usual at his favourite bar, the "Doble SS", playing cards. In the premises there is as always an oppressive silence and suspicion when strangers enter. For years the Vidal shipping company has been able to loot the Antarctic without any intervention on the part of the authorities. They have been protected by regional policy, an antiquated body of laws and political horse trading in Brussels, Madrid and the capital of the province Santiago de Compostela to save the Galician fisheries industry. Now the game is presumably up for "Tucho". The shipping company has been fined EUR 17.8 million for illegal fishing. When the authors meet "Tucho" in Ribeira in October 2016, a criminal case is pending. There the Guardia Civil has delivered its first blow. The court of justice has ruled that the Spanish authorities have so-called jurisdiction in the case. That means that the shipping company's owners and employees can be penalized in Spain, even though the criminal acts they are charged with having committed have taken place in international waters. The Vidal family has appealed the ruling to the Supreme Court.

"I have nothing to say," "Tucho" says from his seat on the outdoor patio of the Doble SS.

A few kilometres away, in a garden, the *Thunder*'s fishing captain Juan Manuel Patiño Lampon is preparing a fishing line. It is a magnificent villa with chandeliers and heavy furniture, situated in seclusion on a quiet street. According to the rumours, Lampon has started working for himself as an inshore fisherman. He does not look up from the line bins; he repeats only a monotone "never, never, never" when we ask to speak with him. Several of the other officers of the *Thunder* from Ribeira have been hired by other vessels. "Don't bother my head with this," or "I'm never going to talk" are the brief messages they give over the phone.

The *Bob Barker*'s first mate Adam Meyerson has been made captain of the Sea Shepherd's campaign ship, the newbuilding the *Ocean Warrior*. The ship, with a price tag of USD 12 million and a maximum speed of all of 30 knots, is the environmental movement's first specially built vessel and will be used in the fight against the Japanese whaling fleet, which has begun new missions in the Antarctic.

Captain Siddharth Chakravarty of the *Sam Simon* is taking a break from Sea Shepherd indefinitely and has started his own project, Enforceable Oceans.

When he left Hobart in search of the *Thunder*, Peter Hammarstedt hoped that Operation Icefish would be a turning point for Sea Shepherd. The Swedish captain wants a closer form of collaboration with the authorities, but Sea Shepherd's violent past makes that extremely difficult.

"It's better to cooperate with Interpol than to be hunted by them," he told us during one of our many conversations.

Hammarstedt's dream project has been to lend out Sea Shepherd's ships to poor coastal nations that don't have the resources to patrol their own waters. A few months after the sinking of the *Thunder*, Hammarstedt was back in the Gulf of Guinea. There he met Mike Fay, the American explorer who is a special advisor of the president of Gabon, and who promised to help Hammarstedt during the chase. Together they planned Operation Albacore, a step forward on the road to making Sea Shepherd a kind of coast guard force. In April 2016, the *Bob Barker* set out on a new mission. On board there were Sea Shepherd activists, fisheries officers and heavily armed soldiers. For five months, the *Bob Barker* patrolled the waters of Gabon and São Tomé in search of pirate fishermen. One of the vessels seized was a tuna fishing vessel owned by a shipping company in Galicia. In the cold storage rooms the soldiers and officers found thousands of fins from illegally caught shark.

In October Hammarstedt was invited to a conference on fisheries crime in Indonesia. In attendance were the officers and police who took part in the hunt for "The Bandit 6". Sea Shepherd had been invited in from the cold.

A few weeks later, CCAMLR decided that an area of 1.55 million square kilometres by the Ross Sea in Antarctica was to be protected for the next 35 years. It is the world's largest protected marine region.

At Christmas in 2016 the newspaper *La Voz de Galicia* reported that the Vidal family had won its Supreme Court appeal so the Guardia Civil will most likely have to drop the criminal case against the family. The reason for this is that the illegal fishing has taken place in international waters and the Vidal family can therefore not be punished by the Spanish courts. The open sea is still a wet Wild West and the toothfish is, in practical terms, up for grabs.

"Tucho" Vidal will be spared having to spend the years of his retirement in prison, but the fine of EUR 17.8 million for illegal fishing was still in effect when this book went to print.

When he read the news, Peter Hammarstedt sat down at his computer.

"The decision by the Spanish Supreme Court is as disappointing as the hard work of INTERPOL and Spanish law enforcement is inspiring. The ruling unfortunately sets the precedent that Spain is a safe place for criminals to organize and launder the theft of fish worth millions.

"However, the monster that is the Galician Mafia is still severely wounded, and while it licks its wounds, it does so knowing that if they resume their toothfish poaching operations in the future, then they do so under the watchful eye of police – who now understand their *modus operandi* better than ever before – and a proven commitment by Sea Shepherd to shut them down on the High Seas that the Spanish Supreme Court has surrendered to poachers," he wrote in a message published on Sea Shepherd's website.[1]

Then he wrote a message to the authors of this book:

"Kjetil & Eskil, had I been convinced that governments and courts of justice solved problems, I wouldn't be doing the kind of work that I do."

* * *

After the *Thunder* and the *Viking* sank, the *Perlon* was sold for scrap metal and the *Kunlun*, *Songhua* and *Yongding* were detained by authorities; most who had followed the chase of the "The Bandit 6" assumed that the pirate sextet was out of the game for good.

In March 2017 a ship agency in Sao Vicente on Cabo Verde received a letter from the company Pesca Cisne in Punta Arenas, Chile, regarding a vessel that had been detained on the island since Peter Hammarstedt spotted it by accident almost two years earlier.

"As you know, we are the new owners of the ship, which will be called *Pesca Cisne 1*. The vessel is currently docked in Sao Vicente and we would like to engage your services as our ship agent," the letter written in Spanish read.

When it was chased in the Southern Ocean in 2015, the same vessel was called *Songhua* and was owned and operated by the Vidal family in Ribeira. The company in Chile who has now, according to the letter, bought the vessel, has since the late 1980s been owned by the family of Florindo González Corral from the small and unassuming town of O Carballiño in Galicia.

ACKNOWLEDGEMENTS

One November day in 2014, we were discussing ideas for new articles for the Norwegian national daily newspaper *Dagens Næringsliv*. The conversation went something like this:

"Do you remember the two fishing vessels that were wanted by Interpol?"

"Yeah ..."

"What was it that actually happened?"

The work that led to writing this book began with one of journalism's most fundamental questions. And although we weren't aware of it, Peter Hammarstedt had just set his course for the Banzare Bank in search of the *Thunder*, the *Viking* and "The Bandit 6". The documentary article about Hammarsted's pursuit of the *Thunder* and our search for the ship's owner in Galicia was one of the most read pieces in *Dagens Næringsliv* in 2015. A book deal followed, along with trips to five continents to speak with people who were involved in the story of the search for "The Bandit 6".

It has been a long journey and there are many people who have helped us out along the way.

First, we give thanks to our bosses at *Dagens Næringsliv*, Gry Egenes, Frode Frøyland and Espen Mikalsen, who gave us the opportunity to work on the story for the newspaper – and who later granted us leave so we could write this book.

Our wonderful colleagues Kenneth Lund and Morten Iversen deserve a solid pat on the back for their interpreting and reporting assistance.

We owe a huge thanks to Frode Molven, editor at Vigmostad & Bjørke, for his belief in the project, especially when our own belief failed us. Rita G. Karlsson, at Kontext Agency in Stockholm, has done a fantastic job of selling the book to the rest of the world. Thank you!

The Sea Shepherd captain Peter Hammarstedt contributed above and beyond the call of duty. When we had received 500 emails, we stopped counting. Sid Chakravarty, Simon Ager, Alex Cornelissen and Michelle Mossfield at Sea Shepherd also deserve our thanks for making a contribution far beyond any reasonable expectation.

We give a huge thanks to all our sources who came through for us in Spain. A special thanks goes to journalist Victor Honorato and María José Cornax from the environmental organization Oceana. Victor accompanied us on our first trip to Ribeira, knocked on doors and made uncomfortable phone calls. María answered all of our more or less intelligent questions about the pirate syndicates, Spanish bureaucracy and the Spanish authorities' unwillingness to take any action against the fisheries mafia in Galicia – up until the moment when they moved in with the big guns in 2015, to a large degree thanks to the tireless efforts of María and Oceana.

Special thanks also go to Tor Glistrup, Eve de Coning and Gunnar Stølsvik in Norway who gave us our first introduction to the work of combating international fisheries crime.

We are particularly thankful to Alistair McDonnell from

Interpol's Project Scale and Glen Salmon at AFMA in Australia who guided us, dug through archives and answered questions as far as their job descriptions would permit.

We have travelled far and wide in conjunction with the work on this book, but the trip to São Tomé and Príncipe is the one we remember best. We thank our interpreter Alex and the untiring manager of Sweet Guest House. The same holds for the adventurous and newlywed couple Aleksandra Dorann and Olof Van Winden. What a party!

In Oslo, the team at Visualdays, along with Tore Namstad, Morten Haug Frøyen and Anne Walseth all deserve our thanks for their advice, encouragement and overall goodwill.

The captain of the *Kunlun*, Alberto Zavaleta Salas from Peru, also merits a particularly honourable mention. He was the only officer on the pirate vessels who was brave enough to be interviewed on the record.

We have saved our biggest thanks for last: Fernando Manuel Toledo Oregon, the fearless optimist who travelled with us to Latin America when the book project was on the brink of falling apart, who certainly saved us from being robbed in Valparaiso and whose resolve did not waver when we knocked on the door of "Mr. Big" in Galicia. *Muchas gracias*!

And to Anne Grete Arntzen, Hilde Andersen and our children: thank you for putting up with all our madness.

The writing of this book was made possible by funding from the Fritt Ord foundation and the Norwegian non-fiction writers association (NFF). We are incredibly fortunate to have you. Thank you.

We will conclude with a well-known phrase: this is a documentary in which we describe real-life events to the best of our abilities. Any errors, omissions or misunderstandings are not the fault of our sources, but wholly our responsibility as the authors.

Eskil Engdal and Kjetil Sæter
Oslo, December 2016

NOTES

2 "THE BANDIT 6"

1 Industrialized illegal fishing for the Patagonian toothfish began on a large scale off the coast of Chile and Argentina around 1990. When the authorities tightened up control measures and quotas, the fleet of trawlers and longline fishing vessels moved towards the British overseas territory of South Georgia, where the fishing was very good. When they were being hunted by the British in the mid-1990s, many of the same stakeholders popped up, first around the South African Prince Edward Islands, and subsequently in the French southern territories of the Kerguelen and Crozet Islands and the Australian Heard and McDonald Islands. After they were chased away by South African, French and Australian authorities, respectively, the first vessels were observed in international waters near the ice edge of Antarctica in January 2002.

2 Descriptions of the chase, Peter Hammarstedt's preparations and his thoughts along the way, are based on interviews with Hammarstedt carried out in Bremen in April 2015, Southampton in January 2016 and Stockholm in September 2016. Background materials also include numerous emails, telephone conversations and WhatsApp messages from January 2015 and up until the time when the book went to press, transcripts of dialogue, sound recordings made on the bridge of the *Bob Barker* and information from the *Bob Barker*'s ship's log. The authors also spent two days with the crew on the *Bob Barker* when they arrived in Bremen on 27 April 2015. At that time the majority of the crew had been at sea since 3 December of the previous year.

3 The *Thunder, Viking, Kunlun, Yongding, Songhua* and *Perlon* have changed names multiple times in the course of recent years. When Hammarstedt made his "The Bandit 6" poster, the *Kunlun, Yongding* and *Songhua* had other names – respectively, the *Chang Bai, Chengdu* and *Nihewan*. In the text the authors have consistently chosen to refer to each ship by a single name. The names chosen are the names the ships had when they were being chased in the Antarctic in 2014/2015.

4 The Commission for the Conservation of Antarctic Marine Living Resources (CCAMLR) is based in Hobart in Tasmania and manages the so-called krill convention, which went into effect in 1982 and is a part of the Antarctic Treaty System. Twenty-four nations and the EU are members of CCAMLR, which provides annual guidelines, advising on the amount of fish that can be harvested in the area.

5 Interpol operates with several types of wanted alerts, which they call notices. The latter can be red, blue, green, yellow, black, orange or purple, depending upon the information Interpol is requesting. A Purple Notice was issued for the *Viking* and the *Thunder*, in which Interpol and the nation ordering the notice requested information from Interpol's 190 member nations about a specific modus operandi – how the criminals were operating and how they tried to conceal their violations of the law.

6 George Forster (1777): *A Voyage Round the World*.

7 In the USA and Canada, Patagonian toothfish is sold as Chilean Sea bass, which is completely misleading since the fish is not a sea bass, and neither does it have any special connection to Chile. It was the American fish wholesaler Lee Lantz who came up with the name when he tried to market the fish in the USA in the late 1970s. The Chileans call the same fish *bacalao de profundidad*, in France it is called *legine australe*, in Spain and Japan it goes under the name of *mero*, while it is called *merluza negra* in Argentina, Peru and Uruguay. The Atlantic toothfish, which lives even closer to the Antarctic ice edge, is a closely related breed.

8 The quote is credited to the British restaurant critic and author Adrian Anthony Gill and cited in the article "How Prince Charles' letters (almost) helped save the Patagonian toothfish", written by Geoffrey Lean and printed in *The Telegraph*, 15 May 2015.

9   The Banzare Bank was named after Douglas Mawson's expedition in 1929: The British Australian New Zealand Antarctic Research Expedition.

3 OPERATION ICEFISH

1   The notices are controversial and, ironically, it is in France, where Interpol has its headquarters, that Watson may reside in exile undisturbed. Furthermore, the American authorities choose to overlook the notices.

2   There are several versions of this quote, cited in interviews with Paul Watson. The two James Bond actors Sean Connery and Pierce Brosnan are both members of Sea Shepherd's advisory board. Richard Dean Anderson, better known as MacGyver, Christian Bale, who played Batman in a number of movies, and William Shatner, who played Captain Kirk on *Star Trek*, have all previously been members of the same advisory board.

3   Paul Watson made a number of appearances in the Norwegian media in conjunction with the operation in Lofoten. He appeared on the programme "Antennetimen" of the Norwegian Broadcasting Corporation (NRK), and he wrote a long letter to the newspaper Nordlys, in which he called himself an ambassador for the nation of sea mammals. Portions of the letter were printed in translation in Nordlys on 11 January 1993.

4   *Whale Wars* was a weekly documentary series that premiered in the autumn of 2008 and followed Sea Shepherd's campaigns against the Japanese whaling fleet in the Southern Ocean. By 2015, Animal Planet had broadcast seven seasons of the series comprising a total of 63 episodes.

5 HOT PURSUIT

1   The doctrine of "hot pursuit" (the right to continuous pursuit) on the high seas grants a coastal state the right to pursue a vessel in international waters if there is suspicion that the crew has committed a criminal act within the nation's territorial waters. The right is set out in the UN Convention on the Law of the Sea. In order for a pursuit

to be defined as continuous in practical terms today the target cannot disappear from the pursuer's radar screen.

6 OPERATION SPILLWAY

1 Project Scale is a part of Interpol's division that combats environmental crime. The project was started 26 February 2013, and the first director was the lawyer Eve de Coning from Norway. Project Scale is funded by Norway, the USA and the Philadelphia-based Pew Charitable Trusts.

2 The centre of operations, also called CCC, is manned 24 hours a day, 365 days a year as a contact for member nations in need of immediate information or facing a critical situation. The headquarters are located in Lyon, but Interpol also has operation centres in Buenos Aires and Singapore.

3 Illegal, unreported and unregulated fishing is often referred to as IUU fishing. Such fishing activity is illegal both if it violates laws established by a coastal state, and if it violates rules set out in the many international conventions regulating fishing in international waters. Fishing is considered unreported if there is a failure to report, if an incorrect report is made to the nation in which the vessel is registered, to the harbour where the fish is brought ashore or to a fisheries organization administrating fishing activities in international waters. Unregulated fishing is legal, but must take place in an unregulated area or for an unregulated species, or where there is no body of rules protecting the fish stock.

4 The descriptions of the work leading up to Interpol's Project Scale are based on a large number of documents and reports, as well as interviews with people who participated in the work: Tor Glistrup, Gunnar Stølsvik and Eve de Coning from the Norwegian fisheries authorities, Stuart Cory from the National Oceanic and Atmospheric Administration in the USA, Alistair McDonnell from Interpol's Project Scale, Gary Orr from the Ministry from Primary Industries in New Zealand and Glen Salmon from the Australian Fisheries Management Authority.

5 As a fisheries officer on isolated South Georgia in the 1990s, Alistair McDonnell had seen how overfishing in the British maritime zones in

the South Atlantic was on the verge of obliterating the toothfish stock. At its peak, the annual catch amounted to 100,000 tons of toothfish. Three fishing vessels were put under arrest by the British authorities before the fleet of trawlers and longline fishing vessels gave up.

7 THE ICE

1 The bay was named after the general manager of the "Whalers Mutual Insurance Association" (Hvalfangernes Assuranceforening), Olaf Prydz. It was mapped for the first time in 1935 by the Norwegian whaler Klarius Mikkelsen on the ship *Thorshavn*. The following year the bay was explored extensively by a Norwegian expedition led by the whaling ship owner Lars Christensen, who outfitted nine scientific expeditions to the Antarctic. Christensen himself was on four of them.

2 Malaysia Airlines' Flight 370 was on the way from Kuala Lumpur to Beijing on 8 March 2014 carrying 227 passengers and 12 crew members when it suddenly disappeared from radar screens above the Gulf of Thailand. At least 57 ships and 48 aircraft took part in the rescue operations, which were carried out in an enormous geographic region. A few days after the airplane disappeared, the authorities announced that the Boeing 777 aircraft had probably crashed some place in the Indian Ocean west of Australia. It wasn't until 17 months later that the first piece of wreckage from the crashed plane was found, a part of the wing that washed up on the coast of the French island of Réunion.

3 AMSA's search and rescue incidents 2013–2014: www.amsa.gov. au/search-and-rescue/amsas-role-in-search-and-rescue/search-and-rescue-stories/2013-14/index.asp (accessed 28.09.2016).

8 *VESTURVON*

1 The story about the *Vesturvon* is taken from a number of newspaper articles that appeared in the Norwegian newspaper Sunnmørsposten in 1969, the website Vagaskip.dk and the authors' interview with one of the ship's first shipmasters: Jóhan Páll Joensen from the Faroe Islands.

2 Alec Gill (2003): *Hull's Fishing Heritage*. Wharncliffe Publishing.

9 THE PIRATE CAPITAL

1 This information was found in the archives of the Coalition of Legal
Toothfish Operators, Inc. (COLTO), during a visit to their secretariat
in Perth, Australia, June 2016. COLTO is the interest organization
for the legal fishing fleet, and the members represent 90 per cent of
the legal fishing of toothfish.

2 From 2000 to 2003 according to Interpol, the *Thunder* was owned
by three different companies, each of which had a connection to
ship owners in Spain: Vistasur Holding, Southern Shipping Ltd. and
Muñiz Castiñeira S.L.

3 On 22 September 2006 the *Thunder* was blacklisted by CCAMLR.
During the years leading up to Sea Shepherd's finding the *Thunder* at
the Banzare Bank in December 2014, the ship was observed at least
19 times around Antarctica or on its way to or from the Southern
Ocean by surveillance planes, patrol vessels and legal fishing vessels.
It was also inspected or refused entry by port authorities in Malaysia
and Indonesia on five occasions.

4 Glen Salmon interviewed by the authors on Skype, 31 August and 1
September 2016.

5 Salmon's anonymous voyages along the coast of Malaysia were the
start of a collaboration which would culminate in the end of «The
Bandit 6». 11 nations in Southeast Asia and Oceania, including
Australia and Malaysia, are part of the regional cooperation RPOA-
IUU (The Regional Plan of Action to Promote Responsible Fishing
Practices Including Combating Illegal, Unreported and Unregulated
Fishing), which was established during a large-scale Minster confer-
ence in Bali in 2007.

6 In Glen Salmon's archives there are more than 50 reports from the
Australian surveillance planes and patrol boats that have observed
suspected toothfish pirates in the Indian Ocean and in the Southern
Ocean. The reports have been shared with the authorities in Indonesia, Malaysia and Thailand, where the fishing vessels usually slipped
in on quiet days on the weekends. The Australian authorities have
also sent more than 60 formal letters to countries where the blacklisted vessels are flagged and where the crews come from. The letters

were sent from Australian embassies and consulates to nations such as Nigeria, Spain, Mongolia, Chile, Russia, Tanzania and Honduras. (Source: Glen Salmon.)

10 THE STORM

1 Matthew Fontaine Maury (1806–1873) was an American naval officer, hydrographer, historian, oceanographer, meteorologist, cartographer, author and geologist. In 1855 he wrote *Physical Geography of the Sea*, the first comprehensive book on oceanography.

2 In the Antarctic convergence zone cold water from the Southern Ocean meets warmer water from the southern regions of the Pacific Ocean, Atlantic Ocean and Indian Ocean. The phenomenon is found throughout the entire Antarctic at approximately 58 degrees latitude. The cold water sinks below the warm water and the mingling of water types produces abundant marine life, particularly the Antarctic krill, which is the most important food for penguins, whales, fish and birds. Due to the enormous amounts of krill in this area, the Antarctic krill is referred to as "the most successful animal on earth".

11 THE SECRET CHANNEL

1 Alistair McDonnell and Mario interviewed by one of the authors in Lyon, 9 August 2016. Due to the nature of his job as an intelligence agent, Mario does not want his surname made public.

2 At this time, fisheries officers and legal professionals from Australia, New Zealand, Norway, Canada and the USA took part in the telephone conferences.

3 Interpol is the police's global headquarters for collaboration across national borders. The need for such a central agency arose simultaneously with the emergence of commercial air traffic and private motoring. Suddenly it was simple for criminals to escape across national borders. The precursor to the Interpol of today was established in Vienna in 1923, but the organization was hijacked by Hitler, who appointed Nazi generals as presidents, including Reinhard

Heydrich, one of the architects behind the Holocaust. After the war Interpol was relocated to Paris and later to Lyon, where the organization now has its global headquarters. Interpol has 190 member nations. Only the UN has more. Interpol has no authority over the member nations and to ensure the organization's political neutrality, Interpol is not to become involved with crime of a political, military, religious or racial nature.

4 Specialists on digital investigation from the Royal Canadian Mounted Police were involved in Project Scale from the beginning. They participated in Interpol's first fisheries crime operation, Operation Stingray, and in Operation Spillway – the search for the *Thunder* and the *Viking*.

5 Interpol's work to combat fisheries crime is two-fold. Project Scale, the group of investigators and analysts who are led by Alistair McDonnell, is based in Lyon. Project Scale is supported by an expert group of inspectors, legal professionals and bureaucrats who are not employees of Interpol, but whose daily activities are carried out in ministries and directorates in their respective nations. The expert group is called the Fisheries Crime Working Group and is headed by the Norwegian Gunnar Stølsvik. The nations that played the most active part in the chase for the *Thunder* were Norway, Australia, New Zealand, USA, South Africa, Canada and eventually Nigeria.

6 Tor Glistrup interviewed by the authors in Bergen, 26 May 2016.

12 THE LONGEST DAY

1 Roald Amundsen (1912): *Sydpolen. Den norske sydpolsfærd med Fram 1910–1912.* Jacob Dybwads forlag, Kristiania.

2 Approximately 100,000 British and German soldiers took part in the unofficial Christmas cease fire on the Western Front in 1914. Gifts were exchanged and dead soldiers lying in no-man's land were buried. In several places football matches were also played, which later came to be a kind of symbol of humanity in an inhumane war. A young corporal in the 16th Bavarian reserve infantry regiment strongly disapproved of the cease fire. His name was Adolf Hitler.

3 On 4 June 1989, the People's Liberation Army marched on Tiananmen Square in Beijing, to quash the students demonstrating for greater freedom and democracy. The estimates of the number killed in Beijing on that day range from 241 to 5,000.

4 John Wesley Carlos from Harlem, New York was one of the founders of the Olympic Project for Human Rights (OPHR), which demanded that Rhodesia (today called Zimbabwe) and the apartheid regime of South Africa be banned from Olympic participation in Mexico in 1968. They also demanded that the IOC president step down and that more Afro-American coaches be hired. After winning the bronze for the 200 metres, during the award ceremony he wore black socks and a black glove that he raised into the air in solidarity with impoverished Afro-Americans in the USA. The IOC president responded by throwing Carlos off the American team and banning him from the Olympic village. When Carlos returned to the USA, where the civil rights struggle was raging, both he and his family received death threats.

13 THE SHIPMASTER

1 Alberto Zavaleta Salas interviewed by the authors in Lima, 17–19 April 2016.

2 The description comes from the red list of threatened species published by the International Union for Conservation of Nature (IUCN). www.iucnredlist.org/details/183775/0 (accessed 26.09.2016).

3 The descriptions of Chimbote's decline have been taken from several sources. The most important is the authors' interview with Alberto Zavaleta Salas and the report "Looting the Seas", a prize-winning investigative journalism project carried out by International Consortium of Investigative Journalists (ICIJ) and published by the Center for Public Integrity in 2012. Various sections of the report have been cited in a number of newspapers. www.publicintegrity.org/environment/natural-resources/looting-seas (accessed 28.09.2016).

4 The *Kunlun* has been mentioned in debates and speeches made in the Australian parliament several times. The first case the authors know of was on 10 September 2003, when Senator Kerry O'Brien

from Tasmania asked the Minister for Agriculture and Fisheries Ian Macdonald whether the Australian authorities had succeeded in preventing the *Kunlun*, which at that time was named the *Dorita*, from landing its illegal toothfish catch in Japan, Hong Kong, China, Mozambique and Kenya. Minister Macdonald replied that the Australian authorities had tried, but that Japan, Hong Kong and Kenya had accepted fish from the vessel. Out of the five nations, only Mozambique confirmed having refused toothfish from the *Dorita*.

5 Most of the observations of "The Bandit 6" (and other suspected pirates) on the way to and from Antarctica are available to the public on the website of RPOA-IUU, a regional collaboration for combating illegal fishing in Southeast Asia and Oceania. http://rpoa-iuu.org/index.php/iuu-vessel/iuu-vessel-list.html (accessed 28.09.2016).

6 The authors have communicated with Shipmaster Juan Manuel Núñez Robles on the *Yongding* using a chat program and over the phone several times in the spring of 2016.

7 The crew of the *Viking* posted this photo of the Christmas party on Facebook.

14 DESOLATION ISLAND

1 The article "Poaching Vessel 'Thunder' Deliberately Avoids French EEZ While Sea Shepherd Continues Gillnet Retrieval" published on Sea Shepherd Global's website, 27 December 2014. www.seashepherdglobal.org/news-and-commentary/news/poaching-vessel-Thunder-deliberately-avoids-french-eez-while-sea-shepherd-continues-gillnet-retrieval.html (accessed 28.09.2016).

2 During the *Bob Barker*'s search for the *Thunder*, Project Scale sent 51 messages to 49 different countries through Interpol's secure communication channel I-24/7, according to the head of Project Scale Alistair McDonnell. Based on the two ships' position and speed, Interpol officers were able to calculate when the ships could be at a port or within a country's exclusive economic zone (EEZ), which extends 200 nautical miles out from the coast. When the *Thunder* and the *Bob Barker* approached the Kerguelen Islands, it was the first time they were near an EEZ.

3 The seafarer Binot Paulmier de Gonneville, born in Dieppe, travelled in 1503 from Honfleur in Normandy towards southern waters and claimed to have discovered an unknown country, a six weeks' sail east of the Cape of Good Hope. It has later been assumed that this was either Madagascar or the areas around Ilha de Catarina in Brazil. In the seventeenth and eighteenth centuries there was a widespread belief in France that de Gonneville was the person who had discovered Australia.

4 The confiscated pirate ship the *Osiris*, named after the god who watched over the kingdom of the dead in ancient Egypt, was among the vessels sent out to guard these waters. On 23 August 2013, the *Osiris* also found the *Thunder* while she was fishing illegally in a CCAMLR zone between the French Crozet Islands and the South African Prince Edward Islands, but since the *Thunder* was fishing in international waters, the vessel was not boarded.

5 Due to shrinking quotas and poor revenues for the shipyard's law-abiding fleet, the family Vidal from Ribeira in Spain decided to bank on the fishing of toothfish, in that they had recognized its enormous financial potential. First, the family formed a partnership with a French company that had the licence to fish toothfish around the Kerguelen Islands, but Vidal's skilled fishing captains found so much fish that the French company saw no reason to share the profits in the following season. When they dissolved the partnership Vidal decided to fish in French waters nonetheless. The *Arvisa*, the Vidal syndicate's first toothfish vessel, was caught, fined and later confiscated by the French authorities. Later also the Vidal ship the *Apache*, formerly the *Caroline Glacial* and owned by Norwegians, was confiscated near the Kerguelen Islands. In 2005 the French had chased the last pirates out of their waters. A Vidal ship escaped. The tiny and nimble *Dorita* would many years later up end up on Peter Hammarstedt's "The Bandit 6" poster under the name the *Kunlun*.

15 THE PHANTOM SHIP

1 At the authors' request, Lloyd's List did a search for the *Thunder*'s IMO number on 16 March 2016. The seven-digit IMO number, assigned by Lloyd's Register Fairplay, is unique for each ship and is

to follow the ship throughout its entire lifetime, also through recon-
structions and change of name, shipyard or flag state.

2 Taken from Paul Watson's Facebook page. Published 30 December
2014. www.facebook.com/paul.watson.1426/posts/101533827008
63362 (accessed 28.09.2016).

3 Candidate for mayor Rune Ellingsen of Røst, Lofoten referred
to Paul Watson as a "terrorist" and "warlord" in an interview with
Avisa Nordland 10 June 2015. www.an.no/kommunevalg/rost/
ordforerkandidat-pa-linje-med-al-qaida-og-is/s/5-4-108295
(accessed 28.09.2016). Paul Watson responded to Ellingsen's
comments in an interview with the same newspaper, published on
1 July 2015, with the following question: "Does Ellingsen think
this is a James Bond movie?" www.an.no/nyheter/planter-og-dyr/
skipsfart/tror-ellingsen-at-dette-er-en-james-bond-film/s/5-4-
120047 (accessed 28.09.2016).

4 On 2 December 2014, the day before the *Bob Barker* sailed from
Hobart to search for "The Bandit 6", the article by researchers Indi
Hodgson-Johnston and Julia Jabour from the University of Tasmania
"Sea Shepherd's toothfish mission bites off more than it can chew" was
published on the website *The Conversation*. http://theconversation.
com/sea-shepherds-toothfish-mission-bites-off-more-than-it-can-
chew-34856 (accessed 28.09.2016).

5 Stuart Cory interviewed by the authors by telephone, 22 September
2016. Cory is a special agent at the National Oceanic and Atmospheric Administration in the USA.

16 THE WALL OF DEATH

1 The descriptions of what took place on the *Thunder* before, during
and after the chase are to a large degree based on long interviews with
crew members who were on board, and the crew's explanations to,
respectively, the *Thunder*'s insurance company and the authorities of
São Tomé and Príncipe. Those who have told us about the journey
wish to remain anonymous out of fear of reprisals on the part of the
ship owner.

2 After the pirates understood that the Australian authorities had them
under aerial surveillance, the majority chose to avoid the Sunda Strait

between Sumatra and Java and instead take the long way around up the Strait of Malacca and around the northern end of Sumatra on the way to the Southern Ocean. In this manner they hoped to avoid being seen by the Australian P-3 Orion aircraft. But the four-engine aircraft have a long range and sophisticated surveillance equipment and many were detected nonetheless. (Source: Glen Salmon.)

17 THE WORLD RECORD

1 G. Bruce Knecht (2006): *Hooked: Pirates, Poaching, and the Perfect Fish*. Rodale Books.

2 The *Viarsa 1*, owned by the company Viarsa Fishing Company, was an anagram for Vidal Armadores SA, the parent company of the family syndicate Vidal in Ribeira, Spain.

3 The polite rejection Sea Shepherd later received from the editors of the Guinness Book of World Records informed them that there is a condition of notification of the intention to set a new record before actually doing so.

4 The *Antillas Reefer* tried in 2008 to acquire a licence for fishing tuna in Mozambique, but while the authorities of the country were processing the application, the vessel poached large quantities of shark. When the ship was taken, there was shark meat, shark oil, shark liver, shark fins and shark tails for a value of five million dollars in the cold storage rooms. The ship and the catch were confiscated and after a lengthy court battle the Vidal company that owned the *Antillas Reefer* was sentenced to pay a fine of 4.5 million dollars, money that Mozambique has never received. The *Antillas Reefer* was owned by the company Gongola Fishing JV (Pty) Ltd, controlled by the Vidal family syndicate in Ribeira, Spain.

5 The article "Mozambique leads the charge against *Thunder*", was published on Sea Shepherd Global's website, 12 January 2015. www. seashepherdglobal.org/icefish/campaign-updates/commentary/ mozambique-leads-the-charge-against-thunder.html (accessed 28. 09.2016).

6 Robert William "Bob" Barker was for 35 years a television host for the USA's most famous game show, *The Price Is Right*, which is still running on the TV network CBS.

18 "THE ONLY SHERIFF IN TOWN"

1 Graham MacLean interviewed by the news portal Stuff.co.nz in New Zealand. The article, "Sea Shepherd: Navy's toothfish poaching operation 'cowardly'", was written by Michael Field and published on 20 January 2015. www.stuff.co.nz/national/65226107/Sea-Shepherd-Navys-toothfish-poaching-operation-cowardly (accessed 26.09.2016).

2 Comment made by Paul Watson on Sea Shepherd's website: "The 'likes of Sea Shepherd' succeed where the Navy fails", published 20 January 2015. www.seashepherd.org/commentary-and-editorials/2015/01/20/the-likes-of-sea-shepherd-succeed-where-the-navy-fails-683 (accessed 26.09.2016).

3 Minister of Defence Gerry Brownlee interviewed by Radio New Zealand (RNZ), 15 January 2015. The interview was also published on RNZ's website the same day under the title "Govt defends poaching operation". www.radionz.co.nz/news/national/263716/govt-defends-poaching-operation (accessed 28.09.2016).

4 The article "Sea Shepherd announces plans to take over chase from New Zealand Navy", published 15 January 2015. www.seashepherd.org.uk/news-and-commentary/news/sea-shepherd-announces-plans-to-take-over-chase-from-new-zealand-navy.html (accessed 28.09.2016).

19 THE FLYING MARINER

1 Warredi Enisuoh was interviewed by the authors over the telephone and by email on many occasions in 2015 and 2016.

2 The authors have access to the documents from the *Thunder*'s registration in Nigeria.

3 Republic of Liberia, Truth and Reconciliation Commission, Volume II, Consolidated final report, published July 2009.

4 The authors have tried on a number of occasions to make direct contact with both Dew Mayson and Henry Macauley. Both have confirmed by email that they have a relation to the company Royal Marine & Spares, but that they did not know about the fishing vessel the *Thunder* before they were contacted by the Nigerian authorities and the authors after the search for the *Thunder* had commenced.

Both claim that Royal Marine & Spares, which was an oil service company that is no longer in business, must have been exploited by the *Thunder*'s owners and agents.

5   The Overseas Security Advisory Council (OSAC) at the Bureau of Diplomatic Security of the US State Department publishes an annual Crime and Safety Report. The descriptions of Lagos come from OSAC's reports in 2014, 2015 and 2016. The reports are available on OSAC's websites.

6   The authors established contact with one of the *Thunder*'s Nigerian consultants on the social network LinkedIn. The man, who claimed to be Managing Director at Maritime Consultants Limited, gave the following answer to the authors' question about the *Thunder*'s ship's documents: "Thanks for thinking of me, but I'm not interested."

20 A BLOODY NIGHTMARE

1   On 1 January 2015, Chakravarty was contacted by Gary Orr from the Ministry for Primary Industries in New Zealand. Orr was one of the fisheries officers who participated in Interpol's Operation Spillway. He informed Chakravarty of the importance of securing evidence in a professional manner so it could be used in a potential criminal case.

2   Siddharth "Sid" Chakravarty interviewed by the authors in Jakarta, 2 and 3 March 2016. Chakravarty has also responded to questions in a long series of emails from the authors in 2015 and 2016.

3   The Storegg Bank was discovered on 9 January 1934 by the Norwegian-owned ship the FLK *Solglimt*. The ship was searching for new whaling grounds when they discovered the plateau that suddenly rose out of the depths of the ocean, from 5,100 metres to 310 metres.

21 *LA MAFIA GALLEGA*

1   "Luis" and his colleague interviewed by the authors in Barcelona on 2 February 2015 and 7 June 2016.

2   Two of the lawyers are currently employed at the law firm Abogados Marítimos y Asociados in Panama, a country where anyone can purchase anonymity as long as they have the financial means. "The Panamanian lawyers having acted as registered directors do not run

the business of such companies nor are they involved in their corporate affairs. We were and are NOT aware of the matter disclosed in your letter as we are concerned with the registration of the companies and with their compliance with the laws of Panama in that regard only." Written by one of the members of the board of Estalares, the lawyer Iria Barrancos Domingo, in an email to the authors dated 17 May 2015.

3 On 20 April 2010, the environmental organization Oceana published a report in which they documented that the conglomerate of companies controlled by the Vidal family has received EUR 9.9 million in subsidies from the provincial government of Galicia, the Spanish fisheries authorities in Madrid and the EU from 1997 to 2009. During the same time period, vessels controlled by the same syndicate were fined, confiscated and observed dozens of times in connection with illegal fishing.

4 From the article "Spain doles out millions in aid despite fishing company's record", written by Kate Willson and Mar Cabra, and published by The International Consortium of Investigative Journalists on 2 October 2011. www.icij.org/projects/looting-seas-2/spain-doles-out-millions-aid-despite-fishing-companys-record (accessed 13.11.2016).

5 The sentence has been discussed in a number of publications, including the article "Spanish fishing firms fined £1.62m", written by Ryan Hooper, and published by The Independent on 26 July 2012. www.independent.co.uk/news/uk/home-news/spanish-fishing-firms-fined-162m-7978843.html (accessed 28.09.2016).

23 BUENAS TARDES, BOB BARKER

1 The Melville Bank was discovered and mapped by scientists on board the ship the R/V Melville in 1978. The ship was named after the American engineer, rear admiral, author and explorer George Wallace Melville (1841–1912).

25 RAID ON THE HIGH SEAS

1 The UN Convention on the Law of the Sea (UNCLOS), in laymen's terms called the Law of the Sea, regulates traffic and financial activity

on the high seas and coastal states' rights in own territorial waters and exclusive economic zones (EEZ). A coastal state has full sovereignty in its own territorial waters, which extend 12 nautical miles from the coast. A coastal state can also establish an economic zone with exclusive rights to exploit all the natural resources up to 200 nautical miles from its coast. The rest of the ocean is fair game; it belongs to nobody, but all of the 168 nations that have ratified the convention have made a commitment to secure the open ocean from pollution and destruction. There are also a number of regional conventions that regulate fishing on the high seas, such as CCAMLR, which regulates fishing around Antarctica.

2 The next day, the director of Sea Shepherd Paul Watson posted his indignant commentary "The Aussies came, they saw, they did nothing!" on the organization's website. www.seashepherd.org/commentary-and-editorials/2015/02/27/the-aussies-came-they-saw-they-did-nothing-688 (accessed 26.09.2016).

26 OPERATION SPARROW

1 Assistant Managing Director Héctor Villa González of General de Control e Inspección Secretaría General de Pesca, a division subordinate to the Ministerio de Agricultura, Alimentación y Medio Ambiente (MAGRAMA), interviewed by the authors in Madrid on 6 June 2016.

27 EXERCISE GOOD HOPE

1 Eve de Coning was interviewed by the authors on several occasions in Oslo in 2015 and 2016.

2 The descriptions of the military drill Exercise Good Hope were taken from the website of the South African Navy. www.navy.mil.za/archive/1503/ (accessed 26.09.2016).

3 A fishing vessel was almost sunk by the battleships that took part in Exercise Good Hope. The battleship mixed up the fishing vessel and a radio-controlled boat that was supposed to be a target for a shooting exercise at sea off Cape Agulhas. The crew of the fishing vessel almost died of fright when three large calibre grenades suddenly landed in the water 15 metres in front of the vessel in the darkness of night.

The shipmaster immediately switched on all the lights on the ship and screamed over the radio that there were ten men on board.

28 THE BIRD OF ILL OMEN

1 The letter from Prince Charles to the (then) Minister of the Environment Elliot Morley, dated 21 October 2004, was made public by the British government on 13 May 2015. The letter can be accessed here: www.gov.uk/government/publications/prince-of-wales-correspondence-with-the-minister-for-environment (accessed 25. 09.2016).

2 The quote is cited many places but originally stems from an article by the Associated Press. Here is a version of the article "Whaling clash sparks accusations", published by *The Wall Street Journal*, 7 January 2010. www.wsj.com/articles/SB126283509683519109 (accessed 28.09.2016).

3 Article from Sea Shepherd's website, "The time is right for Bob Barker to rescue the whales", published 5 January 2010. www.seashepherd. org/news-and-media/2010/01/05/the-time-is-right-for-bob-barker-to-rescue-the-whales-265 (accessed 27.09.2016).

29 THE WANDERER

1 From a documentary piece about J. Michael Fay in the magazine *Outside*, written by Michael McRae, published 21 October 2011. www.outsideonline.com/1887471/how-nomad-found-home (accessed 28.09.2016).

2 J. Michael "Mike" Fay interviewed by the authors on Skype, 25 August 2016.

31 THE THIRD SHIP

1 David Carter interviewed by the authors in Melbourne in June 2016.

32 "YOU ARE NOTHING"

1 The article "Attempted suicide on board poaching vessel *Thunder* as Nigeria strips registry" was published on Sea Shepherd's

website 26 March 2015. www.seashepherdglobal.org/news-and-commentary/news/attempted-suicide-on-board-poaching-vessel-thunder-as-nigeria-strips-registry.html (accessed 27.09.2016).

33 THE SNAKE IN PARADISE

1 After the officers of the New Zealand battleship the HMNZS *Wellington* tried boarding the *Kunlun* in early January, the authorities in Wellington requested that Interpol issue a notice on the ship. On 21 January 2015, Interpol published a Purple Notice on the *Kunlun*.

2 www.facebook.com/paul.watson.1426/posts/10153640142298362 (accessed 27.09.2016).

34 THE ARMPIT OF AFRICA

1 Portions of the account about Equatorial Guinea's history are based on the documentary *Djevelens håndtrykk*, ("The Devil's Handshake") written by Eskil Engdal following a reporting trip to the country, and published in *Dagens Næringsliv* 15 September 2012.

2 The US Department of Justice initiated a civil case against Teodor Obiang Nguema at the US District Court in the Central District of California 24 October 2011. The US authorities want to collect more than USD 70 million from Obiang. The case from which the quote is taken is available here: www.opensocietyfoundations.org/sites/default/files/obiang-doj-doc1-20111026_0.pdf (accessed 28.09.2016).

3 The story of the fate of the *Fantome* is to a large extent taken from the book *The Ship and the Storm: Hurricane Mitch and the Loss of the Fantome*, written by Jim Carrier and published by International Marine/Ragged Mountain Press in 2000.

36 A WEIRD DREAM

1 Simon Ager, interviewed by the authors in Bremen, 28 April 2015, and on Skype, 14 January 2016.

2 Adam Meyerson, interviewed by the authors in Bremen, 28 April 2015.

38 THE ISLAND OF RUMOURS

1 Wilson Morais, interviewed by the authors in São Tomé and Príncipe, 3 and 4 February 2016.

41 THE LUCK OF THE DRAW

1 The story of the *Perlon*'s final expedition in the Southern Ocean is based on interviews with Glen Salmon of the Australian Fisheries Management Authority (AFMA) and Naval Captain Khairul Nizam Misran at the Maritime Crime Investigation Department of Malaysia.

42 THE ESCAPE

1 www.seashepherd.org/news-and-media/2015/09/09/interpol-wanted-poaching-vessel-kunlun-and-its-illegal-catch-escape-from-thailand-1744 (accessed 04.11.2016).

46 THE MAN FROM MONGOLIA

1 Peter Pham, "Ship of fools", *The Washington Times*, 7 May 2008. www.washingtontimes.com/news/2008/may/7/ships-of-fools/.

47 THE LAST VIKING

1 Rear Admiral Achmad Taufiqoerrachman, interviewed by the authors in Jakarta, 3 March 2016.

48 OPERATION YUYUS

1 The Guardia Civil was founded as a national police force in 1844, has 80,000 employees and is Spain's oldest and largest police force. The organization performs both military and civil tasks. Investigator Miguel works at the Guardia Civil's Servicio de Protección de la Naturaleza (SEPRONA), the division that combats environmental crime. Due to the fact that his job includes undercover police work, Miguel does not want his surname made public. The authors interviewed him in Madrid, 7 June 2016.

2 The name of the operation, "Yuyus", was investigator Miguel's idea. The first assignment he received when he assumed his post in the

Guardia Civil's environmental crime division in 1998 was to investigate a man who was smuggling Senegal parrots, which are also called the "yuyu" in Spanish. Phonetically Miguel thought the pronunciation sounded like IUU – Illegal, Unreported, and Unregulated fishing.

3   The instant messaging service Telegram was developed and financed by the brothers Nikolaj and Pavel Durov, who made a fortune on the Russian social network VK – known as the Russian version of Facebook. In conjunction with the conflict in Ukraine and the protest movement Euromaidan, the Durov brothers had a falling out with the Russian authorities, according to Pavel Durov because VK had refused to provide Russian intelligence with personal information about the social network's users. The Durov brothers went into self-imposed exile and started Telegram. "The No. 1 reason for me to support and help launch Telegram was to build a means of communication that can't be accessed by the Russian security agencies," Pavel Durov said to the website TechCrunch in February 2014. techcrunch. com/2014/02/24/telegram-saw-8m-downloads-after-whatsapp-got-acquired/ (accessed 22.10.2016).

4   Angel Vidal Pego was observed in Phuket by a criminal investigator from New Zealand who was there to help the Thai authorities investigate computers and other digital equipment on board the *Kunlun*. The information has been confirmed by Gary Orr of the Ministry for Primary Industries in New Zealand. Orr, who was New Zealand's man in Operation Spillway, was interviewed by the authors over the phone on 22 September 2016.

5   ARTAI Corredores de Seguros was the insurance broker for at least four of "The Bandit 6" – the *Kunlun*, *Songhua*, *Yongding* and *Thunder*. ARTAI had contact with the ship owners and did the rounds with the insurance companies to procure the best offers. It was usual for one insurance company to underwrite the ship, while another underwrote the cargo – the toothfish. At least three large European insurance companies have sold insurance to "The Bandit 6" ships after they were black-listed for illegal fishing activity and at least two companies continued to sell insurance while the ships were wanted by Interpol. British Marine has insured all six of the pirate vessels, but cancelled the insurance when they were confronted, by the authors

among others, early in 2015. The Spanish company Murimar Seguros was the insurance company for the *Thunder* when the ship was sunk. The world's largest insurance company, the German Allianz, underwrote the Vidal ship the *Tiantai*. There has been an extreme amount of secrecy around the insurance policies of the pirate ships. Since March 2015 and up to November 2016 the authors have on repeated occasions tried to schedule interviews and asked for comments, but none of the insurance companies have communicated anything more than "no comment". When the authors visited the busy office of the insurance agency ARTAI Corredores de Seguros in Vigo on 10 October 2016, there was nobody there who was willing to talk.

6 In the EU body of laws prohibiting illegal, unreported and unregulated fishing (IUU fishing), which went into force on 1 January 2010, accomplice liability is loosely defined in article 39. The first paragraph reads as follows: "Nationals subject to the jurisdiction of Member States (nationals) shall neither support nor engage in IUU fishing, including by engagement on board or as operators or beneficial owners of fishing vessels included in the Community IUU vessel list." It is the word "support" which is relevant to the companies that sold insurance to "The Bandit 6" ships. All the vessels were on the EU's blacklist.

49 THE *TIANTAI* MYSTERY

1 From the time the refrigerated cargo ship was bought by the Vidal family through a company in Panama in 2011 and up until the shipwreck in 2014, the vessel operated under at least four different names: the *Baiyangdian*, *Keshan*, *Luoyang* and *Tiantai*. The *Baiyangdian* was flagged in Tanzania, while the *Keshan* was flagged in Mongolia. It is unclear whether the identities *Luoyang* and *Tiantai* were authentic or pure fabrications. The authors have consistently chosen to use the name the *Tiantai* in their descriptions, as this was the name of the ship when they first learned of it.

2 The account of the fate of the *Tiantai* is based on the maritime declaration following the shipwreck, Alberto Zavaleta Salas' statement to the Guardia Civil, a number of reports from the South Asian collaboration to combat illegal fishing (RPOA) and interviews with Captain

Peter Hammarstedt of Sea Shepherd, Glen Salmon of the Australian Fisheries Management Authority AFMA, Captain Alberto Zavaleta Salas on the *Kunlun*, investigator Miguel of the Guardia Civil and three insurance investigators in Spain who wish to remain anonymous.

50 A DIRTY BUSINESS

1 www.interpol.int/News-and-media/News/2015/N2015-160 (accessed 04.11.2016).
2 www.nytimes.com/2015/10/06/world/us-announces-plans-to-combat-illegal-fishing-and-other-steps-to-protect-oceans.html (accessed 04.11.2016).
3 The *Maya V* was confiscated in 2004; the 200 tons of toothfish sold at an auction for 2.3 million dollars and the money went to the Australian state. The fishing captain and captain were fined 30,000 Australian dollars.
4 Professor Denzil Miller and Alistair Graham interviewed by the authors in Hobart, Australia, in June 2016.

52 THE MADONNA AND THE OCTOPUS

1 Florindo González Corral interviewed in O Carballiño Spain, 7 October 2016.

53 THE FINAL ACT

1 www.seashepherdglobal.org/news-and-commentary/commentary/spanish-supreme-court-surrenders-southern-ocean-to-toothfish-poachers.html (accessed 29.12.2016).

ZED

Zed is a platform for marginalised voices across the globe.

It is the world's largest publishing collective and a world leading example of alternative, non-hierarchical business practice.

It has no CEO, no MD and no bosses and is owned and managed by its workers who are all on equal pay.

It makes its content available in as many languages as possible.

It publishes content critical of oppressive power structures and regimes.

It publishes content that changes its readers' thinking.

It publishes content that other publishers won't and that the establishment finds threatening.

It has been subject to repeated acts of censorship by states and corporations.

It fights all forms of censorship.

It is financially and ideologically independent of any party, corporation, state or individual.

Its books are shared all over the world.

www.zedbooks.net
@ZedBooks